RICH DAD'S

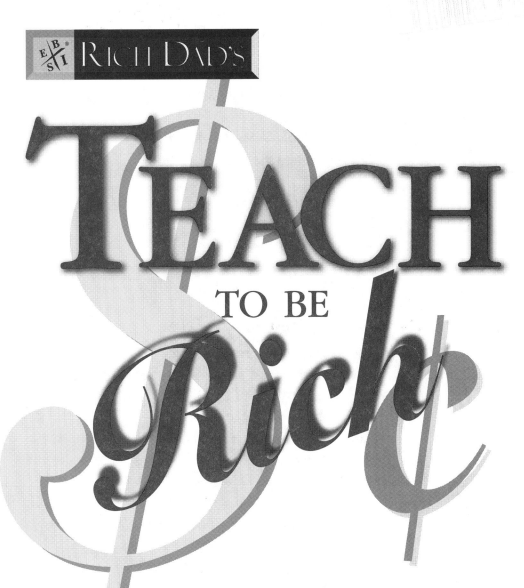

TEACH
TO BE
Rich

Because the best way to learn
is to teach what you want to learn
and
the best way to get rich is to
help others become rich.

Other Bestselling Books by
Robert T. Kiyosaki & Sharon L. Lechter

Rich Dad Poor Dad
What the Rich Teach Their Kids About Money
that the Poor and Middle Class Do Not

Rich Dad's CASHFLOW Quadrant
Rich Dad's Guide to Financial Freedom

Rich Dad's Guide to Investing
What the Rich Invest In that the Poor and Middle Class Do Not

Rich Dad's Rich Kid Smart Kid
Give Your Child a Financial Head Start

Rich Dad's Retire Young Retire Rich
How to Get Rich Quickly and Stay Rich Forever

Rich Dad's Prophecy
Why the Biggest Stock Market Crash in History is Still Coming...
And How You Can Prepare Yourself and Profit From it!

Rich Dad's Success Stories
Real-Life Success Stories from Real-Life People
Who Followed the Rich Dad Lessons

Rich Dad's Guide to Becoming Rich Without Cutting Up Your Credit Cards
Turn "Bad Debt" into "Good Debt"

Rich Dad's Who Took My Money?
Why Slow Investors Lose and Fast Money Wins!

Rich Dad Poor Dad for Teens
The Secrets About Money — That You Don't Learn In School!

Rich Dad's Escape from the Rat Race
How to Become a Rich Kid by Following Rich Dad's Advice

Rich Dad's Before You Quit Your Job
Ten Real-Life Lessons Every Entrepreneur Should Know
About Building a Multi-Million Dollar Business

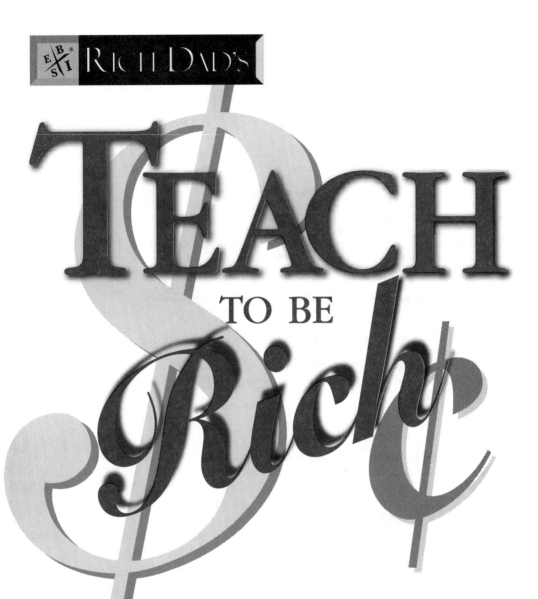

RICH DAD'S

TEACH
TO BE
Rich

Because the best way to learn
is to teach what you want to learn
and
the best way to get rich is to
help others become rich.

By Robert T. Kiyosaki with Sharon L. Lechter, C.P.A.
The Authors of *Rich Dad Poor Dad*

Published by
RICH PRESS
an imprint of Rich Publishing, LLC

This publication is designed to provide competent and reliable information regarding the subject matter covered. However, it is sold with the understanding that the author and publisher are not engaged in rendering legal, financial, or other professional advice. Laws and practices often vary from state to state and if legal or other expert assistance is required, the services of a professional should be sought. The authors and publisher specifically disclaim any liability that is incurred from the use or application of the contents of this book.

Although based on a true story, certain events in the book have been fictionalized for educational content and impact.

If you purchased this book without a cover you should be aware that this book may have been stolen property and reported as "unsold and destroyed" to the publisher. In such case neither the author nor the publisher has received any payment for this "stripped book."

Copyright © 2006 by Robert T. Kiyosaki with Sharon L. Lechter.
All rights reserved.

CASHFLOW, Rich Dad, Rich Dad's Advisors, Rich Dad's Seminars, EBSI, B-I Triangle are registered trademarks of CASHFLOW Technologies, Inc.

Visit our Web site at www.richdad.com

TABLE OF CONTENTS

DEDICATION

*Teach To Be Rich is dedicated to CASHFLOW Clubs
and their members all over the world...*

There Are Only Two Kinds Of People In The World

Rich dad often said, "There are only two kinds of people in the world. People are either *givers* or *takers*." He went on to say, "*Givers* give because they have to give. They like giving. They feel good giving. *Takers* will only give if they get something in return. Most people go to work only because they expect to get paid. If they were not paid, they would not work. *Takers* will only do you a favor if they can get something in return. If they do not get something in return, they want what they gave back or they will resent you forever."

Ever since the success of The Rich Dad Company many *givers* as well as *takers* have crossed our path. At first it was hard to tell the difference between a giver and a taker... but after awhile it became easier. Many people came by offering their services... but only for a fee. Or they came by saying, "I want to help." Later we found out what they meant was, "I want to help (myself to your success)."

As for those of you who have visited our discussion forums, you may have noticed that many critics come to the site only to take from the message, our supporters, and the mission. Many come to the site only to solicit business for their businesses or investments. Others come to take by discrediting The Rich Dad Company or me personally. These people are also takers... not of money but of good will. On top of that, most of them are liars. Some of the comments are that there really is no rich dad. First of all, there really was a rich dad... just as there really was a poor dad. Secondly, how would they know if there was one or was not one? I don't know them and they don't know me. Thirdly, does this person have nothing better to do than tear down another person or organization? Fourthly, it is sad that so many people are willing to believe everything they read. How can people be so gullible to believe what they read or hear... and that includes what they read or hear from me? And fifth, whether there was a rich dad or not, whether I am telling the truth or not, the financial lessons are still lessons. At the end of the day, the most important question to be asked is "Are these lessons important to my life?" And if they are, "How am I going to use these lessons to make my life better?"

In other words, there are many ways takers can take. If you look at your own life, you may notice that you have friends or family members who are either takers or givers.

My Favorite Givers

Still others who were drawn to The Rich Dad Company asked for nothing. They did not get into the discussion if there was a rich dad or not, if Robert Kiyosaki was for real or not, and silently went on to support rich dad's message. Instead of getting into the fray of taking from the good will of rich dad's message, or coming and saying "I'm here to help… (myself)," many just got on with the mission and began using the CASHFLOW® games as teaching tools. That is why I created the original CASHFLOW game… as a teaching tool for people who want to teach. Once people learned the game, they could learn more by teaching others the game. In other words, instead of *taking*… I wanted people to be givers, to *teach themselves* and go on to *teach* as many people as possible.

The CASHFLOW game was first commercially available in late 1997. The problem was how to sell it. The game experts said it should be priced at $39. The problem was, at the time, it cost us nearly $50 per game just in production costs. Second, the real problem was that the game was too difficult for the average person. The same game experts said that the average person in America has actually gotten more illiterate and our instructions were too difficult for most people to read and follow. They said "If someone brought us *Monopoly*® today, we would have to turn it down because the instructions are too difficult. People have become accustomed to games that are easy to play."

With those bits of information from the game experts, we raised the price to $200 per game to insure that only people who really wanted to learn and increase their financial IQ would purchase the game. If we tried to sell the game for $39, not only would we lose money on each game, the returns from unhappy game players would be staggering. In simple terms, we would go broke attempting to be a *game company* rather than a *financial education company*.

In 1997, *Rich Dad Poor Dad* was self-published. *Rich Dad Poor Dad* was written as a brochure to educate people on the value of the board game. In other words, we used the book as a qualifying tool, to identify people who want to learn. The marketing strategy worked better than our wildest dreams. In the year 2000 *Rich Dad Poor Dad* made *The New York Times* bestsellers list. Soon after that, Oprah Winfrey invited me on her program for the whole hour. Obviously, the push from Oprah was immense. Since she is syndicated all over the world, the book was soon on bestseller lists all over the world. Soon I was known for my book not my board game. Today as I write, *Rich Dad Poor Dad* has been on *The New York Times* bestsellers list for over five years.

On February 1, 2004, *The New York Times* ran nearly a full page article on the board game. The CASHFLOW game was finally being recognized. During the interview, *The New York Times* reporter, asked, "Do you know how many CASHFLOW Clubs you have?"

"CASHFLOW Clubs?" I asked. "What clubs?"

"You have clubs all over the world," said the reporter. "I have found clubs in Israel, England, Africa, Singapore, Australia, China, New Zealand, Canada, Japan, Mexico, South America, and even in Russia and the old Soviet Union. Didn't you know about them?"

"No, I didn't." I said.

Thanks to *The New York Times* reporter, we as a company are now focusing on the givers and not the takers. That is why this book has been written, written as a support document for anyone who wants to raise their own financial IQ and their financial well-being by teaching others to do the same.

In Sunday School I learned to "Give and you shall receive." In physics classes I learned one of Sir Isaac Newton's Laws that "For every action there is an opposite and equal reaction." That is why this

book is dedicated to the givers — the thousands of people, most of whom I have not met — who are quietly and diligently teaching the CASHFLOW game to their friends and family members… teaching them some of the same lessons my rich dad began teaching me years ago, when I was just nine years old.

To the givers, the teachers who teach the CASHFLOW game, I say thank you for carrying on the mission. That is why this book and The Rich Dad Company's future endeavors will be focused on people like you in mind.

What We Do With The Money

One of the final questions *The New York Times* reporter asked was, "Two hundred dollars for a game is a lot of money. What do you do with the money?"

In response I said, "First of all, we have had less than 1% in returns of the games. That means almost all of the people who have purchased them feel they got their money's worth. Secondly, how do you value an expense? If I purchase something cheap and it is of no value, then even if it was low priced… it was not worth the price, and a waste of money. Thirdly, if a person turns their financial life around and becomes a financial success, what is that worth? And fourth, if this person who purchases the game teaches 10 people, then what has the cost per person been?"

"Nice sales pitch," the reporter said. "So what do you do with the money?"

"We believe in giving back," I replied. We fund our Foundation for Financial Literacy, a not-for-profit organization that donates money to worthy educational causes. We have also spent millions developing a website www.richkidsmartkid.com, a free, non-commercial site available to parents and schools throughout the world at no charge. On this site we have developed financial education games and a curriculum for children kindergarten through 12th grade. We have had this 'giving back' aspect as part of our business since we founded the company."

In conclusion, if we expect others to be givers, we as a company also need to be givers.

So this book is dedicated to the CASHFLOW Clubs all over the world and their members. Thank you for being givers more than takers. I trust this book will assist you in furthering your financial education and the financial education of others. As rich dad said, "Anyone can be rich by being greedy. Having a high financial IQ means knowing how to be a generous person." So thank you for being givers.

FOREWARD

A Sunday School Lesson That Should Be Taught In School

When I was in Sunday School, I was taught:

1. If you *give* someone a fish…

    you feed that person for a day.

2. If you *teach* a person to fish…

    you feed that person for life.

Since the current educational systems in our schools teach us little to nothing about money, millions of people are getting their financial advice from people who sell people fish, but do not teach people to fish. Put sell and fish together and it spells *selfish*.

This book has been created to do what our schools do not do, that is to teach people to fish.

> *"All these people who think that food stamps are debilitating and lead to a cycle of poverty, they're the same ones who go out and want to leave a ton of money to their kids."*
>
> —Warren Buffett

PLEASE READ this overview before reading this book.
It will give you an idea of what this book is about.

Five Reasons Why Schools Are Failing You

Is the current system of education preparing you and your children for the real world? The following are five reasons why I believe the school system is failing all of us.

Reason #1: The World Has Changed And Education Has Not

The following are dates of important events that have led up to the reasons why the number one fear in America is running out of money during retirement.

1929 **The Stock Market Crash**

This stock market crash ended the "Roaring 20s" and led to the Great Depression. This experience, financially as well as emotionally, scared my parent's generation. This experience may be the reason why my mom and dad insisted we go to school to get good, safe, secure jobs, with a pension. Security was paramount.

1933 **President Franklin Delano Roosevelt introduces the New Deal and, in 1935, Social Security.**

Socialism took root in America and in England. In England, after the war, instead of reelecting Winston Churchill, a war hero, they elected a pro-labor candidate. Labor unions flourished on both sides of the Atlantic after the war, promising to protect the worker from the financial catastrophe of the Depression.

Also in 1933, Adolf Hitler was elected Chancellor of Germany. He was elected by the German middle class, who were angry at having their savings wiped out by inflation. This is happening again today.

1964 **President Lyndon Johnson promotes the Great Society and, in 1965, Medicare.**
President Johnson tried to fight two wars. One was the war in Vietnam and the other was the War on Poverty. He lost both wars.

Today, Medicare is a bigger financial problem than Social Security. As of 2004, the bill for Social Security was $10 trillion and Medicare was $64 trillion. The $74 trillion dollar total is more money than all of the stock and bond markets in the world.

1971 **President Richard Nixon takes us off the quasi-gold standard.**

In 1971 *savers became losers* because they were now saving a currency instead of saving money. The problem with saving a currency is that a currency is designed to go down in value. Between 1995 and 2005, the U.S. dollar lost nearly 50% of its value when compared to gold. In 1995 gold was approximately $275 an ounce. By 2005 gold was over $500 an ounce. That meant the U.S. dollar lost nearly half of its purchasing power in the world market.

1974   ERISA is passed.

ERISA stands for the Employee Retirement Income Security Act. This ultimately led to what we now know as the 401(k). 1974 is a significant year because, with the passage of ERISA, corporations were no longer willing to take care of workers for life.

1974 signaled the shift away from the protectionism of socialism to the brutal realities of global competitive capitalism, also known as *globalization*.

ERISA signaled the shift from pension plans to savings plans. The differences between *pension plans*, often called *defined benefit plans*, and *savings plans*, also known as *defined contribution* plans, is significant. Simply stated, *pension plans* cover you for life and *savings plans* cover you for as long as you have money. That is why 1974 is such a significant year. The problem, today, even *pension plans* are going broke, simply because globalization causes workers to become too expensive as we transition to a more competitive capitalist world.

1980   President Ronald Reagan takes office.

President Reagan and Margaret Thatcher of England were leaders who played significant roles in transitioning their countries from socialism to capitalism.

1989   The Berlin Wall comes down.

When the Berlin Wall came down it signaled that even the communists in Eastern Europe were becoming capitalists.

The World Wide Web came up.

The World Wide Web would change communication and access to information dramatically.

1996   The Telecom Reform Act passed.

One of the primary reasons why so many jobs are being exported overseas is due to the 1996 Telecom Reform Act.

This Act gave rise to companies such as Global Crossing, which laid fiber optic cable throughout the world. The reason this is important is because that Act, in 1996, allowed businesses to hire white-collar workers in low-wage countries such as India and Ireland. Today computer programmers, accountants, and even doctors can be hired in distant lands at much lower wages.

After 1996, the idea of a high-paying job with benefits became a dangerous idea and, for many, an obsolete idea. One of my businesses was recently able to let go of $150 an hour programmers and hire programmers in India for $25 a day, and even less if we hire them by the month.

By the year 2020, it is estimated that another nine million high-paying, white-collar jobs will be exported from America to countries overseas.

2001   China joins the WTO.

The largest communist country in the world became capitalist. Global Capitalism became hyper-competitive.

Today, there are over four billion workers in low-wage countries who are excited about working for $10 a day without benefits or retirement plans. Small wonder the greatest fear in America is running out of money during retirement.

In Summary...

Reason #1 why the current educational system has failed is because the world is changing and the school systems have not. Schools are continuing to prepare students for a world where the worker has job security and retirement security. Today the idea of job security followed by a pension for life is an obsolete employment contract.

In an increasingly hyper-competitive, capitalistic environment, the cost of workers' wages and benefits must come down. The idea of automatic pay raises and security for life is obsolete. Most of us need to be more financial independent rather than dependent upon a company, the government, or a financial advisor to take care of us.

This book has been created to provide some of the basic financial education required to survive in a hyper-competitive, capitalistic world, today and into the future.

Reason #2: Financial Education Is Not Important In School

Today, the educational system focuses on:

1.   Academic Education: the ability to read, write, and compute

2.   Professional Education: learning a trade to earn money

The current educational system does not focus on:

3.   Financial Education: learning how to have money work for you

Today, all three types of education are essential for survival in the world. Whether we are rich or poor, smart or not-so-smart, we all use money. Since money is not a subject taught in school, this leaves financial education up to parents or to people who profit from selling investment services... people who sell fish.

This lack of financial education causes:

1.   Poverty... to be passed down from generation to generation

2.   Three classes of investors:
     a. Non-investors (the poor)
     b. Passive-investors (the middle class)
     c. Active-investors (the rich)

Since money is not taught in schools, it is taught in our homes, which is one reason why poverty is often inter-generational. The following are examples of financial information taught in the three different classes.

1. **The Poor:** They believe in the government supporting them financially. They count on family support, Social Security, and Medicare.

   Most of the poor are ***non-investors***, consuming everything they earn. Most live paycheck to paycheck.

   A major stock brokerage firm defined a poor person as a person with less than $100,000 to invest.

   Many poor people do not own their own home.

2. **Middle Class:** They believe in a good education, a high-paying job or profession, home ownership, and saving for retirement through a pension.

   Most are ***passive investors***, turning their money over to financial experts or people they hope are financial experts. These experts sell fish but do not teach people to fish. That is because many of these so-called financial experts do not know how to fish.

3. **The Rich:** They are entrepreneurs (like Bill Gates and Oprah Winfrey).

   They are ***active investors*** (like Warren Buffett and Donald Trump).

Differences Between Active And Passive Investors

Passive Investor	Active Investor
1. No control	1. Has control
2. Higher risks	2. Lower risks
3. Banker will not lend money	3. Use bank's money (OPM)
4. Insurance agent will not insure	4. Uses insurance
5. Higher taxes	5. May pay zero taxes
6. *Worries* about market crash	6. *Welcomes* market crash
7. Low returns	7. Unlimited returns
8. Plan can run out of money	8. Provides for generations
9. May never retire	9. May retire early

Simply said, *passive investors* turn their money over to financial experts. *Active investors* invest first in becoming financial experts.

The Reason for Writing This Book

This book is created to teach people to fish — to either become a financial expert themselves or be able to tell the difference between good financial experts and bad financial experts. This book is written for you if you want to become an active investor.

Standard Advice For Passive Investors

Standard advice for passive investors is, "Work hard, save money, get out of debt, invest for the long term, and diversify."

In this book you will find out why this standard advice for passive investors is obsolete advice and can often be bad advice.

The Price Of Bad Advice

Between 1995 and 2005, millions of passive investors who followed their financial advisors advice of "Work hard, save money, get out of debt, invest for the long term and diversify" lost $7 to 9 trillion dollars. Many passive investors lost their retirement nest eggs by following this advice and may never be able to retire.

On top of losing trillions of dollars, many failed to participate in the biggest economic boom in the history of the world. Between 1995 and 2005, savers were losers and debtors were winners.

In Summary...

This book is written with the intent of teaching people to fish... to possibly become *active investors* and avoid the pitfalls of being *passive investors*. Since *passive investing* only works for approximately 20% of all *passive investors*, why bother being a *passive investor*? In this book, you will find out why the people getting rich via the passive investment methods are mainly the people selling passive investments. Rather than teach people to fish, most financial advisors only sell fish.

Reason #3: Schools Are Poor Teachers

This is not to say that teachers are poor teachers. This means the education system is a poor teacher.

Most of us know that our current school system is designed for less than 20% of all students. That means 80% of all students struggle in the current learning environment.

The following 1969 study on how we humans learn – The Cone of Learning — explains why so many students struggle to learn in school.

The Cone Of Learning

Point #1: You may notice that, according to this study, *the least effective* way to learn is *via reading*. The second least effective way is via lecture. Our current system of education relies heavily on reading and lecture. This is not to say that reading and lecture are not important. This only points out the lack of long-term effectiveness of those teaching methods.

Point #2: The second most effective way of learning is via simulations or games. This is also known as active learning. Active learning should involve a person's body, mind, emotions, and spirit in the learning process. Much of this book is about the thought processes that went into designing the CASHFLOW game as an educational game, more than an entertainment game. Actually, CASHFLOW was designed to be both fun and educational.

Cone of Learning

After 2 weeks we tend to remember		Nature of Involvement
90% of what we say and do	Doing the Real Thing	Active
	Simulating the Real Experience	
	Doing a Dramatic Presentation	
70% of what we say	Giving a Talk	
	Participating in a Discussion	
50% of what we hear and see	Seeing it Done on Location	Passive
	Watching a Demonstration	
	Looking at an Exhibit Watching a Demonstration	
	Watching a Movie	
30% of what we see	Looking at Pictures	
20% of what we hear	Hearing Words	
10% of what we read	Reading	

Source: Cone of Learning adapted from (Dale, 1969)

Sharon's Note: The Cone of Learning was created over 35 years ago, in 1969, within the educational system. Why hasn't the educational system changed to reflect what has proven to be effective?

This is the first book that actually explains the important financial lessons designed into the CASHFLOW game.

Point #3: The best way to learn is via real life. This book points out that our school system teaches students the skills for success in school or as employees… not for the streets of real life.

In order for a student to be an active investor, they need to have the streetwise skills required for the real world.

Point #4: Cooperation is cheating. You may notice that *Participating in a Discussion* is very high on the Cone of Learning. In school, participating in a discussion during a test is known as cheating.

In the real world, when I take a test, I take along my smartest advisors. In the real world, taking along your advisors is known as collaboration, not cheating.

The CASHFLOW game was designed to be a cooperative learning game. It was designed to have players help each other in understanding the educational lessons embedded into the game.

Again, in school, cooperation is called cheating. In the real world it is known as collaboration, or teamwork. As you can see from the Cone of Learning, cooperative learning is better than satisfy learning.

In Summary…

From this diagram of the Cone of Learning, it is obvious that the best way to learn, other than real life experience, is via simulations or games.

One of the reasons so many people think that investing is risky is because they have no place to practice except in the real world. One of the reasons for writing this book is to encourage people to get together and practice using a game, before investing in real life. To me, it makes more sense to practice and learn with *play money* at home before risking *real money* in the real world.

Also, if you look at the advantages of being an active investor versus a passive investor, you may understand why being an active investor is superior to turning your money over to someone who only sells fish. If you want your money to work harder for you, practicing and learning with a game is better than risking your nest egg in real life… or trusting your money to a person who sells fish, but may not be a real investor.

Reason #4: You Lose Control Of Your Life In School

Teaching students to be employees and to turn their investment dollars over to an expert means a person loses financial control over their entire life.

In this book you will learn why investing does not have to be risky. This book is designed to give you back more control over your life and your financial future.

In Summary...

Millions of people leave school looking for a job in a world with less and less job security and turning over their money to financial experts who cannot guarantee financial security. One reason why American's greatest fear is running out of money during retirement or people fear losing their jobs, is because they have been taught in school to give up control over their own lives.

This book is about taking back financial control of your life.

Reason #5: Genius Is Crushed In School

Personally, I never felt stupid until I went to school. One of the reasons why schools fail people is because schools fail to develop your genius. It is the premise of this book that each of us is born with a genius. Why do I believe this? Well, if you look at the animal kingdom, all animals have a native and unique skill. For example, a bird can fly and a cheetah can run fast. If all animals have a unique God-given gift... why not humans?

Our unique genius comes out only in certain environments. For example, Tiger Woods' genius comes out in the environment of the golf course. His genius may not shine as bright as a jockey. Mick Jagger went to school to be an accountant. But his genius comes out on stage as a Rolling Stone.

Intelligence is finding the environment where your genius can come out and shine. The final section of this book is dedicated to offering ways for you to find your own unique genius. If and when you find your genius, magic will happen.

Creating Magic In Your Life

Why does magic happen? Because when you look at the word genius, it is made up of the words Genie-In-Us. All you have to do is find your magic lamp — that environment where your genie thrives.

In Summary...

Many of our great leaders did not do well in school, but do well in the real world. One reason why they do well is because they found the environment, their magic lamp, where their genius thrived. For example, Thomas Edison was considered a slow learner in school, yet found his genius in his laboratory. Henry Ford did not do well in school either, yet found his genius in his garage.

The intent of this book is for you to find your genius, your magic gift. Once you find your genius, true wealth and success usually follows.

This is what this book is about. If this is what you want, then read on.

INTRODUCTION

Americans' Greatest Fear

Once upon a time in America, all you had to do was go to school, get a good job, work hard, retire at age 62, and play golf for the rest of your life. The company you worked for and the government would take care of you for as long as you lived. Today, the fairy tale is over.

The Great Retirement Rip Off

In 2002, *Rich Dad's Prophecy* was published. *Prophecy* was written about the coming failure of retirement plans and the impact it would have on peoples' lives and the economy.

Three years later, on October 30, 2005, *The New York Times Magazine* ran a cover story with an old man sitting alone on a chair with a headline that read,

> ***"We regret to inform you that you no longer have a pension."***

One day later, on October 31, 2005, the cover of *Time* magazine ran the headline:

> "Millions of Americans who think they will retire with benefits are in for a nasty surprise.
> How corporations are picking people's pockets — *with the help of Congress."*

All three publications, *Rich Dad's Prophecy, The New York Times Magazine*, and *Time* magazine are saying the same thing. The reason *Prophecy* was three years ahead of *Time* and *The New York Times* is simply because my rich dad knew the world had changed thirty years ago.

The World Changed In 1974

My rich dad knew in 1974 that the world was changing. In 1974, Congress passed ERISA, the Employee Retirement Income Security Act, which began a pension reform movement that eventually evolved into the 401(k) and other retirement plans. The significance of ERISA was that it changed the rules... the world of business was no longer going to take care of employees for life. And once the employees left the company, they were on their own... regardless of how long they lived. Unfortunately, most employees didn't realize the significance of these changes at the time. Now the realization is hitting more and more of them.

From Socialism To Capitalism

In the bigger picture, the reason 1974 is a significant year is because that year marked the shift from socialism to capitalism. In a socialistic society, the government is more benevolent and tends to protect the workers. In a capitalistic world, the society is more pro-business than pro-worker.

During the Great Depression America voted in more socialistic leaders. During his four terms as President, Franklin Delano Roosevelt and the U.S. Congress voted in Social Security and other more "people friendly" reforms. Right after World War II, England voted out Winston Churchill, even though he was a great wartime leader, and voted in the Labor Government. My parents' generation was ready for a kinder form of government.

As global competition heated up, and our one-time enemies — Japan, Italy, and Germany — became our competitors, and employee benefits became a hindrance to profits. In 1974, in order to become more competitive, the government started passing laws that allowed employers to start moving away from offering *defined benefit pension plans* and begin offering *defined contribution savings plans* to their employees. These changes occurred over several years. Notice the change of words from *benefit to contribution* and *pension* to *savings*. These changes in the words are the reasons so many workers are or will be in financial trouble when their working days are over. There is a big difference between defined benefits and defined contributions. There is also a big difference between a pension plan and a savings plan. In other words, a 401(k), a popular retirement plan in the U.S., is not a pension plan. The problem is that most workers do not know the difference.

After 1974, my rich dad began to worry about his employees. My poor dad was not aware of the changes going on… which is why he continued to think all a person needed to do was go to school and find a good job with benefits. My rich dad knew the rules were changing and the world was changing. My poor dad still believed business and government would protect and care for workers.

In the 1980s, Ronald Reagan and Margaret Thatcher were elected and the change from socialism to capitalism began. In 1989, the Berlin Wall came down which meant that even the communists were becoming capitalists. In 2001, the biggest communist country in the world, China, entered the World Trade Organization (WTO). Global Capitalism or Globalization officially marked the start of the 21st century. The world had made its shift from pro-worker socialism to pro-business capitalism. Riots started breaking out at World Economic Summits and on September 11, 2001, the ultimate protest was staged and the world changed forever.

The Greatest Fear In America

In 2004, *USA Today* reported that the greatest fear in America was the fear of running out of money during retirement. I believe this is directly related to the 1974 change in the rules of employment.

In 2005, on the Fox Television Network, one of the news programs also did a survey asking viewers what their greatest fear was: the fear of running out of money during retirement or the fear of terrorist attack? The survey found over 60% of those polled were more afraid of running out of money as compared to a little over 20% who were more afraid of terrorism.

Why Fear?

In the year 2000, millions of workers with 401(k)-type retirement plans awoke to the reality that the stock market does not always go up. The following is a graph of the NASDAQ.

NASDAQ 1995-2005

Questionable Advice

In the year 2000, as the market began to crash, many panicked investors called their brokers or financial advisors seeking reassurance… and they received it. The advice was, "Don't worry, this is just a temporary correction. Keep investing for the long term and diversify." In spite of the reassurances, the market kept falling. Today, millions of investors may never be able to retire, or may run out of money during retirement, because of this questionable advice.

What, Me Worry?

Many workers with defined contribution plans, such as the 401(k) plans are in trouble… many will never be able to retire. Even those with the older defined benefit pension plans are in trouble. Many workers at companies such as Ford, General Motors, United Airlines, Polaroid, and others are finding out that their retirements are not as secure as they thought they were. In fact, many are finding out that their pension plans were legally stolen. The PBGC, the Pension Benefit Guarantee Corporation in charge of protecting workers with defined benefit retirement plans, is technically broke and may not be able to protect workers who, at one time, were smug in thinking they had nothing to worry about.

What Is The Answer?

So what is the answer? To me, it seems obvious. Since the problem is a financial problem, the answer is financial education. Then the next question is, "What kind of financial education?" Many people think the tried and true financial advice of "work hard, save money, get out of debt, invest for the long term, and diversify" is good financial advice… and it has been good advice for some people. Yet if you look at the facts, millions of investors who followed that advice were the ones who lost $7 to 9 trillion dollars between the year 2000 and 2004.

Two-Time Losers

To make matters worse, those millions of investors who followed that advice not only lost trillions of dollars, they failed to make trillions of dollars in what *The Economist* magazine said was the biggest financial boom in the history of the world. In other words, those who followed the advice of "work hard, save money, get out of debt, invest for the long term and diversify" were two-time losers between 1995 and 2005.

At the risk of sounding like a braggart, those people who followed my rich dad's advice, advice found in Rich Dad books and products, did very well. They participated in the biggest financial boom in history. Those who followed their financial advisors' advice of "invest for the long term in a well-diversified portfolio of mutual funds" were some of the investors who lost trillions of dollars.

It Is Time To Change Again

Does this mean that my investment advice is better than the financial advisors'? My answer is "No." Am I resting on my past success?" Again, the answer is "No."

In the summer of 2005, I sent out a warning to anyone who would listen via the Rich Dad web site, a warning that said "All Booms Bust." I even went on national TV and radio explaining my point of view that the real estate boom had turned into a bubble and was probably going to burst.

Many of my friends who are in real estate called me in anger, demanding I stop saying what I was saying. Many other friends, who are also in real estate, called and congratulated me. Several said, "I can't wait for the bust. I'm looking forward to bargain hunting."

I Am NOT A Real Estate Broker

The reason I can say what I say is that I am not a real estate broker. I do not sell real estate, or stocks or bonds or mutual funds. I am an entrepreneur and an investor. My income comes primarily from passive income from my businesses and investments. I do not sell investments. If I have anything to sell it is financial education… not financial advice or investment products, which means I am not beholding to anyone selling stocks, bonds, mutual funds, or real estate.

Financial Education From Sales People

After 1974, millions of workers needed financial education. Unfortunately what they found was financial advice.

My rich dad said, "One of the reasons so many people are confused or worried about losing their money is because they get their financial education from sales people… not rich people." If you take a moment and think about it, you may find some truth in my rich dad's words. For example:

1. **From a banker we learn the financial wisdom of "Save money."**

   What a banker does not tell you is that for every dollar you put in the bank, the banker can lend out $20 or more. In addition, the banker pays you only 1 to 5% interest for your money ($1) but then can lend the $20 — at 10%, 20%, 30% or more interest.

2. **From financial planners you learn the financial wisdom of "Invest for the long term."**

   What they do not tell you is that they collect a commission over the long term. The longer you keep your money in, and the more money you put in, the more in commissions or fees their mutual fund company makes. They get paid whether the investment they put your money into makes money or loses money. When I buy a piece of real estate or a business, I pay a commission once, not forever.

High Prices, High Risk, For Low Returns

We all know that people with limited financial training pay the highest prices for the worst investments and receive the lowest returns. Worst of all, they invest in investments they actually think are safe, but are in reality the riskiest of all investments. Once again, that is because they receive their financial education from sales people.

Definition Of Poor People

Since 1974, millions of people have realized they need to plan for retirement. This occurred just as global competition picked up and wages started to come down. Today, millions of workers do not earn enough money to be able to afford the rising cost of living, raising a family, taking care of aging parents, let alone saving for retirement.

In 2005, an internal memo was found from a well-known financial planning and investment banking house that read, "The definition of a poor person is a client with less than $100,000 to invest." The memo also went on to state that the company would only hire employees who had five or more friends and family members with over a $100,000 to invest. If having less than $100,000 in cash to invest is the new definition of 'poor,' then the U.S. is filled with poor people.

Obsolete Advice

The introduction to this book began with *"Once upon a time…"* The reason it began with those words is because once upon a time, the advice of "Work hard, save money, get out of debt, invest for the long term, and diversify" was good advice. It worked for my parent's generation, the World War II generation, but it will not work for my generation, the baby boomers, and the generations to follow. The world has changed and is changing faster and faster.

Seeking Investment Advice

During my book signings, people often come up to me and ask such things as, "I have $25,000. What should I do with it?" Or "I'm coming into some money from an inheritance. What should I invest in?" Or "Can you recommend someone to talk to about investing my money?"

Shaking my head, I half jokingly (yet half sadly) say, "The first thing I would do is not tell people you have money to invest. If you don't know what to do with your money, there are millions of people who do. And their answer is to turn your money over to them."

As I said, the big problem is people are getting their financial advice from sales people, not rich people.

The Million-Dollar Questions

To me, the more intelligent questions are:

1. "How do you know good financial advice from bad financial advice?"

2. "How do you know a good investment from a bad investment?"

3. "How do I know if the investment advice is right for me?"

This book, *Teach To Be Rich*, has not been created to give you the answers to those questions. This book has been created to allow you to find — and teach others to find — *your own answers* to these million dollar questions.

This book is not aimed against financial sales-people. We all are sales-people with something to sell. Most of us need to sell something in order for money to come in. For example, a doctor sells his or her medical training, a secretary sells his or her time, a financial sales person sells his or her financial advice and investment products.

For clarification, The Rich Dad Company sells financial education, not financial advice. Nor does The Rich Dad Company sell investment products such as stocks, bonds, mutual funds, or real estate. This keeps us free to say what we want to say. We have been approached many times by financial institutions, wanting us to recommend their products and services; but we have, as a matter of policy, turned them down. Obviously, we could have made a lot more money recommending their advice, products, or services, but we felt we would have compromised our educational core. We welcome joint ventures with major investment companies that support their educational programs, not their financial advice or products divisions.

Everyone Is Looking For Money

One of the ironies of the world today is that almost everyone is looking for money. Everyday I am solicited to donate money to a charity, invest in this or that investment, or buy a hot new product. In spite of the numbers of people looking for money, there are millions of people with money, who have no idea where to put their money. These people would find great opportunities if they could learn the difference between a good investment and a bad one.

Once again, this book is not against sales-people. This book is created to assist you and those you teach to:

1. Increase your financial literacy.

2. Be able to separate fact from fiction.

3. Know what is best for you, not the sales person.

4. Be better able to reduce risk and increase returns.

5. Be able to ask more financially intelligent questions.

6. Be better able to deal with financial sales people.

7. Take greater control of your financial future.

8. Maybe become richer than your wildest dream, by helping people, not taking from them.

A Vow Of Poverty

For those of you who have read my other books, you may already know that I come from a family of teachers. In my family, teaching is the most noble of all professions. In fact, in many religions, the most respected profession is that of a teacher. The problem is, because it is held as a noble profession, it is also considered un-noble to teach for money. In fact, in my family, being a teacher almost meant taking a vow of poverty. In fact, I think it is a crime how little we pay our teachers.

The good news is that if you teach yourself and others to be rich, you can become richer, regardless of how big or small your paycheck is.

Do I Have To Be Rich…
Before I Can Teach Others To Be Rich?

My professional teaching career began in 1984. At the time, I was not rich. In fact, I was nearly broke, having lost my second business. By 1994, my wife, Kim, and I were financially free. We became rich simply because we practiced what we taught. We were teaching others how to have money work hard for them so they did not have to work hard for money. Although we did not earn much money for ten years, our money earned a lot of money over those same ten years. That is how we became financially free.

During the time I was not rich, I simply began my seminars telling people the truth. I told them about my successes and failures. More importantly, I talked about the lessons I had learned. I was brutally honest with them as well as with myself. I also told them about what I was doing, my plans, what I was investing in, and when I expected to be financially free. As I said, in 1994, Kim and I exited the Rat Race, financially free for the rest of our lives, barring any unforeseen economic disasters.

Do I Have To Have Teacher Training To Be A Teacher?

Personally, I studied and learned a lot about teaching, education, and the different ways different people learn.

I would not be accepted as a teacher inside the traditional system of education, because I was not trained by the system. As you may know, I did not do well in school and did not like what I was taught — or the way I was taught. So I had to learn new and different ways of teaching. That is why I do not teach inside the system of education. I am a teacher outside the system. The good news is that I make millions of dollars as a teacher outside of the system.

So I would say that teacher training is important. But not as important as the desire to teach, and more importantly, to help others to learn.

A Teaching Tool

Much of this book is about the CASHFLOW board game I developed in 1994, after I was financially free. I created the game to be a teaching tool… to assist people in teaching the financial lessons my rich dad taught me. This book is about the embedded lessons I hid inside the game…

lessons that can only be discovered by playing the game a number of times.

The CASHFLOW board game was designed to make teaching the subject of money easier. As we know, the subject of money and getting rich is not a simple subject. In fact it is a complex subject with many twists and turns. For the first time, in this book, I reveal some of those twists and turns I embedded into the game. Once you come to understand those twists and turns, the financial wisdom wired into the game is transferred to you and then you can share that wisdom with those you teach.

So after studying this book, and playing the game a number of times, a person who teaches the game to others learns priceless new lessons about teaching, money, and people. This is ultimately what makes you richer. By learning the intricacies hidden in this game, then teaching them to others, my rich dad's wisdom is transferred to you.

Why Teach To Be Rich?

As many of you know, I have not taken a vow of poverty. I love making a lot of money, driving foreign cars, wearing Italian suits, and flying in private jets. I also love teaching. For me, the secret to becoming richer was simply teaching others what I wanted to learn.

We all know of the Golden Rule, which is "Do unto others as you would have them do unto you." Or the other rule, "Give and you shall receive." These rules are designed into my games. But the true power of the game is not released until a person becomes a teacher of the game, a teacher with a sincere desire to help others increase their financial IQ. That is why studying this book, learning the CASHFLOW games 101 and 202, and then teaching others is a vital part of The Rich Dad Company's financial education program. We would rather do business with *givers*… not *takers*.

A Lesson From Sunday School

When I was in Sunday School I was taught, "Give a man (or woman) a fish and you feed them for a day. Teach a man (or woman) to fish and you feed them for life." It is unfortunate that too many financial services companies only teach their employees to *sell fish*, rather than teach people to fish. Notice that if you put the words *sell* and *fish* together, you get the word *selfish*.

The Rich Dad Company was created to be a financial education company rather than a financial advice company. What we sell is financial education, not financial advice or investment products such as stocks, bonds, mutual funds, real estate, or business opportunities. Our perfect customer is a person who wants to teach people to fish, not sell fish to people.

The Cocoon

Most of us have heard the metaphor of a caterpillar spinning a cocoon and emerging as a butterfly. This is also called a metamorphosis.

School is a cocoon. My own personal experiences with school are:

1. In 1969, I entered the U.S. Navy Flight School in Pensacola, Florida and two years later emerged as a pilot.

2. In 1974, I entered the Xerox Corporations sales training school, in Leesburg, Virginia, and emerged as a salesman, a profession essential to being an entrepreneur.

3. In 1974, I signed up for a real estate investment school, in Honolulu, Hawaii and emerged as a real estate investor.

You may have noticed that 1974, the year I left the Marine Corps, was a very important year for me. That was the year I chose to enter my rich dad's educational cocoon versus my poor dad's cocoon. Of all the schools I entered, those two schools I entered in 1974, Xerox sales training school and rich dad's school, have made me the most money… much more money than my college education. Most important is that the education from those two schools allowed me to become financially free, completely out of the Rat Race of life.

In 1974, rather than go back to school to get my Masters degree and then my Ph.D., the educational cocoon my poor dad recommended, I choose to learn to be an entrepreneur and an investor, and entered my rich dad's cocoon.

Choose Your Cocoon Carefully

My poor dad, as the head of education for the State of Hawaii, sincerely believed in the power of education. He constantly said, "Go to school and get good grades, so you can get a good job."

My rich dad also believed in the power of education. The problem was, it was not the same education my poor dad believed in. Instead he said, "Be careful in choosing the school you attend. Entering school is like entering a cocoon. Before you enter, you better be sure you want to be what you become when you leave school."

Some of the rich dad's examples were:

1. When people go to school, they usually enter as kids and come out as employees.

2. When students enter art school, they enter as a student and emerge from the cocoon as an artist.

3. When young people enter the Marine Corps boot camp, they enter as kids and exit as Marines.

4. After students complete flight school, they exit as pilots.

5. After finishing medical school, students emerge as doctors.

"The problem is," said rich dad, "most schools do not teach you anything about money. Most schools teach you to work for money rather than learn how to have money work for you. Most schools teach you to work for the rich rather than teach you to be rich." Pausing, he said, "That is why you need to first choose what you want to become before you choose what school you attend."

That conversation with rich dad took place in 1974, as I was leaving the Marine Corps. That was when I decided to work for Xerox to learn how to sell, and signed up for a real estate investor program so I could learn how to invest my money (and my banker's money) wisely.

The Cause Of The Greatest Fear In America

America, once the richest country in the world, is in trouble today. It is now the largest debtor nation in the world. America has many people with a lot of money, but who do not know what to do with their money. That is the primary reason why so many people are more afraid of running out of

money during retirement than are afraid of terrorist attacks.

In a few years, the first of approximately 75 million of the baby-boom generation adults will begin to retire and expect to collect the money they contributed into the government system. Unfortunately, there is not enough money.

The math is simple. If there are 75 million baby boomers and they each collect a $1000 a month in Social Security and Medicare benefits, that equals $75 billion a month we are not paying today… but have agreed to pay in the near future. In 2004, it was estimated that the total bill for Social Security is $10.4 trillion and for Medicare it is $62 trillion… and growing. This is more money than all the money in the stock and bond markets of the world. Obviously there is a financial storm brewing and the winds will only increase in speed as the baby boomers age and need more medical care.

When hurricanes Katrina and Rita hit, those storms tore off the roof and exposed to the world the shocking poverty that exists in America, once the richest country in the world. I remember a television reporter interviewing a young couple as Hurricane Rita approached, asking them why they were not evacuating, especially after they knew of the devastation and death caused by Katrina. Their reply, "We cannot afford to put gas in our car."

You Cannot Teach Poor People To be Rich

While it is not realistic to save everyone from the financial hurricane that lies a ahead, it is possible to save some people. As my rich dad said, "You cannot teach a poor person to be rich. You can only teach someone who *wants to learn to be rich*, to be rich." You may notice that the key words are *wants to learn to be rich*. He did not say people who *want to get rich quick* or people who *want a hot tip on what to do with their money*. The key words are *wants to learn to be rich*. He also said, "Many people want money but very few people want to learn to be rich. That is why there are so few rich people."

That is why this book was created only for people who *want to learn* and *want to teach* others who want to learn and want to teach. In my opinion, a grassroots financial education program is the best way to prepare for the financial hurricane that is brewing. If you are waiting for the government, the school system, your mutual fund company, your banker, or your financial expert to protect you and your family from the coming storm, you might also want to invest in some cots, candles, canned goods, water, and blankets.

Remember, there is a big difference between learning to fish and selling fish. The reason so many well-educated people ask, "What should I do with my money?" is simply because our schools do not teach us much about money. Because *they do not know how to fish*, these people wind up *taking financial advice from people who sell fish* but do not teach people to fish. This book is about learning to fish and teaching others to fish. We sell financial education. We do not sell fish.

INTRODUCTION TO PART I

A Fool And His Money

As I have mentioned, at my book signings someone always comes up to me and asks, "I have some money. What should I do with it?"

My standard reply is, "The first thing I would do is stop telling people you have some money." I go on to say, "If you do not know what to do with your money, then there are a lot of people who do."

Many of us have heard the saying, "A fool and his money are easily parted," Or, "A fool and his money are one big party." Part I of this book is about why there are so many fools and the parties being held with the fool's money. The problem is the fools are not invited to their own party.

School Smarts vs Street Smarts

As we all know, there are two kinds of people… people who are *street smart* and people who are *school smart*. It is often those who are *school smart* who ask the question, "What should I do with my money." Those who are street smart either do not have any money or are the ones taking the money from the fools.

A Gift from Rich Dad…

BONUS DOWNLOAD:
The **Ten Personal Controls**
that can make you rich

It's FREE…
you can access the download at:
www.richdad.com/tencontrols

Two Schools Of Thoughts

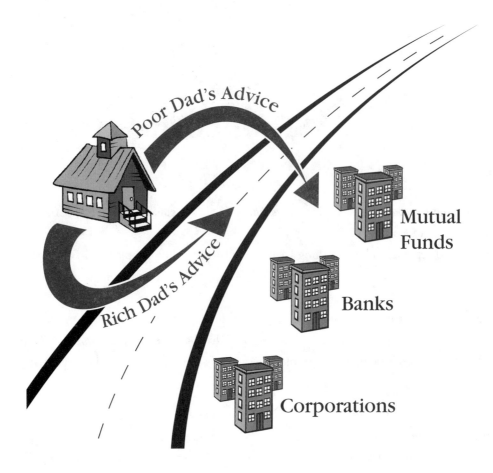

School Smarts vs Street Smarts

My poor dad was school smart.
My rich dad was street smart.

My Poor Dad's Advice

My poor dad was a great man and a great teacher. He dedicated his life to education… eventually becoming the Superintendent of Education for the State of Hawaii. His advice was "Go to school, get good grades and find a high paying secure job with benefits." When it came to money, his advice was, "Save money, buy a house, and get out of debt." When it came investing he said, "Investing is risky." Which is why he said, "Turn your money over to financial experts." He was a well-educated, school-smart man who did not know what to do with his money.

My poor dad saw the street as a dangerous place… a place to be avoided. He believed that big corporations, government, banks, and financial institutions — those with school smarts — should protect people from the harshness of the street, once the student left school.

My Rich Dad's Advice

My rich dad was also a great man and a great teacher. He dedicated his life to building businesses and investing his own money. His advice was, "Get a college degree, become an entrepreneur and invest your own money." In his mind, being an employee was risky and turning your money over to strangers was also very risky.

My rich dad also saw the street as a dangerous place… but not a place to be avoided. Instead of avoiding the street, he trained his son and me to thrive and survive on the street, in spite of the dangers. He said, "There are many smart people on the street. Some are good and some are bad. Your job is to be one of the good people and be able to tell the difference between the good and the bad people." Instead of training us to seek financial *security*, he trained us to seek a life of financial *freedom*, on the street.

Security vs Freedom

Those of you who have read my books may already know that security and freedom are not the same thing… in fact they are exactly the opposite. As my rich dad often said, "The more you seek security, the less freedom you have." He also said, "The people with the most security are in prison. That's why it is called maximum security."

The Problem With Security

The problem with security is when it runs out. As we all know, many corporations, such as Ford, General Motors and United Airlines, have pensions plans that are in trouble. The government's safety nets — Social Security and Medicare — are in trouble. Many workers' retirement plans, such as 401(k) plans, are in trouble because the financial experts working for the giant financial institutions have not proven to be experts. Soon millions of educated, hard-working people will be hitting the streets, the very place they hoped they could have avoided.

One of the problems with being on the street is that a person may have professional freedom but not have financial security. For example, self-employed maids may have the professional freedom to set their own hours, they may make a lot of money, but if they become sick or injured, their income stops. There are millions of people in America and billions in the world who are surviving on the street, but have no financial security.

The Three Types Of Education

Many who have read my books already know there are three basic types of education required for success in today's world. They are:

1. Academic education: the ability to read and write

2. Professional education: learning a skill to earn money

3. Financial education: learning how to have money work for you

As you know, our schools do a pretty good job on academic and professional education, but fail in the financial education category. This is why so many people are afraid of the street. When they leave school, most people only know how to be employees or professionals, such as doctors or lawyers. They

also learn to turn their money over to financial experts. The problem is, in the last few years, many people have found out that their financial experts were not really experts.

Two Kinds Of Financial Education

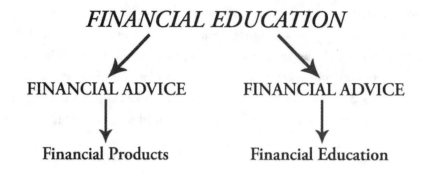

A few days ago, a stockbroker from a large financial services company called me and invited me to a financial education seminar. Being a person who is always interested in improving my financial education, I signed up for the seminar.

There were about thirty people in the room, ranging in age from 25 to 85. All were well-dressed and seemed to be educated and affluent. The seminar leader, a senior broker from New York, talked about opportunities in China and in oil and gas, the hot topics of the day. At the end of the seminar, he mentioned the financial products they recommended. They just happened to be oil and gas drilling funds and funds specializing in China. At the end of the evening, the guests were making appointments to come back in to find out more about oil and gas investments and China.

My point for mentioning this seminar is because in the current world of financial education, most of the education is not about education. Most financial education is a sales pitch. A company brings you in and then narrowly focuses you on the products they have for sale.

The Rich Dad Company also has a sales pitch. But our pitch is to recommend getting financially educated before buying financial products.

Unfortunately, most people would rather be told what products they should invest in rather than invest in their financial education. They want answers, not education. That is why so many people ask me, "What should I do with my money?"

The Biggest Boom In History

Between 1995 and 2005, millions of investors who turned their money over to experts *lost* trillions of dollars. Between 1995 and 2005, investors who followed my rich dad's advice *made* trillions of dollars. Between 1995 and 2005, according to *The Economist* magazine, the biggest financial boom in history took place.

Those who followed the financial experts' advice and saved money, got out of debt, and invested for the long term, primarily in a well-diversified portfolio of mutual funds, not only lost trillions of dollars, they failed to make trillions of dollars.

In other words, between 1995 and 2005 people who followed my poor dad's advice got poorer and people who followed my rich dad's advice got richer. Those who avoided the street and turned their money over to the experts working for banks and large financial institutions lost, and those that were financially educated and street smart won.

Desperate People

In 2008, the first of 75 million baby boomers are eligible for retirement. That means many will be hitting the street, the very place they have been working hard to avoid. Some will thrive on the street. But as they get older, millions will become financially desperate as their ability to work (and their savings) runs out.

While I am concerned about my generation, the baby boomers, I am more concerned with the children and grandchildren of the baby boomers. It is these younger generations who will ultimately have to make the hard decision to support poor baby boomers in their final years or support their own children. I saw one estimate that Social Security taxes will have to be increased by 300% on the younger generations to pay for the baby boom generation's retirement. In other words, there will be multiple generations of financially desperate people, all doing their best to avoid life on the street.

Become Your Own Financial Expert

Rich dad often said, "You cannot teach a poor person to be rich. You can only teach someone who wants to be rich, to be rich."

This book does not pretend to be the savior of people in poverty or people destined for poverty. This book is not written for people who expect a company, the government, or some financial expert to save them. This book is written for people who know there is a financial storm brewing and want to save themselves, their families, and their friends. In my opinion, the best way to ride out the financial storm that is coming is to become rich by learning to be rich and teaching others to be rich.

There are many ways you can become rich. Some are: be born rich; marry someone who is rich; get lucky by winning the lottery; or be gifted such as a pro athlete or movie star. I was not blessed with any of these avenues to wealth. The way I became wealthy was by investing in my financial education before I invested my money. In other words, I became my own financial expert rather than turn my money over to a person I hoped was a financial expert.

The Next Financial Boom

In every disaster there are *victims* and *victors*. For example, when Hurricane Katrina hit, there were many victims of that storm. There are also going to be many victors, people who benefit because of the storm.

The same is true with any disaster. When I write about the coming financial storm, I do not view the coming disaster through the eyes of a financial victim. Personally, I see the coming financial disaster as a financial boom, without me personally exploiting the victims.

One of the reasons why there were so many financial victims between 1995 and 2005, was because millions of investors were following financial experts' advice, "Work hard, save money, get out of debt, invest for the long term and diversify." People who followed that advice were the financial victims of that 10-year period.

People who followed my rich dad's advice made trillions of dollars in the biggest financial boom in the history of the world, without having to exploit the victims of bad financial advice.

How could this happen? How can there be victims and victors without the victors exploiting the victims? It happened because those who followed my rich dad's financial advice were in different markets. They were not in the stock market. They were in the real estate and commodity markets.

That is why one group can become victors without exploiting victims.

So the victims were investors who didn't know there were other markets to invest in. All they knew about were the financial products their financial advisor advised them to invest in. And those financial products are the only ones the advisor is allowed to sell. (That is why most victims do not hear about other investment vehicles.)

It is unfortunate that millions of investors are still in the stock market, many in mutual funds, following their financial expert's advice of investing for the long term. They are victims of poor financial advice. By 2020, just as they give up on the stock market and sell their stocks, the stock market cycle should head back up again.

The Biggest Big Change

The biggest change of all is not the change of 20-year asset cycles. The biggest change of all is that we are no longer in the Industrial Age, and as of the year 2000, we officially entered the Information Age. So the biggest problem of all is that millions of people still have Industrial Age ideas about money. For example, in the Industrial Age, companies and government could afford to take care of people, keeping them off the street, when their working days were over. Those days are gone.

In just a few years, the United States went from the richest nation in the world to becoming the largest debtor nation in the world. This change, more than the 20-year asset cycle, will cause a financial storm unlike any the world has seen before.

When this storm hits, millions of educated, hard-working people — people with money today — will become the next financial victims… many landing on the very street they worked so hard to avoid.

This book is written in four parts. All four parts are written for people who want to be financial victors in the coming years. In my opinion, the best way to become a victor is to become your own financial expert by developing your financial genius. In other words, my advice is to invest first in your financial education before you invest in financial products. Then you will have a better chance of knowing good advice from poor advice and a good investment from a bad investment.

If becoming your own financial expert sounds like too much work, then this book, all four parts of it, is not for you. For people who do not want to study, learn, and teach others, then it is best to look for a financial expert who you hope really is a financial expert and ask, "What should I do with my money?" I am sure they will have an answer for you.

Author's Note: Obviously, those who are *not successful* on the street wish they had a big company or the government or a family member to take care of them. Yet, those who are successful on the street tend to love it. Freedom is far better than security. Not only is life on the street *the road to freedom*, it is also the place where entrepreneurs and investors find the best financial opportunities. I have found that once a person finds success on the street, they never want to go back to the world of security.

Chapter One

THE THREE GOLDEN RULES

Most of us have heard of the Golden Rule. Yet when it comes to money, many people do not realize there are two other golden rules. So in total there are three golden rules and they are:

Golden Rule #1: "Do unto others as you would have them do unto you."

Golden Rule #2: "He who has the gold makes the rules."

Golden Rule #3: "A fool who has gold works for those who make the rules."

My poor dad subscribed to Golden Rule #3. He did not know he subscribed to it, yet he emphasized it every time he advised his children to "Go to school, get good grades, get a safe secure job, work hard, save money, get out of debt, and invest in safe stocks, mutual funds, and bonds."

When most financial experts offer financial advice, they too are generally following Golden Rule #3. That is why most financial experts say, "Work hard, save money, get out of debt, invest for the long term, and diversify."

My rich dad did not subscribe to Golden Rule #3. That is why he did not believe in working hard for money, saving money, getting out of debt, investing for the long term, and diversifying. When it came to money, he believed in the first two Golden Rules.

Simply said, my poor dad was poor because he followed Golden Rule #3. My rich dad was rich because he followed Golden Rules #1 and #2.

Most people struggle financially because they are taught to follow Golden Rule #3 at home, at school, and by many so-called financial experts.

By the end of this book you will know why the financial advice of "Work hard, save money, get out of debt, invest for the long term, and diversify," is not smart financial advice — if you want to be rich. It is not smart financial advice because it is a derivative of Golden Rule #3. If you truly want to be rich, the first two golden rules are smarter rules to follow.

Why The Rich Are Getting Richer

In January of 1998, I was watching a very popular national morning television show. The two attractive male and female hosts, smile their toothy smile into the camera and say, "This morning, we have our network's investment expert in the studio to give us her financial advice for the start of the new year."

The camera then cuts away to an extremely attractive young woman who smiles into the camera and says, "For 1998 my advice is to work hard, save money, get out of debt, invest for the long term,

and diversify."

The female host smiles and says, "That is such good advice. I hope everyone follows it."

The male host, frowning a little in an attempt to appear more thoughtful and intelligent, asks, "What do you recommend they invest in?"

The attractive young woman smiles her perfect smile and says "I recommend a well-diversified portfolio of mutual funds, with an emphasis on the technology sector."

"Great advice," the male and female hosts say in unison. Once again, they smile to the camera and thank the financial expert for her advice and for appearing on the program.

A year later, in January of 1999, the scene is the same. Once again the two attractive hosts invite the same attractive financial expert on stage to offer her financial advice for the start of the new year. And once again her advice is, "Work hard, save money, get out of debt, invest for the long term, and diversify." As a special extra tip she adds, "Be sure to maximize your 401(k), especially if your employer has to match your contribution. And if you have any other money, invest it in the stock market. You know the stock market goes up on average at least 10% per year."

"Fantastic advice." says the attractive female host.

"I'm going to call my broker right after the show," nods the male host. "I have some extra money sitting in a savings account that I can put to work in the market. Any tips?"

"Well, I think mutual funds are a smart investment. They offer lower risk and greater diversification. I also like individual technology and telecom stocks," said the financial expert. "But more important than what you invest in, always invest for the long term, buy, hold, and diversify. That is what smart investors do."

You may recall that in 1999, the stock market was out of control. It was a mania, a bubble. People who had never invested before were in the market and were suddenly experts. I read a story of a fireman in Los Angeles who quit his job as a fireman so he could devote all his time to his mutual fund portfolio. He even started an investment advisory service after investing for less than a year. There is a saying that goes, "When shoeshine boys are offering stock tips, it is time to sell." Well, I did not meet any shoeshine boys in 1999, but the woman at the checkout counter of my local supermarket did tell me about the mutual funds she was in. When she passed on her hot tip as she scanned my cat food, I knew the boom was about to bust.

In 1999, the dot-com bubble was a balloon… a giant hot air balloon. So-called smart investors were literally throwing billions of dollars into companies that had no value… companies that were no more than concepts scribbled on a cocktail napkin. All someone needed to add were the words dot-com after their company name and people who had no business investing were throwing money at the venture.

A business magazine ran an article under the banner "Get Out And Network." Under the headline was a photograph of young college kids, male and female, exchanging business cards with older people, presumably older people with money to invest. The article described networking parties where young so-called entrepreneurs with a concept for a dot-com company could mingle and present their ideas to investors. According to the article, a number of these college kids raised millions of dollars for their ideas and quit school to build their companies. Talk about the blind leading the blind.

In January of 2000, the scene at the television station was the same… same two attractive hosts and same attractive financial expert. Once again the financial expert smiles to camera and says, "Work hard, save money, get out of debt, invest for the long term and diversify."

One of the hosts asks, "People say there is a bubble in the stock market. Do you think it is time for people to sell?"

"Oh, no," says the financial expert. "Professional investors don't try to time the market. They simply buy and hold… they invest for the long term."

"Shouldn't they take some of their profits and convert to cash?" asks the male host.

"Oh, no," says the financial expert. "You may want to sell a few shares, but I would not keep it in cash. I would simply diversify more."

> *"The dumbest reason in the world to buy a stock is because it's going up."*
> —Warren Buffett

In January of 2001, the scene repeats itself… and the advice is the same. "Work hard, save money, get out of debt, invest for the long term, and diversify." This time there is a little nervousness in the air. The market has been heading down, not up. Still the attractive young financial expert reassures millions of people that "Investing for the long term is the smart thing to do." She also adds, "This is the time to buy more. Smart investors know to *buy the dips*. Prices are lower so buy now before they go back up."

In January of 2002, the scene is the same and so is the financial advice. The only thing different now is that people realize the stock market is crashing. Scandals are in the news. Even though it is crashing, the financial expert reminds them to sit tight and invest for the long term. This time she adds, "The events of September 11th are tragic and have affected the market. Just sit tight and remember to be a long-term investor."

By the January of 2003 show, most people realize that the stock market has officially crashed. Although the market has crashed, the two hosts welcome the attractive financial expert to the show. Once again, the advice remains the same.

"So you don't recommend selling?" asks the male host.

"No, I don't," smiles the financial advisor. Turning to the camera she says, "If you sell when prices are lower, then you lose. You do not lose any money as long as you do not sell. So sit tight and remember to invest for the long term."

In January 2004, it is déjà vu all over again. Same television show, same people, same smiles, same financial advice. I thought about writing in and recommending they just play reruns of earlier programs.

> *"Wall Street is the only place that people ride to in a Rolls Royce to get advice from those that ride the subway."*
> —Warren Buffett

Big Losers

As mentioned, between January of 2000 and December of 2003 it is estimated that millions of investors lost $7 to 9 trillion dollars following the advice of "work hard, save money, get out of debt, invest for the long term, and diversify." More than just losing the money, many of these investors were investors who could not afford to lose. Many investors were baby boomers who were counting on their investments for their retirement. They could no longer afford to *invest for the long term*. They were out of time. Not only were millions out of time, millions were out of work, or working for less money and holding down more jobs.

As stated before, there are three Golden Rules. Millions of people lost trillions of dollars because they did not realize their financial experts subscribed to Golden Rule #3 which states, "A fool who has gold works for those who make the rules."

My rich dad simply said, "Golden Rule #3 is about fool's gold."

As Goes GM, So Goes America

At the same time that millions of little investors were losing their retirement, so were many giant corporate investors. During this same period of time, it became apparent that many big corporate pension plans, such as General Motors, were under-funded.

There is an old saying that goes, "As goes General Motors, so goes America." There is some degree of wisdom in those words even today. Today General Motors' problems are not production problems. General Motors has a problem of too many retirees who have been promised a paycheck for life as well as medical benefits for life. In other words, General Motors' problem is not really from competition from other car makers. General Motors' problems are caused by having too many older workers who are no longer working. They are expecting to be cared for, for the rest of their lives... as they were promised.

The same is true for the United States. We are a nation of hard working, productive people. The big problem looming on the horizon, as already mentioned, is the millions of workers close to retirement. In fact, the first of approximately 75 million baby boomers is set to retire in 2008, just three years away from the writing of this book.

This is not only an American problem. It is a problem in many wealthy countries. In July of 2005, the government of Japan informed its younger workers that they will have to pay more in taxes to pay for the older workers' retirement. We in American may be getting the same news in a few years.

It is a sad day when General Motors' and Ford Motor Company's corporate bonds are rated as junk bonds. If the same rating is applied to the Treasury Bonds of the United States, there will be global economic chaos. So maybe the saying should be, "As goes GM, so goes the *world*."

The plight of General Motors' retirees is also the plight of employees from other giant companies in the airlines and the steel industries. The problem of inadequate pension funds is so great that the PBGC, the Pension Benefit Guarantee Corporation that insures the pensions of workers, is technically bankrupt. Instead of receiving the pension they expected, many retirees are currently taking a cut in retirement pay. Many are having to go back to work because of this.

There is now a cry from those retirees for the government to bail out the PBGC. How can the government do that when it can't bail out its own Social Security retirement plan? And if the government bails out the PBGC, will that mean the government will also have to bail out the millions of people with failed 401(k) plans?

In 2004, after his re-election, President George W. Bush began his campaign to *privatize* Social Security. In other words, turn the Social Security System into a government 401(k) plan. While I applaud his courage for taking on the problems of the Social Security System, I am afraid the people of America are not as courageous as he is. The people of America still live in hope that someone will take care of them financially and medically when their working days are over.

Missing The Biggest Boom Of All

In my opinion, worse than losing money, the tragedy of following the advice of "invest for the long term... buy, hold, and pray" is that the investor, the fool and his gold all failed to make money. The investors who followed Golden Rule #3 via their financial expert's advice missed out on the biggest financial boom in history.

While millions of investors were losing $7 to 9 trillion dollars between 2000 and 2003, other investors were making trillions of dollars.

The June 18, 2005 issue of *The Economist* said, "Measured by the increase of asset values over the past five years, the global housing boom is the biggest financial bubble in history."

In other words, looking back at the 10 years between 1995 and 2005, the decade where millions of people were invested in the stock market, especially mutual funds, and losing money, the biggest financial boom in history was taking place simultaneously. The reason they missed the boom was due to bad financial advice and being in the wrong market. The millions of people losing trillions were in the stock and bond market and were missing the boom that was taking place in the real estate, commodity, and currency markets.

In January of 2005, the same two attractive hosts welcomed their financial expert back on program. Once again, the attractive financial expert turns to the camera, smiles and says the same thing.

And that is why rich dad said Golden rule #3 was about *fools' gold*. If you followed the widely-accepted financial advice of "*work hard, save money, get out of debt, invest for the long term and diversify*", from 1995 to 2005, you were a fool who lost his gold and missed out on the biggest financial boom in history.

All Booms Bust

Before going further, I think it best to state that this book is *not* about real estate, oil and gas, gold, currencies or any investment in particular. This book is dedicated purely to financial education. While this book will be mentioning investments, such as real estate, currencies, and oil and gas, these asset classes are mentioned primarily as props or backdrops to clarify different points I think are important to make.

Assets Do Not Make You Rich

My primary objective in this book is to illustrate the power of good financial education versus bad financial education. Simply said, "Good financial education makes you rich and bad financial education makes you poor."

This book is about your personal responsibility to know if your financial education is making you richer or poorer. It is not stocks, bonds, mutual funds, real estate, gold, or oil and gas that make a person rich or poor. I know just as many people who lost money in real estate as people who lost money in the stock market. I also know of people who made fortunes in the stock market as the market crashed. In other words, *assets do not make you rich*. Ultimately, it is a person's financial IQ, their financial intelligence, not the asset, that makes a person rich or poor.

This book is being written in 2005. As I write, the world is in a panic buying real estate like there is no tomorrow. It is a bubble and no one knows when the bubble will burst. Just as in the dot-com era, people are saying, "This time it is different. The real estate bubble will not burst." For their sake, I hope they are right. Personally, I am a little bit older, wiser, and more cynical. In my reality, all booms bust. They have throughout history so why should this time be different? Just as novice investors rushed into the stock market in 2000, just before the crash, novice investors are rushing into the real estate market in 2005, just as the pros are getting out.

So once again, my reasons for writing this book are *not* to write about the glories of real estate, or

to criticize stocks, bonds, or mutual funds. My reasons for writing this book are in the interest of simple financial education and to point out how good financial education can make you rich and how a poor financial education can make you poor. This book is about teaching yourself and others to become rich, regardless of what asset you are investing in and whether the market is going up or down.

Why *Teach To Be Rich* **Works:** When you teach others to be rich, you are employing Golden Rule #1. That is why teaching others to be rich works in making you rich. It is also known as being generous, not with your money, but with your knowledge of money. If you are generous with your knowledge of money, you will gain more knowledge. And it is financial knowledge, your financial IQ, not money, that ultimately makes you rich. In fact, you will learn in this book that the higher your financial IQ, the less money it takes to become rich. And on the flip side, the lower your financial IQ, the more money it takes to become rich.

After raising your financial IQ you can begin to apply Golden Rule #2: "He or she who has the gold makes the rules." When you control the rules, it is definitely easier to become richer. And because they make the rules, the rich are becoming richer.

Another reason the rich are getting richer is because they do not have to follow the advice "Work hard, save money, get out of debt, invest for the long term, and diversify." This advice is good advice for the poor and the middle class; but not good advice for anyone wanting to become rich and, more importantly, remain rich. One must raise his or her financial IQ so they can see beyond common advice, and the best way to raise one's financial IQ is to teach others to raise theirs. And that is why *Teach To Be Rich* works. It is the first and only Golden Rule.

Chapter Two

IF I AM SO SMART WHY AM I NOT RICH?

In 1979, I was sitting quietly in the warm sun, gazing out at the ocean just beyond the white sand of Waikiki Beach. I had just come in from an early morning of surfing and was taking a short break before heading home. Tourists were beginning to arrive and hurriedly staking their claim in the sand. After spreading their towels and lathering themselves with suntan lotion, they would lay down to bake in the sun. In less than an hour, I knew the famed beach would be covered with bodies from all over the world. It was a ritualistic beach transformation I had witnessed for years… local surfers leave and tourists arrive.

In 1979, although I was living in paradise, my life was a mess. I had never been so miserable and depressed in my life. My nylon surfer wallet business was failing; I had no income, and owed nearly a million dollars to investors. Up to this time in my life, I had for the most part been successful. I had experienced setbacks before, but the loss of my once very successful business was a monster bigger than I could handle. More than the loss of money, and more than the embarrassment of facing friends, family and creditors, I had lost confidence in myself. I doubted myself. I was my own worst critic. My spirit was shattered. I now knew what the word *failure* meant.

Sitting in the sun with my surfboard at my side, I asked myself, "If I am so smart, why am I not rich?" I asked that question because, up to this point in my life, I thought I knew what to do. I thought I had all the answers. After all, I had been guided by my two good fathers, my real dad and my best friend's dad. I had gone to a very good school and had a college degree. I had also volunteered to serve as a military pilot in Vietnam rather than trying to hide from military service as many men my age did. I was successful in the corporate world with the Xerox Corporation, and my first big entrepreneurial venture, the nylon wallet business, was a great success until it failed. Yet with all my academic training, military training, and real-world business training, here I was 32 years old and a financial failure.

Once again I asked myself, "If you're so smart, why aren't you rich?" Again there was no reply. There was no answer. So I sat there silently watching the waves and the tourists staking their claims to their patch of the beach. Suddenly out of nowhere, I heard myself talking… at least it sounded like me. It seemed I was answering my own question and the reply was, "You will not become rich until you teach others to be rich."

With that I sat straight up in the sand and said out loud, "Teach?"

My outburst — "Teach?" — startled the couple baking in the sun in front of me. They raised their heads to see if I was all right, gave me a funny look, and returned to their face-down position, worshiping the sun.

"What do you mean teach?" I silently asked myself. "What do you mean I will not become rich

until I teach others to be rich?"

Just then, two boys chasing each other ran into my surfboard. One boy fell and cried. The other just laughed at his brother's wailing. Standing and helping the little boy up, I continued to ask for further clarification… I wanted to know what I meant by "You will not become rich until you teach others to be rich." But there was no answer.

Sitting for about ten more minutes, I hoped I would hear more. But all I heard were the sounds of music from the radios belonging to the sunbathers and the waves rolling up and over the beach. Finally I stood, dusted off the sand, picked up my board and headed home. I never heard that voice again… but I also never forgot what I heard.

Follow In Your Father's Footsteps

My dad, the man I call my poor dad, was a great teacher. He was dedicated to the profession of teaching. Late in his life, he was recognized as one of the two greatest teachers in Hawaii's 150 years of public education. It was this recognition that, I believe, brought peace to his troubled soul, just before he passed away. One of my most cherished possessions is the newspaper article about this recognition.

While growing up, many people would ask, "Are you going to become a teacher like your dad? He is a great teacher you know… and it would be good if you followed in his footsteps." Most of the time I would reply, "No, I do not want to be a teacher like my dad. I have no plans on following in his footsteps. I don't like school and I don't want to work there. I know school is important, but once I graduate from school, I never plan on going back." That usually ended the conversation.

Most of my family on my father's side was involved in the educational system of Hawaii. It almost seemed like nepotism. Because of this, I often felt trapped by the school system. At home, I was surrounded by teachers and at school I was surrounded by teachers.

Even on the athletic field, I was once again surrounded by my family of teachers. One of my dad's brothers was a great football star in high school and college, and could have gone on to the pros if he had not been wounded in Italy during World War II. So even when playing high school football, my coaches would report my progress back to my uncle or compare me to my uncle. I used to get sick and tired of having my coach say to me, "You're not as big as your uncle and not as fast," or "You don't have the killer instinct your uncle had."

So in 1979 at the age of 32, the last thing I wanted to hear was "You will not be rich until you teach others to be rich." Being a teacher was a profession I had spent my life avoiding. Not just because of my family but because I truly did not like school. I found school boring. On top of that, every time I asked my teacher, "How does this subject apply to the real world?" I never got a satisfactory answer. The most common answer I got was, "If you don't get good grades you won't get a good job." To which I would reply, "What if I don't want a good job? What if I don't want to be an employee? What if I just want to be rich?" Again, there never really was a satisfactory answer. Carrying my surfboard home that day in 1979 was a very disturbing day. I did not want to become a teacher… yet, I had received the answer to my question.

Rich Dad's Advice

Putting the idea of becoming a teacher aside, I headed home to get ready for lunch with my rich dad. In 1979, I had very big financial problems to handle so I would often meet with rich dad to figure out how to get out of the mess I had gotten myself into. My business was failing. I had many

money problems and problems with my partners. Before I could think about becoming a teacher, I needed to figure out how to pay nearly a million dollars back to investors and to the government.

If you have read my other books, you may already know that my rich dad was my best friend's father. He began teaching me, or mentoring me, when I was nine years old. All through school, he spent countless hours teaching his son and me his financial philosophies. He also had his son, Mike, and me work for him, after school and on weekends. Even though he paid us little, if he paid us at all, the lessons he taught his son and me helped us become financially successful adults. In other words, my real dad was a great teacher and so was my rich dad. The difference was, they taught very different subjects and had very different philosophies, especially when it came to the subject of money.

In 1979, with my business a mess and deeply in debt, my rich dad became an even more important teacher to me.

Lunch With Rich Dad

After a quick shower, I sat down to prepare my presentation to rich dad. I knew as soon as we sat down for lunch, he would ask, "What were your sales for the month?" The reason rich dad wanted the sales figures was that he had constantly reminded his son and me that "Sales equals income." He also said, "One of the reasons why people have low incomes is because they either cannot sell, or have nothing of value, such as a skill or talent, to sell."

I also needed to have my expense numbers, which meant I had to keep track of everything my business and I spent. Rich dad often said, "Expenses are more important than income." He also said, "Another reason so many people struggle financially is because they focus on income, how much they earn, rather than what they spend money on." He would repeatedly say, "Poor people are poor because they spend their *time* and *money* poorly."

Our lunch meeting was at his favorite restaurant. There were many tables available since it was a Saturday. As soon we sat down and got over the pleasantries, such as "How was the surf?" rich dad immediately asked "Do you have your sales report?"

As the meeting progressed, I remembered the idea I had earlier that morning, the idea that *I would not be rich until I taught others to be rich*. As I did my best to justify my low income and high expenses, I realized that rich dad was teaching me to be rich. "Was that why he was rich?" I asked myself. "In teaching me to be rich was he also teaching himself to be richer?"

Suddenly being more open to the idea of teaching, I stopped the lesson and asked rich dad "Are you learning as you are teaching?"

Rich dad chuckled, smiled, and said, "Of course. I'm not doing this just for you. I'm doing this for me. I learn something every time I teach. We may not be learning the same things, but I, too, am learning. There have been many a time I've been teaching you or Mike and suddenly a new idea pops into my head, or I see something completely differently. There has been many a time I have solved my own problems helping you solve your problems."

"So teaching me to be rich helps you become richer?" I asked.

"Absolutely," rich dad said with a grin. "Are you only realizing this now?"

"Yes, only now," I replied sheepishly. "I thought you were only doing this for me. I thought you were just doing me a favor."

Rich dad roared out loud. "I'll let you in on a big secret then," he said grinning from ear to ear.

"What secret?" I asked.

"Teach what you want to learn," rich dad said, smiling.

"Teach what I want to learn?" I said softly. "That means if I want to be a better golfer, I should teach golf?"

"Yes," nodded rich dad.

"But what if I am a lousy golfer?" I asked skeptically.

"Well, then you shouldn't teach golf," smiled rich dad. "Look, you have to be honest and responsible to be a teacher. If you teach what you are not interested in, or teach just to make money, then there is a lack of integrity."

"Integrity?" I asked. "Why is it a lack of integrity?"

"Integrity means whole," replied rich dad. "Have you ever had a teacher that taught a subject that he or she was not interested in… they only taught the subject because they were paid to teach?"

"I've met many of them," I said. "I've had many teachers who taught subjects they either did not really believe in, didn'tknow much about, or were not passionate about."

"And that is what I mean by a lack of integrity. Something was missing."

"So if I am passionate about learning then I could be a good teacher, even if I do not know much about the subject… yet."

"The more I teach, the more I learn. The more I learn, the better teacher I become."

"So passion is important in teaching?" I asked.

"Absolutely," said rich dad. "Passion to learn and a passion to help others. If you have those two traits, you have the potential to be a great teacher."

"So I would not make a great calculus teacher because I am not passionate about calculus and I do not know how calculus helps the average person."

"I did not need to study calculus to become rich," smirked rich dad. "All you need to become rich is to be able to read, write, do simple math, and have some common sense. Of the four, common sense is the most important. I've met many people who went to school and became very smart but lose their financial common sense."

As rich dad talked, my mind thought back to my dad, an academically brilliant man, a great teacher, who lost his job in his fifties, and was struggling financially in his so-called golden years. If not for Social Security, he would have been in dire financial straits.

"My dad was a great teacher," I said.

"I know," said rich dad. "He was a great teacher because he was passionate about helping kids learn. The problem was he taught kids subjects many of them would never use in the real world. When your dad lost his job, he found out how useless much of what he knew was in the real world of business. The problem with too many academics is that they have lost touch with the real world. School teachers are preparing kids for a world that no longer exists… like a world of job security and guaranteed pensions for life. By the year 2015, the world will wake up to how far behind and out of touch with the real world the world of education has been. Your dad is an early example of how ill prepared for the real world many people are."

"So even though I am a financial mess today, by going over my mistakes today at age 32, I'll be better prepared for the future?" I asked.

"Of course," said rich dad. "One of the reasons I spend my time with you is because I care about you. My concern is that you might end up like your dad. You know that your mom and dad are your

most influential teachers. The problem with your dad is that he is encouraging you to learn the same things he learned… subjects that only work inside the world of education. If you want to be rich or financially free at a young age, you will not learn what you need to learn in school."

"But I'm 32 and broke," I whined. "Most of my classmates have higher paying jobs. They are making more money than me."

"Yes, but they have jobs or professions. You are learning to be rich. If you want to be rich or financially free, you need to study different subjects. Besides, you should be grateful you messed up early in life. You don't want to get older, like your dad, when you wake up to a financial disaster."

"Can an older person learn?" I asked, hoping that there was hope for my dad.

"Sure, but it is harder," said rich dad. "There is some truth in that saying, 'You can't teach an old dog new tricks.' The older you are, the harder it is to change. It can be done… but it takes more work."

"But… " I said.

"Enough about your dad," said rich dad. "You are here and your dad isn't. You cannot teach someone who does not want to learn… or is not interested in what is being taught. Unfortunately, your dad is living in the past. He was an 'A' student in school but not today. He was successful when he was younger and but not when he is older. He is good man who spent his life learning and teaching subjects he could *not* use to make money with in the real world. Thank God the government is there to take care of him. If not for Social Security and Medicare, you would have two people to take care of financially, you and him… and right now you can barely take care of yourself. So enough about your dad. Right now I am interested in you because you are interested in learning… and so am I. Now back to learning from your mistakes."

Risking having my head bitten off, I pushed the subject one more step. "So at 32 years old, if I want to get richer faster, I need to teach other people to be rich?"

"That is one way," replied rich dad. "Teaching is not for everyone… but in your case I think you could be a pretty good teacher. It runs in your family. It starts with a desire to help others. Do you want to help others get rich?"

"Yes… I really do."

"Then teach," smiled rich dad. "But first you need to learn. Nothing is worse than a teacher who teaches a subject they do not know or are not passionate about."

Sitting at the lunch table with rich dad, I now understood what the voice I heard meant when it said, "You will not be rich until you teach others to be rich."

"OK, let's go over your expenses," interrupted rich dad.

As I fumbled through my briefcase for my monthly financial statement, the idea of teaching others was sounding more and more like a good idea.

Why *Teach To Be Rich* Works: Most of my life I was the class clown. I was never the teacher's pet. I did not like school and did not like what I was being required to learn. Hence, I never took my education seriously. I was always flunking out (or nearly flunking out) of school.

It was not until I decided to teach that my desire to learn increased. I realized that if I was going to teach others, I had a responsibility to them, for I was dealing with their minds. I did not want to be one of those people who mindlessly repeats back what they have been taught to say, for example, "If you don't get good grades you won't get a good job." Or, "Tomorrow you will take

your final calculus exam. If you fail this exam, you fail the entire year." Or " Work hard, save money, get out of debt, invest for the long term, and diversify." Instead of being a parrot, mindlessly repeating back what everyone else was saying, I wanted to be more like my rich dad and research what I was saying before I said it. I also did not want to be like most teachers who are told by the government or their administrators what they had to teach, even if they did not believe in what they were teaching. I also did not want to be a teacher who needed money and taught for the money.

Once I began to do my research, both into money and into how we learn, my eyes were opened to a world very few people ever see or know about. The more I researched, the more I learned; the more I learned the more I knew I did not know… so the more I researched. Because teaching is a huge responsibility to the student, I became a student for the first time in my life. When I became a student, I began to learn, and the more I learned, the smarter I became; and the smarter I became the richer I became, financially and spiritually. Most importantly, through teaching I found my life's purpose… and that purpose is to be a student who teaches other students to be free from the slavery of money and from those who seek to control their money.

When I was a kid, I swore I would never be a teacher. Thank goodness we are allowed to change our minds.

From 1979 to 1984, I studied education, how we learn, and how best to teach. In 1984, I began my professional career as a teacher. By 1994, I was financially free. Today I continue to study and to teach, and the money continues to pour in. I believe this happens because, as teachers, we follow Golden Rule #1 and Golden Rule #2. The Rich Dad Company does not subscribe to Golden Rule #3 as most teachers and financial experts do.

Chapter Three

WHY GOING TO SCHOOL
DOESN'T MAKE YOU RICH

In 1979, after deciding to be a teacher, I would often sit quietly and search my mind for memories of my family and their relationship to money. I knew that if I could recall my family's relationship to money, I would better understand my relationship to money. Sitting quietly one evening, I was reminded of my earliest memory of money and, unfortunately, it was not a pleasant memory. In fact, it was a painful one.

When I was seven years old, I remember waking in the middle of the night and finding my mom crying. She was sitting at our dining room table with a stack of envelopes in front of her. Walking towards her I asked, "What's wrong, Mom?"

Startled, she tried to wipe her tears away and hide the envelopes. "You frightened me," she said. "You should be in bed."

"Why are you crying?" I asked. "Is something wrong? Are you OK?"

"It's nothing that concerns you," said my mom. "You're too young."

"Too young for what?" I asked.

"To understand," said Mom, now beginning to smile and put on a brave face. "This is a problem adults have. It's not a problem for someone your age. You'll find out soon enough."

"Find out what?" I asked tired of being treated like a kid. "I already know something is wrong, so you may as well tell me."

My mom then showed me her monthly bank statement. In those days, the statement came on gold-colored paper. The number entries were typed by hand. The numbers started in black and a few lines down changed to red. "What do the numbers in red mean?" I asked.

"The color red means I wrote checks but I do not have enough money in my checking account to cover those checks," said my mom softly. "It means I'm overdrawn at the bank and the bank wants to know when they will receive their money. If I do not pay them, they will send the checks back to the people I wrote them to."

Not really understanding the whole problem, I asked, "Does Dad know?"

Mom nodded and said, "Yes, he knows we are short of money... but I try not to tell him too much. You know he's in school and he's working when he can. As soon as he graduates he'll find a good job and we won't have this problem anymore."

At the age of seven I felt an intense anger at my dad for not making enough money and making mom cry. I also felt extremely helpless, unable to help my mom. That single event changed my life's direction. From then on, I wanted to know why my dad could not provide enough money for our family. I began my search for answers and, two years later, I met my rich dad.

The year this occurred was 1954. In 1979, as I contemplated the idea of teaching, I reflected back

upon this incident with my mom. As I sat quietly, a short jolt of pain ran through my heart and I wished I could reach out and hug her as a grown man. Mom had died a few years earlier, a year before I went to Vietnam in 1972, and I still missed her a lot.

In 1979, I realized that if I was going to transition to teaching, I needed a reason to teach and my mom was my reason. I knew that for me to be successful I needed to be passionate about what I was going to do. The memory of my mom sitting at the dining table late that night was my reason. It provided the energy to begin my new profession in education.

The reason my mom was important to me was because mom suffered financially for years. Our family never had enough money. Even after my dad graduated from school and got the high-paying jobs, our family continued to struggle financially. My dad spent much of his adult life going back to school so he could get a higher government rating which meant an incremental pay raise. Yet, no matter how many pay raises he got, our family was always short of money… always in the red.

In 1979, the year I decided to become a teacher, my dad — now nearly 60 years old — was out of work. Although highly-educated and a good, hard-working man, he had run for Lt. Governor against his boss, the governor of the State of Hawaii, at the age of 52 and lost. The governor and his political party put my dad on notice that my dad would never get a job in state government again… and he never did.

In 1979, I decided to follow in my dad's profession but not in his footsteps. I vowed I would never be a teacher who worked for the government. Instead, I would be a teacher who taught people to be entrepreneurs and investors so they could possibly become financially free… rather than always need a job and money like my father did. In other words, I would begin to teach others the same lessons my rich dad was teaching me.

Passion Is Essential For Success

In 1979, it was the memory of both my mom and dad's financial struggles that gave me the passion to begin learning to teach and learning about money. If you look at anyone successful, I am certain you will find a person who has passion. As my rich dad said, "Passion is essential for success."

Although I never heard the message, "You will not be rich until you teach others to be rich" again, I knew what I had to do. At the age of 32, I embarked upon my new career as a student of learning. I also recommitted to become a better student of the lessons my rich dad had been trying to teach me for years. Instead of being the class clown, which I had been for most of my life, even through the military academy and through flight school, for the first time I wanted to take my education seriously. Through my mom and dad, I found a passion for learning I had never known before.

Why Let Money Run Your Life?

To me, it never made sense to let money dictate the boundaries of one's life. Having two dads gave me a perspective on life few people enjoy. My mom and dad suffered financially all their lives, no matter how much money they made. They constantly said, "We can't afford this or we can't afford that." Instead of figuring out how they could afford what they wanted in life, they let money dictate by saying "We can't afford it." They lived as frugally as possible, scrimping, saving, and never getting ahead financially.

My rich dad, on the other hand, got richer and richer although he never really had a job. He was

an entrepreneur and an investor. Although he did not have the advantages of the formal education my mom and dad did, he never let money, or his lack of it, get in the way of what he wanted to have in his life. He never said "I can't afford it." In fact, he forbade his son and me from ever saying those words. He would say, "Poor people say 'I can't afford' it more than rich people. That is why they are poor." Then I would go home and hear my mom and dad say, "We can't afford this," or "We can't afford that" over and over again and again. Reflecting on these differences I began to realize that money or the lack of money has nothing to do with one's education. It has more to do with one's basic attitude about money, an attitude we often learn from our family and from our teachers.

Although I knew it was too late to teach my mom and dad not to let money dictate their lives, I knew it was not too late to learn to teach others how to be masters of money rather than slaves to money. So in 1979, at the age of 32, my real education began.

Old And Out Of Money

As I began my new career, I began to realize that education had not just failed my mom and dad. Education's failure to teach us much about money was taking a devastating toll on millions of people.

For most of my life, I had often wondered why our school system teaches us to *work for money* but *teaches us very little about money*… but I never did much about my question. Once I decided to learn and look into the problem of money and education, I was shocked by some of the statistics I came across… interestingly some of the best information is provided by the government itself.

I once saw some statistics from the U.S. Department of Health, Education and Welfare. They found that for every 100 people, at the age of 65, the lack of financial education is apparent. At age 65:

> 1 – was wealthy

> 4 – were well off

> 5 – were working because they had to

> 36 – were dead

> 54 – were broke surviving off of family and the government.

Rich Dad Poor Dad

When I looked at these statistics, I realized my rich dad was that one person out of 100 who, at age 65, was in the wealthy category. My poor dad, a smart, hard-working, honest, highly-educated man, would be in the bottom category, one of the 54 that needed a government pension, Social Security and Medicare to survive. If not for government support, he would have had to move in with one of his children. My mom was in the group that passed away before the age of 65. Looking at these stats and comparing them to my family history, I realized that if I did not make some changes, I would either be dead or broke before age 65.

Young And In Financial Trouble

Today, the lack of financial education is not just affecting older people. Today, the lack of financial education is also affecting young people. The American Bankruptcy Institute states, that, during 2001, more young people declared bankruptcy than graduated from college. And our school system continues to teach us little, if anything, about money.

Why The Gap Gets Bigger

Most of us know that there is a growing gap between the *haves* and *have-nots*. As you can tell from the statistics, many people may find out at age 65 that they are in the have-not category, even though they were in the *have* category while working.

As I began my new career as a teacher, one of the next questions I wanted answered was why there was this gap between my rich dad and my poor dad at age 65, and if there always was a gap. My studies found that the gap between the *haves* and *have nots* is a relatively new human event… and it is growing.

Why The Gap Is Growing… Not Shrinking

Most of us know that humans have evolved through four socio-economic ages. They are:

1. The Hunter-Gatherer Age

2. The Agrarian Age

3. The Industrial Age

4. The Information Age

During the Hunter-Gatherer Age, humans were nomadic and lived in tribes. Although there was a chief, the chief had the same basic standard of living as the rest of the tribe. His hut or tent may have been bigger, but it was still a hut or a tent.

During the Agrarian Age, suddenly there was a king who lived on the hill in a fortress known as a castle. Ninety-nine percent of the people worked on the king's land and paid taxes to the king. So basically, there was one rich guy and his friends who lived very well, and everyone else was poor. So while there was a gap, most people were poor.

The Industrial Age, which began around 1500, gave rise to a new class of people, the middle class. The good news: A person's self-determination, education, and hard work could pull them out of the poor class and into the middle class, and possibly the rich.

The Information Age, which officially began in year 2000, ushered in a new kind of wealth. Young entrepreneurs such as Bill Gates, Steven Jobs, Michael Dell and Sergey Brin started companies, from nothing, that were soon worth more than General Motors. While some people are becoming billionaires or earning multi-million dollar salaries, the middle class is eroding and some of the middle class is sliding into the 20% of the population that is poor. Today, a person competing for your job may live in India or Ireland and is willing to work harder for much less money. In other words, in the Information Age, the income gap between the rich and everyone else is not just big… it is enormous and widening.

What Age Are You In?

Growing up in Hawaii, it saddened me to learn about the native Hawaiians losing their culture and land to people of European ancestry. I also learned that many indigenous people, such as the American Indians, Africans, and even Europeans, lost land to the Europeans. At first I thought it was racist. Yet, the more I learned, the more I realized it was not so much an issue of race as it was a difference in the Ages. The Hawaiian's culture operated in the Hunter-Gatherer Age and the Europeans

operated in the Industrial Age. In other words, it was more modern *information* that made one group the conqueror and the other the conquered. It was *information* that caused one group to gain wealth and caused the other group to lose wealth. The same thing is happening today.

Today, people with Industrial Age financial information are being left behind or even wiped out financially by those with Information Age financial information. Examples of Industrial Age ideas are:

1. "Job security."

2. "The company will take care of you once you retire."

3. "Social Security and Medicare will take care of you."

4. "Save money."

5. "Invest for the long term."

6. "Get out of debt."

7. "Turn your money over to an expert… someone you can trust."

Today, millions of people are falling behind financially because their information is obsolete. Their minds are filled with ideas from an age that has passed. In the Information Age, you will need Information Age financial education if you want to survive and get ahead. If you operate with Industrial Age financial information, you will probably be wiped out or left behind by those who have Information Age financial education.

Agrarian Age School System

Our school system is stuck in the Agrarian Age. That is why we have such a long summer vacation. It is not because the kids needed a break from school, but because, during the Agrarian Age, parents needed their kids to work on the farm during the summer harvest months. Today, even though fewer than 5% of us work on farms, our schools still think that kids need a long summer break in order to harvest the crops.

The problem with an educational system that is stuck in the Agrarian Age is that it continues to educate children for a world that is long gone. On top of that, it teaches at the same slow pace of the Agrarian Age. The education system cannot change fast enough in the Information Age. It has been said that by the time a child graduates from college, most of what they have been taught is obsolete. That is how fast information is changing in the Information Age.

Learning Is More Important Than Knowing

In the Information Age, how fast one can *learn and change* is more important than what a person knows. This book is about teaching and learning to be rich at a higher rate of speed. Why? Because the world is changing at a higher rate of speed.

Today, an investment opportunity appears and is gone in a split second. One of the reasons so many people got wiped out in the stock market crash was simply because they invested at a snail's pace, investing for the long term. In the Information Age, gaining wealth and keeping your wealth will mean you need to be faster, not slower. Instead of parking his or her money, a person needs to keep that money moving. As Bob Dylan sang years ago, "The Times They Are A-Changin'"… and they are changing faster and faster.

If you want to become wealthy and financially secure, investing with Agrarian or Industrial Age ideas will probably not work. In the Information Age you will need more information, more up-to-date information, and more speed. That will require learning faster because, in the Information Age, learning is more important than what you know… because what you already know is probably, obsolete.

In the Information Age, not only will the gap between the *haves* and *have-nots* grow… it will grow wider and wider… faster and faster.

Why *Teach To Be Rich* Works: In 1989, two events occurred that changed the world. In that year, the Berlin Wall came down. That signaled the end of the Industrial Age where people lived and operated behind walls. That same year, the World Wide Web went up. The Information Age had officially begun. The rules of the world have changed, but not everyone has noticed.

In the Industrial Age, we were taught to win by *competing*. Once the wall came down and the web went up, the new rules said that the way to win was by *cooperating*. With the advent of the Internet, people were less willing to allow people to exploit other people for personal gain. Also, people were demanding more accountability and transparency, which is why so many big corporations such as Enron, Arthur Anderson, and WorldCom were taken down.

Instead of taking the wealth of others, the new rules of the Information Age state that we had better start helping others keep their wealth and gain more wealth, which is why companies such as eBay have done so well. That company has helped many little people become rich (like the big people), and that may be one reason why it has done so well.

In the Industrial Age, *might was right*. If you were rich and powerful you could make the rules that made you rich. In the Information Age, the rules have changed. Instead of being greedy, if we earnestly assist others in becoming richer, we can become richer. After all, that is the first Golden Rule.

The Industrial Age was a *resource-based* era. That meant that only a few people could have wealth. For example, if you had oil on your land, you became wealthy. But your neighbor didn't. That is because, in a resource-based economy, there is a limited amount of materials. In the Industrial Age, economics was based upon the ideas of Thomas Malthus and is known as Malthusian Economics. Malthus, who was not an economist but a preacher, taught the world that *economics is the allocation of scarce resources*. The assumption of that economic theory was that there was not enough to go around and if I shared with you, I deprived myself. In other words, it was a *you **or** me* world, not a *you **and** me* world. That is why the Industrial Age was an age of power and greed and the Golden Rule that followed had been, "A fool and his gold work for those who have the gold and make the rules."

In the Industrial Age, the way to get rich was to make sure there were a lot of poor people. Poor people are always happy with a secure job. I found out that this need for workers who were poor is one reason why our schools do not teach us about money. If we knew about money, we would not be workers seeking job security. Instead of teaching people about money, the school system teaches people to work for the rich and then turn their money back over to the rich. This is Golden Rule #3 in action. This is how the rich got richer in the Industrial Age.

The Rules Have Changed

In the Information Age, the primary resource is *information*. The good thing about information is that the more we share information the more information expands; when it is shared it does not decrease… it multiplies. If I share an idea with you, the idea expands.

And that is why *Teach to be Rich* works. In the Information Age, the more I share, the richer I become because I have more rich people around me. After all, it is easier to get richer faster if there are more rich people around.

Remembering The Golden Rules

This book is about more than money and getting rich. It is really about the three Golden Rules.

This book began in the 1970s, when I came to terms with the realization that in order for me to become rich, I had to teach others to be rich. After all, it is the Golden Rule #1, "Do unto others as you would have others do unto you." It is also known as The Law of Reciprocity. In the Industrial Age, the way to get rich was by being greedy. In the Information Age, the way to get rich is by sharing. In other words, the rules have changed. So, for many people, the best way to get rich is by teaching and sharing what you know with others.

Golden Rule #2 states, "He or she who has the gold makes the rules." One of the reasons my poor dad had so very little power was simply because he was poor. He had no money. In the 1970s, I realized that if I was going to teach people about money, I had better practice what I preached. That is why I did not write *Rich Dad Poor Dad* until 1997, when I could prove that I had money and, more importantly, could hold on to my money. Between 2000 and 2003, while millions were losing trillions of dollars, some of those who followed my rich dad's advice made fortunes. I know I did.

One of the reasons so many financial experts have lost credibility with people is simply because, when the market crashed between 2000 and 2003, not only did those financial experts lose money, so did the people following their advice. In other words, in the Information Age, you'd better practice what you preach. In the Industrial Age, it was easy to lie. Things were not as transparent. Today in the Information Age, if you lie or cheat, or do not practice what you preach, the chat rooms and bloggers of the world will expose you.

Unfortunately, as we all know, there still are many people without gold telling people how to find gold. They are commonly known as financial advisors. Most of these financial advisors work for those who have the gold.

This leads to Golden Rule #3 which is, "A fool and his gold work for those who make the rules." Throughout history, many of the rich forgot about Golden Rule #1. Instead of teaching people how to be rich, they taught people to work for the rich and to blindly turn their gold over to the rich… for safe keeping.

Chapter Four

IS THERE A CONSPIRACY IN EDUCATION?

After deciding to become a teacher, I called my real dad and invited him to lunch. On the appointed day and time, he and I sat down in his favorite downtown Honolulu restaurant and I asked him, "Why did you decide to become a teacher?"

"Our family has had generations of medical doctors," he began. "Before my father, your grandfather, emigrated from Japan to Hawaii, our family had produced a long line of doctors."

"So what happened?" I asked.

"Your grandfather broke the chain when he emigrated from Japan to Hawaii," said dad. "He did not really emigrate from Japan… he ran away from his father. His father sent him to medical school in Tokyo, but instead of spending the money on his schooling, your grandfather spent the money on women and good times."

"So his father came looking for him?" I asked.

"Yes, he did. And when your grandfather heard that his father was coming after him, your grandfather changed his name and hopped on a boat heading for Hawaii. So he never became a doctor, yet he expected me to become a doctor."

"So what happened?" I asked. "Why didn't you go to medical school?"

"Well, I was going to be a doctor until one day I noticed my classmates disappearing. As the student body president of my class, I went to the principal and asked him where my classmates were going."

"And what did you find out?" I asked.

"It took some digging, but I found out that the owners of the sugar and pineapple plantations had a secret agreement with the school system to flunk 20% of each class every year," my dad said in a disturbed voice.

"Why would they do that?"

"So the plantations would always have a steady supply of uneducated workers who would work for low wages. They feared that a well-educated person could find a higher-paying job and would not work for the plantations at low wages."

"And that is why you became a teacher instead of a doctor?" I asked.

My dad nodded, "I felt it was important to do my best to give every child an equal opportunity to receive the best education possible."

Long after our lunch was over, I could not get my dad's words out of my head. It was not that I did not believe him, because I did. My dad was an extremely honest man. I just could not believe that people with money and power would stoop so low as to manipulate the education system just to insure a steady stream of low-paid labor. At the age of 32, I was finding out that Golden Rule #3 was alive and well.

Why The Rich Invest In Universities

In 1980, continuing on my quest to become a teacher of money, I traveled to Kirkwood Meadows, in California near Lake Tahoe, to spend a week with Dr. R. Buckminster Fuller, considered to be one of the greatest geniuses to have ever lived. The week was marketed as the Future of Business, so I was there to learn more about money and business. It turned out that more of Dr. Fuller's talk was on education than on business. He began talking about the same thing my dad had told me about… about how the rich contributed large sums of money to universities in order to find the brightest minds in the country and have them work for them.

Dr. Fuller said, "Harvard should be called J.P Morgan's School of Accounting and The University of Chicago is John D. Rockefeller's executive recruiting center." Dr. Fuller went on to say that many top universities are named after rich entrepreneurs such as Stanford, Duke, and Vanderbilt Universities.

As the conference went on, he said something to the effect of, "From the days of the kings and queens, the rich and powerful have controlled education." He went on to say that the kings knew that the way to conquer people was to keep people divided, keep them separated, and keep them from talking to each other. When the king found an exceptionally bright person, the education system would make them a specialist. For example, if a young person was good in math, that young person would be encouraged to be a mathematician or an accountant. If they were bright in science, they would be channeled into a field of science. By making them specialists via education, they spoke different languages, and could not talk to the other smart people. That kept the king in power because his brightest young people could not talk to each other, and none of them had the whole *generalized* picture he and the royal family had.

Today, you see this practice in business. That may be why so many entrepreneurs did not finish school. Instead of becoming specialists, they knew they had to be generalists who hired specialists such as accountants, attorneys, and engineers. Again, this is Golden Rule #3 in action. Or, as Dr. Fuller said, "To conquer… divide; and to keep conquering… keep dividing." That may also be why, in school, kids are taught to take tests alone, rather than to cooperate. We all know that two minds are better than one, except if you want to keep people divided and conquered.

At the end of the week-long seminar, Dr. Fuller encouraged us to become *generalists* so we would have a more comprehensive view of the world and be able to see the big picture of what was really going on.

After leaving the seminar I realized that it was because my dad was so highly specialized and that was why he was having trouble outside the school system. In fact, after the seminar with Dr. Fuller, I realized that people like my dad thought it important to be a specialist — *knowing a lot about a little* — rather than to be a generalist — *who knows a little about a lot.* Since I did not do well in school and I wanted to be an entrepreneur, I decided I would become a generalist who hired specialists. That is why, today, I make more money than most specialists who did well in school.

As I boarded the plane to head back to Hawaii, I remember feeling terribly uneasy that two men I respected, my dad and Dr. Fuller, had said basically the same thing about how the rich manipulated the educational system in order to ensure Golden Rule #3 prevailed.

The School System Is Broken

From 1979 on, I began to run into many people who were concerned about education. Most knew something was wrong, but no one knew how to change the educational system, which some say is the largest business in the world. Even though people acknowledged that the system was doing a horrible job educating kids, most parents did not want the system changed. When I talked to some of them about changing the system, a common response parents was, "You can change it after my child is out of school." Or "My kids are out of school and they did fine. So what's the problem?"

Many teachers wanted change, but many were like my dad, worn out from teaching kids and from fighting the system. And, of course, there were many businesses that were getting rich from all the tax dollars flowing into the educational system — and they definitely did not want the system changed. On top of that, there were the teachers' unions and they had another agenda that did not include educating kids.

So, while almost everyone I talked to about education agreed the system needed to be changed, most people were resigned to the idea that it could not be changed. They knew it was broken, but no one had the power or desire to fix it.

Teacher Of The Year

Then in the early 1990s, I began to hear of a teacher named John Taylor Gatto, one of the more outspoken and controversial critics of the system. Mr. Gatto was named New York State Teacher of the Year on three occasions. Then, suddenly, he quit the system — while still New York State Teacher of the Year — *claiming that he was no longer willing to hurt children.* He made his announcement in the *Wall Street Journal* in 1991. Needless to say he rattled a few remaining believers in the educational system, the few who believed that schools were doing a good job and kids were getting a great education.

He had also been included in *Who's Who in America* to 1996 and given the Alexis de Tocqueville Award for his contributions to the cause of liberty. Some of his books include, *Dumbing Us Down: The Hidden Curriculum of Compulsory Schooling* (1992); *A Different Kind of Teacher* (2000); *The Underground History of American Education* (2001); and others.

Curious, I began to read some of his books and transcripts of his speeches. It wasn't long before I realized he was saying the same thing my dad and Dr. Fuller were saying… that the rich had taken control of the school system and turned school into a factory to produce workers and consumers of products they produced.

Mr. Gatto has a lot to say that is important. Rather than attempt to duplicate what he is saying, if you are interested you can go to his website and find out more. For the scope of this book, I will simply include a few quotes and my comments on his statements.

Hijacking The School System

Gatto Quote:

"Between 1906 and 1920 a handful of world famous industrialist and financiers, together with their private foundations, hand-picked University administrators and house politicians, and spent more attention and money toward forced schooling than the national government did. Andrew Carnegie and John D. Rockefeller alone spent more money than the government did between 1900 and 1920. In this fashion the system of modern schooling was constructed outside the

public eye and outside the public's representatives.

"Now I want you to listen to a direct quote, I have not altered a word of this, it's certainly traceable through your local librarians. From the very first report issued by John D. Rockefeller's General Education Board — this is their first mission statement — 'In our dreams, people yield themselves with perfect docility to our molding hands. The present conventions of intellectual and character education fade from their minds and unhampered by tradition we work our own good will upon a grateful and responsive folk. We shall not try to make these people or any of their children into men of learning or philosophers, or men of science. We have not to raise up from them authors, educators, poets or men of letters, great artists, painters, musicians, nor lawyers, doctors, (he's really covering the whole gamut of employment isn't he?) statesmen, politicians, creatures of whom we have ample supply (whoever the pronoun we is meant to stand for there). The task is simple. We will organize children and teach them in a perfect way the things their fathers and mothers are doing in an imperfect way.'"

My Comments:

In other words, between 1906 and 1920, the rich and powerful hijacked the educational system without the public knowing about it. The rich and powerful decided to mold the minds of young people. In fact, in another speech, John Taylor Gatto states that the Western system of education comes from Prussia and the purpose of Prussian education was not to create people who could think, but rather create people who would follow orders and become good employees and soldiers.

"Current finance classes can help you do average."
–Warren Buffett

To me, it is arrogant of people like John D. Rockefeller to think they can do a better job at teaching a child than a parent. No wonder Dr. Fuller was often critical of John D. Rockefeller and people like him.

American Workers Live In A Constant State Of Panic

Gatto Quote:

Mr. Gatto quotes an article from *Foreign Affairs* magazine, written by Mort Zukerman, owner of *U.S. News and World Report.* Mr. Zukerman attributes the economic superiority of the U.S. to certain characteristics of the American worker and what the American worker is taught in school. Mr. Zukerman says, "Workers in America live in a constant state of panic, a panic against being left out, they know that companies owe them nothing, there is no power to appeal to management's decision. Fear is our secret supercharger, it gives management the flexibility other nations never have." Zukerman says that even after six years of economic expansion, American workers including management workers fret they might not survive. In 1996, almost half the employees of large firms feared being laid off. This is double the number fearful of being laid off in 1991 when things were not nearly as good as they are now. This keeps wages under control.

My Comments:

Any boss knows that fear is a powerful motivator. I often wonder how an employee can actually believe there is such a thing as job security. If a person had the proper financial education, they could be striving for financial security rather than job security. Once again, it is fear and a lack of an adequate education that causes many people to follow Golden Rule #3.

School Was A Lie

Gatto Quote:

"School was a lie from the beginning and continues to be a lie. You hear a great deal of nonsense these days about the need of a high tech economy for well educated people, but the truth staring you in the face is that it requires no such thing. As our economy is rationalized into automaticity, and globalization, it becomes more and more an interlocking set of subsystems coordinated centrally by mathematical formulae which simply cannot accommodate different ways of thinking and knowing. Our profitable system demands radically incomplete customers and workers to make it go. Educated people are its enemies, so is any non-pragmatic morality."

My Comments:

My interpretation of what Mr. Gatto is saying is that the rich needed customers and workers to grow the economy. So the educational system is a lie. It was never meant to educate. Its purpose was to impose Golden Rule #3, to create people who would *work* for the rich, *buy* from the rich, and *give* their money back to the rich, for the long term, so the rich could use the workers money to make the rich richer. It is for this reason, Golden Rule #3, why I believe the subject of money is not taught in school.

Retarded Maturity

Gatto Quote:

"The secret of American schooling is that it doesn't teach the way children learn — nor is it supposed to. Schools were conceived to service the economy and the social order rather than kids and families — that is why it is compulsory. As a consequence, the school cannot help anybody grow up, because its prime directive is to retard maturity. It does this by teaching that everything is difficult, that other people run our lives, that our neighbors are untrustworthy, even dangerous. School is the first impression children get of society. Because first impressions are often decisive ones, school imprints kids with fear, suspicion of one another, and certain addictions for life. It ambushes natural intuition, faith, and love of adventure, wiping these out in favor of a gospel of rational procedure and rational management."

My Comments:

Personally, I especially liked this statement. His comment on *schools not teaching kids the way they learn* is one of the first things I found out in 1979, when I began studying how we learn. Students like me, who did not like sitting and listening, did very poorly in school. I needed activity to learn. I do not my teachers knew how painful it was to be constantly labeled *stupid* or a *problem child* simply because I could not sit still to listen or to read. Today, if I were in school, I would be the poster child for Ritalin.

His comment, *schools were conceived to service the economy and the social order*, was what I found out in 1980, once I began to search for answers about money and why money was not a subject taught in school. I, too, found that the main purpose of schools was to provide workers for the rich, in order to make the rich richer, rather than support workers to be able to provide for their families.

His comment — "*As a consequence, the school cannot help anybody grow up, because it's prime directive is to retard maturity,*" hit home for me personally. My poor dad, the person who did not become a

"It has been helpful to me to have tens of thousands (of students) turned out of business schools taught that it didn't do any good to think."

–Warren Buffett

medical doctor in order to save his classmates, did not realize how ill-prepared he was for the real world until he left the school system and went broke. My dad, although well-educated, did not have the financial maturity to survive in the real world. The only place he could survive was in the government system, a system that took care of him. Once he went against the system, the system spit him out.

Take Something Simple And Make It Difficult

I completely agree with Mr. Gatto when he says, "It does this by teaching that everything is difficult, that other people run our lives, that our neighbors are untrustworthy, even dangerous." In my other books I wrote that school takes something simple and makes it more complex. For example, they take simple addition and subtraction and turn it into calculus. So in school, the road to success is to take something simple and make it complex. In the world of business, the road to success is the opposite. A business person needs to take the complex and make it simple. For example, I do not have any idea how a cell phone works, yet, because it is simple to use, I pay for the use of it. If they made it more and more complex to use, fewer and fewer people would use the cell phone and the cellular phone businesses would go broke.

The part I especially agree with is the line, *that other people run our lives*. When I read that line, I immediately thought of Golden Rule #3. When it comes to money, we are taught to *work* for the rich, *buy* from the rich, and then *turn* our money over to the rich, for the long term. That is why we constantly hear over and over again, "Work hard, save money, get out of debt, invest for the long term and diversify."

In 1974, when the 401(k) plan got its start with ERISA, that law basically said, "Turn your money over to the rich so we can become richer." And millions upon millions of people dutifully did as they were told. Most did so because they were never taught about money in school; they believe that investing is risky, and that someone else is smarter than they are and should be in charge of managing their money.

Between the years 2000 and 2003, a few of these dutiful people suddenly found that their financial experts could not protect them from a market crash, and many had their retirement plans robbed. I say robbed because we all know that money is not really lost. It simply changes hands.

Imagination Is More Important Than Knowledge

When Mr. Gatto said, *"It ambushes natural intuition, faith, and love of adventure, wiping these out in favor of a gospel of rational procedure and rational management,"* I almost cried. I remember in school being forced to color inside the lines of the coloring book. I did not want to color inside the lines. I wanted a blank sheet of paper.

Today, one of the reasons I succeed in business is because I always remember one of Dr. Albert Einstein's sayings, which goes, *"Imagination is more important than knowledge."* Every time I find myself having difficulty solving a problem, be it a financial, business, or personal problem, I remind myself of his quote and shift to the use of my imagination. I have come to realize that problems are only symptoms of rational thinking and an uncreative mind. In other words, *the only reason a problem is a*

*problem is because I am using an **old** solution to solve a **new** problem.* To solve a new problem requires imagination, intuition, faith, a love for adventure.

Is There A Conspiracy?

So is there a conspiracy in education? My answer is that there seems to be one. You can draw your own conclusion.

In 1994, I went to see rich dad in the hospital. He was very ill. As I sat by his bedside, I told him about my dad, Dr. Fuller, and John Taylor Gatto's comments on education. I asked him what he thought about a conspiracy in education against the worker. His reply was, "So what if there is one? What difference does it make?"

"You mean you're not concerned?" I asked.

"It's not that I am not concerned," he said. "The real question is 'What can I do about it?'" Rich dad went on to say, "All my life I have heard of conspiracies. People such as John D. Rockefeller and Andrew Carnegie were often referred to as Robber Barons. I remember the JFK assassination conspiracy. It's probably true. JFK and his brothers pissed-off a lot of people and would not play ball. That's the risk you take in life. So conspiracy in education is just one more conspiracy. So what? Life is full of conspiracies… big ones and small ones. It's human nature."

"What other conspiracies have you heard of?" I asked.

"I think the U.S. Federal Reserve Bank is an interesting conspiracy," smiled rich dad. "It is true that the Federal Reserve Bank is not an agency of the federal government and many people think it is. It is really a private institution that is controlled by some of the richest families in the world, and most are not Americans. And the Federal Reserve determines the money policy, not only of the U.S. but of the world."

"Who are these people or groups of people?" I asked.

"Oh, I don't remember all of them, but one group is the Rothchilds of London and Berlin, and the Lazard Brothers of Paris. The others whose names escape me come from Italy, Germany, the Netherlands, and a few from New York. These are the people who determine the money policies of the world, not just the U.S."

"You mean they make the rules," I said.

"Exactly," smiled rich dad with a sly grin. "Always remember what I taught you about Golden Rule #2: He who has the gold makes the rules."

Nodding I smiled and said, "Got it."

"You see, if you gave more money to the school system than the government did, then I am sure the school system would let you make the rules. That is why Harvard is one of the richest organizations in the world. Many rich people donate money to the school in the hope of influencing the rules and the graduates. It's about personal ego, power, and greed more than a conspiracy against the poor."

There was a long pause as I just sat there and let what rich dad was saying sink in. "So that is why you've always thought it important for me to learn about money and to become rich. You wanted me to have the gold so I could make my own rules."

Rich dad nodded, "You see many people poor people — people without the gold — conjure up all these conspiracies. There is the IRS and taxation conspiracy, The New World Order conspiracy, and

even the United Nations conspiracy."

"Are they really conspiracies?" I asked.

"Probably," smiled rich dad. "Ever since the days of the caveman, humans have been conspiring against one tribe or another, one person or another. Look at the business world. So many people who have no gold are fighting for a higher rung on the corporate ladder or the corner office. They never ask themselves who owns the ladder or owns the building the corner office is in. They conspire against fellow workers and miss the big picture, failing to see who is really in control of the whole game."

"Golden Rule #2," I said in a whispered tone.

Rich dad smiled and continued saying, "Even if there was a conspiracy, it was a conspiracy that did a lot of good. Look at how high our standard of living has risen, even if the rich got very rich and manipulated the system. We all live a better lifestyle today... even the poor. Today the poor live better, travel better, have access to better healthcare than even the richest people did a hundred years ago. A hundred years ago, even if you were a king, you could not fly from California to New York, or from New York to London. Today, even the poor fly."

"So the end justifies the means?" I asked.

"No, I did not say that," said rich dad. "I'm saying that every coin has two sides. You need to look at both sides to see the whole picture."

"So I need to decide which side of the coin I live on?" I asked.

"That's how I see it," said rich dad. "Again, the question is what are you going to do about it? If you have no gold, there is very little you can do. You can complain all you want and you will still have no gold, and no power. That is why I kept hounding you to learn about money, learn about the laws, acquire your wealth, find your gold, become financially free so you can play your own game according to your own rules. Many people want to play by their own rules but they don't have any gold... so instead of going out and getting their own gold, they complain about conspiracies, just like dogs barking at the moon.

"I know there are two sides to every coin and two sides to the bargaining table. If I have the gold I sit on one side of the table, and if I have no gold, I sit on the other side. I just think people should be told the truth."

Two Sides Of The Table

"Most people see only one side of the table all their lives," I said. "Can't they see the other side of the table?"

"No, not if that is the only side they have ever known. Besides, many people are happy being employees — happy to have someone else run their lives, tell them how much money they can make, what to invest their money in, and when they can go on vacation. Not everyone wants what we want," said rich dad. "Being rich and keeping my wealth has not been easy for me. It may be easy for some people, but it has not been easy for me."

"So most people sit on the other side of the table because they want to," I said seeking clarification. "It's the easier side to sit on. That's why so many people are on that side."

Rich dad nodded, "If you want to be the person sitting at the table offering the job, then listen to what I have to say. If you want to be the person sitting at the table asking for the job, then go to school and do what they say. But you will never have the gold if you listen to only what your teachers say. All you'll have is a paycheck and, hopefully, a retirement plan... but that is not real gold, that's

fool's gold."

I could tell he was tiring and needed his rest. It was late and the sun was going down. I could tell his condition was not getting better. So I thanked him, gave him a hug and left the room.

Why *Teach To Be Rich* Works: In 1994, Kim and I sold our educational business and retired. We never had to work for the rest of our lives. Kim was 37 years old and I was 47.

In 1994, all we had coming in was approximately $10,000 a month in passive income, and we had approximately $3,000 a month in expenses. It was not much money when compared to the Rockefellers or Andrew Carnegie. The most important thing I realized was that my real wealth was not measured in dollars. My real wealth was that I had learned how to play the game of money according to the rules of the rich. Rich dad had taught me the game of the rich, a game very few people know.

In 1996, I developed CASHFLOW 101, a board game that teaches the game of money the way the rich play. CASHFLOW is the only game in the world that does that.

By 2005, our passive income has increased to $300,000 a month, not including our paychecks, with approximately $30,000 a month in expenses. Our goal is to have $1 million a month passive income by 2010. How are we going to do it? By playing the game according to the rules of the rich, the same game and skills taught in CASHFLOW 101 and 202.

Why do we want to get to $1 million a month in passive cash flow? Because it is just a game we like to play. Some people like golf and some like tennis. But playing the CASHFLOW game in real life is a fun game; it is far more exciting and profitable than complaining and worrying about all the conspiracies in the world.

Chapter Five
HOW TO BECOME FINANCIALLY FREE

In the summer of 1994, I began designing the educational board game CASHFLOW 101. In November of 1996, the game was played for the first time at an investment seminar in Las Vegas, Nevada.

You will notice that on the game board pictured below, there are two tracks. The smaller circular track is known as the Rat Race. The larger outer track is known as the Fast Track.

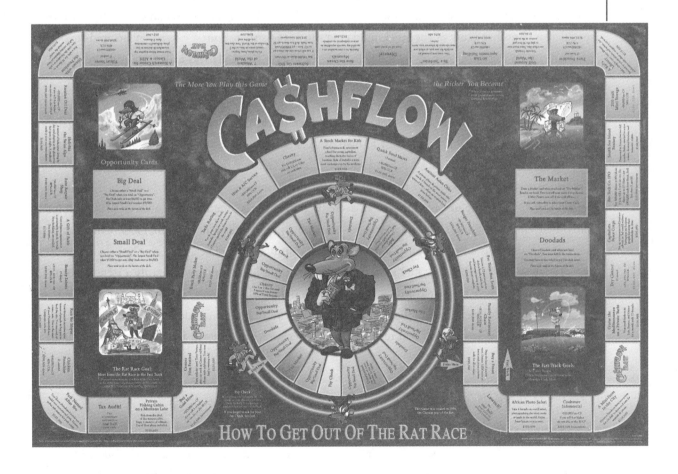

In designing the game, I wanted the player to see and experience the complete, bigger picture of the real world of investments. Simply said:

1. **The Rat Race:** Investments for the poor and middle class

2. **The Fast Track:** Investments for the rich

In *Rich Dad's Guide to Investing*, I wrote about returning from Vietnam and learning that rich dad's and his son Mike's investments were earning very high returns, making them richer and richer… and when I asked if I could invest in, rich dad told me I was not allowed to invest in the same investments, because I was not rich. In 1974, I learned that one of the reasons the rich get richer is because they have access to better investments than the poor and middle class do. It seemed like a Catch-22 — if I wanted to invest to become rich, I first had to be rich.

During my further studies and research into money and investing, I learned that in 1933, Joseph Kennedy, father of former President John F. Kennedy, was one of the creators of what I call the Fast Track. You may recall from history that in 1933 America was in an economic depression. Some people believed, at that time, that one of the causes of the depression was over speculation in the stock market, and many of the speculators were poor and middle class people who could not afford to be speculators. Another cause of the stock market crash was less than honest entrepreneurs and stock promoters who were not playing by the rules. Hence Joseph Kennedy was called upon to create the SEC, the Securities and Exchange Commission, the government body in charge of creating and enforcing the rules of stock market investing.

Obviously, Joseph Kennedy did not create the Fast Track; that is a concept created for the game. But he did create a category of investor known as the *accredited investor*. This class of investor was supposed to have a high financial IQ and money to spare, money to invest and possibly lose. Unfortunately, there is no official financial IQ test, so the only test is primarily how much income a person earns. Today the so-called test of an accredited investor is an annual income of $200,000 for an individual, or $300,000 for a couple, or a net worth over one million dollars. In 1933, when the SEC was created, that was a lot of money, since the average annual salary back then was less than $5,000 a year. Today, a $200,000 to $300,000 salary is an upper middle class salary… hardly a rich person's salary, especially when compared to the multi-million dollar salaries many business executives and entertainment stars receive today. That means more and more people are qualified to invest in Fast Track investments. But the problem remains: How does someone know if they have a high enough financial IQ?

Out Of The Rat Race

In 1984, Kim and I were flat broke. In 1984, I gave up my interest in the nylon and Velcro surfer wallet manufacturing business, and officially began my next career as a teacher. I write about this tough transition in *Rich Dad's Before You Quit Your Job*, a book on my real life lessons as an entrepreneur. Up until the time I entered the education profession, I thought being a *manufacturing* entrepreneur was hard. In 1984, I soon learned that becoming rich and successful as an *educational* entrepreneur was harder than becoming rich as a manufacturer. The education business is not the same business as the manufacturing business and that was one of my lame excuses for being broke in 1984. Obviously, there were other factors that caused our financial and business struggles, and I cover them

in *Rich Dad's Before You Quit Your Job*.

Ten years later, by 1994, Kim and I were out of the Rat Race. We were not rich, but we were financially free at relatively young ages. Kim was 37 and I was 47. We had approximately $10,000 a month in passive income and approximately $3,000 a month in expenses. We were not rich, but barring any financial disaster, we would never have to work for the rest of our lives. And we did it without a government or corporate retirement plan, disability payments, mutual funds, stocks, an IRA or 401(k)-type retirement plans or financial planners — or savings. We definitely did not follow the advice of *work hard, save money, get out of debt, invest for the long term, and diversify*. We did it purely by following my rich dad's lessons on money, business, and investing. Instead of turning our money over to so-called financial experts, as Golden Rule #3 recommends, we became our own financial experts and took control of our own money. If we had not done that, and had instead followed the advice of the financial experts, I suspect that Kim and I would still be in the Rat Race today and worried about how we can afford to retire and live a long life, free from the worry about having enough money to survive on.

Get Out Of The Rat Race

When you look at the picture of the CASHFLOW game board, you will notice sandwiched between the Rat Race and the Fast Track are spaces allocated for different event and opportunity cards.

You will notice that there are Big Deal and Small Deal cards. There are also event cards labeled Market Cards and Doodad cards. The way Kim and I got out of the Rat Race in real life was by first investing in small deals and then big deals. As market conditions changed, as represented by the Market Cards in the game, we were able to take advantage of the market events such as market booms and busts.

Fool's Gold

In real life, most people do not invest in small deals, big deals, or pay attention to the market. Yet in real life, most people are definitely aware of the Doodad cards. On the CASHFLOW game's Doodad cards you can find such tasty treats as a new boat, a cappuccino, designer sunglasses, and other must-have items of consumerism. In other words, Doodads are fool's gold… because Doodad's are what fools think are valuable… such real life items as $100 basketball shoes or designer jeans.

As the game progresses, it becomes painfully obvious that Doodads prevent people from getting rich. After people have played the game several times, you can hear a groan when their playing piece lands on a space requiring them to draw a Doodad card. Many adults do not like the game because the game reminds them of the high cost of their real life love of Doodads. Many parents have said, "Because my kids love playing the CASHFLOW game, every time we go shopping, they now point to the items of consumer necessity, such as new tennis shoes or jeans, and say "Doodads." Some go on to say, "Whenever I look at a new purse or new piece of jewelry, my kids point and say "That's a Doodad." Instead of spending their money on Doodads, they are saving their money to invest so they can get out of the Rat Race." To me, that means the educational lessons embedded in the game are transferring to real life.

In June of 2005, I had the pleasure of meeting one of the smartest young people ever. His name is John Paul and he was just 10 years old. John Paul has read every Rich Dad and Rich Dad Advisor book, and is an avid fan of the CASHFLOW games, both 101 and 202, and both the board games and the electronic versions.

Impressed with his understanding of the Rich Dad messages, I invited him on stage with me. While sitting behind the curtain, waiting for the program to begin, John Paul was having a discussion with Michael Lechter and Garrett Sutton, both Rich Dad Advisors. Michael Lechter is an attorney specializing in Intellectual Property and OPM (Other People's Money). Garrett Sutton is our advisor on legal entities such as corporations and limited partnerships. Both attorneys said, "John Paul has a profound understanding of the law and asked us some very tough questions." Garrett Sutton said, "When I asked him what bad legal entities were, John Paul immediately said, 'Sole proprietorships and partnerships.' Most business people don't know that," said Garrett in amazement. "That is why so many small business owners are sole proprietors or are in partnerships, the worst forms of legal entities possible."

After finishing his talk on stage to an audience of over a 1,000 people, a task most adults would shy away from, I asked him what he wanted for his 11th birthday. Without hesitation he said to the audience, "An investment property with positive cash flow." I doubt this young man will ever know what the Rat Race is.

The Golden Rules

Once again, looking at the game board, you can see other embedded lessons are:

On the Fast Track, Golden Rule #2 is king. Golden Rule #2 is one of the reasons why investors can achieve much higher returns than investors in the Rat Race. On the real-life Fast Track, the players make the rules, according to the rules of higher governing bodies such as the Securities and Exchange Commission (SEC). That is why the Rich Dad's Advisors are such an important aspect of the Rich Dad education and featured in our product line. Simply put, if you're going to invest on the Fast Track, you must have the best professional advice.

The masses of people who invest in the Rat Race really do not need much professional advice, such as legal, accounting, and corporate advice. People who invest in stocks, bonds, REITS, index funds, and mutual funds are investing in what I called "pre-packaged investments." To me, investing in those types of investments is like going to the supermarket and buying selected cuts of meat that are neatly packaged under the guidance of the federal government. If the shopper actually saw how the animal was slaughtered before it appeared in these neat, sanitized packages in the grocer's meat department, many shoppers would become vegetarians. The same is true with stocks, bonds, and mutual funds.

Personally, I enjoy the Fast Track, which is my way of saying I enjoy being on the inside and participating before the packaging of the investment. As an entrepreneur, rather than an employee, I enjoy having control over the rules. I have never liked people telling me when to come to work, how much money I could make, when I could eat lunch, or when I could go on vacation. So investing on the Fast Track fits my true character.

The Fast Track has investments that make money, and other investments that support socially responsible causes, such as investing in libraries or parks in the inner cities. While such investments do not pay much in dollars, they do pay well in the world of the soul, in the form of spiritual money, which is the best kind of money.

As a side note, in *Rich Dad's Before You Quit Your Job*, a book of ten real-life entrepreneurial lessons, I write about the three kinds of money. They are:

1. Competitive money (the money most people work for)

2. Cooperative money

3. Spiritual money

If you would like to learn more about the differences between entrepreneurs and employees and these three types of money, you may want to read *Rich Dad's Before You Quit Your Job*.

Journey To The Fast Track

When designing the board game, I built into the game the same objective my rich dad proposed to me. Years ago he said, "In the real world of investing, the ultimate games of money are played on the Fast Track. If you want to become very rich, you need the financial education that will qualify you to play the game of money at that level."

"Don't I also need money?" I asked.

"No, you don't," smiled rich dad. "If you're in the Rat Race, you need money… but not on the Fast Track. The Fast Track requires a high financial IQ. The higher your financial IQ, the more money you will make, even if you have no money."

"That doesn't make much sense," I said in a confused tone.

"It doesn't make any sense to those who invest in the Rat Race. But once you gain the required financial IQ, a whole new world, a new reality, is presented to you."

Puzzled, I thought in silence for a while. Things did not make sense. Finally I asked, "So when a person is classified as an accredited investor because they have income over $200,000 a year, that really is not a qualification. I mean just because a person has money does not mean they know how to invest on the Fast Track."

"Exactly," said rich dad. "Many high-income people who migrate from the Rat Race to the Fast Track become the victims of the more unscrupulous players who operate on the Fast Track. They have the money, but they lack the financial IQ. In the investment world, there is a standing joke about medical doctors constantly being conned or cheated by hustlers and promoters of Fast Track deals."

"The doctors have the money, but not the education," I added.

"They have the medical education, but not the financial education," said rich dad.

"So financial education is more important than money on the Fast Track."

"Absolutely," said rich dad. "If you have money but no financial education, the money is soon gone on the Fast Track. If you have a strong financial education, you can make a lot of money — more money than most people can dream of — even if you have no money at all."

Approximately 30 years after this conversation with rich dad, I found out that he was telling me the truth. Today, I make more money in a month *without working* than many educated people such as

school teachers do in 10 years, working for money. That is the value of investing in your financial education.

Raising Your Financial IQ

Pictured below is the simple line drawing of a financial statement.

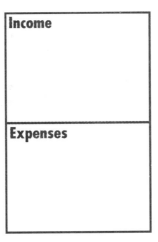

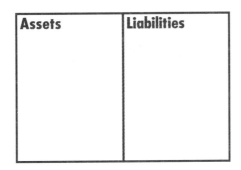

It was a drawing like this that I used to explain rich dad's lessons in *Rich Dad Poor Dad*. If you have not read that book, I strongly recommend you read it, even before finishing this book. From here on, the lessons in this book will assume you have already read *Rich Dad Poor Dad*. It is a simple book with many deeper lessons. And I believe you will find still deeper insights hidden in the original book, once you have finished this book.

Pictured on the next page is the financial statement used in the CASHFLOW games. You may notice that it is more detailed, in-depth, and complex.

I believe this financial statement is what sets my board game apart from other board games. In fact, I often say that the financial statement used in the CASHFLOW game is the *real* game board. In other words, the game board found in the board game is not the real game board… the financial statement is.

The financial statement makes the CASHFLOW game a true educational game. It also makes the game more difficult since there is so much more to learn and more to comprehend. That is why I recommend investing at least four hours the first time you play the game. These first few hours will get you acquainted with the game, a new vocabulary, and the operating systems of the game. After you play the game once, I then recommend you play it at least 10 more times. Each time you play it, you

will find and learn something new — if you are playing it properly and according to the rules. There is a lot of information hidden, buried, and embedded in the game. The only way for you to find the information is to play the game, which is why the slogan on the box says, "The more you play this game, the richer you become." You become richer because your financial IQ goes up each and every time you play the game. Your financial IQ is real gold… rather than fool's gold.

Profession _____ ## Player _____

Goal: To get out of the Rat Race and onto the Fast Track by building up your Passive Income to be greater than your Total Expenses

Income Statement

Income

Description	Cash Flow
Salary:	
Interest:	
Dividends:	
Real Estate:	
Businesses:	

Auditor _____
Person on your right

Passive Income= _____
(Cash Flows from Interest +
Dividends + Real Estate + Businesses)

Total Income: _____

Expenses

Taxes:	
Home Mortgage:	
School Loan Payment:	
Car Payment:	
Credit Card Payment:	
Retail Payment:	
Other Expenses:	
Child Expenses:	
Bank Loan Payment:	

Number of
Children: _____
(Begin game with 0 Children)
Per Child
Expense: _____

Total Expenses: _____

Monthly Cash Flow: _____
(Pay Check)

Balance Sheet

Assets				Liabilities	
Savings:				Home Mortgage:	
Stocks/Mutual's/CDs	No. of Shares:	Cost/Share:		School Loans:	
				Car Loans:	
				Credit Cards:	
Real Estate:	Down Pay:	Cost:		Retail Debt:	
				RE Mortgage:	
Business:	Down Pay:	Cost:		Liability: (Business)	
				Bank Loan:	

©1996-2002 CASHFLOW Technologies, Inc. All rights reserved. CASHFLOW games are covered by one or more of the following US Patents; 5,826,878; 6,032,957 and 6,106,300. RichDad®, CASHFLOW® and Investing 101® are registered trademarks of CASHFLOW® Technologies, Inc.   G101CT17

The Magic Key

In the coming chapters, you will find that the magic key to great wealth is found in the financial statement. Soon you will find that the simple line diagram below holds the key to unlimited wealth, if you are willing to understand the financial power that this overly-simplified diagram represents. The reason I recommend people read or reread *Rich Dad Poor Dad*, to better understand the six simple lessons my rich dad passed on to me. After reading this book, rereading *Rich Dad Poor Dad*, and playing the CASHFLOW game, I believe you will begin to see a world very few people see… a world of unlimited money and wealth.

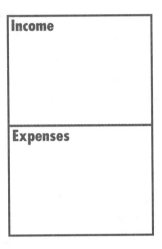

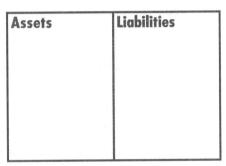

What Some People Do Not Want You To Know

In the next part of this book I will go deeper into the financial statement and you will soon see why I call it the magic key. I will go into Rich Dad lessons I have never discussed before. In Part II of this book you will find out why the philosophy of "work hard, save money, get out of debt, invest for the long term, and diversify," is not good advice, but really a *sales pitch* from the most powerful people on earth — the people who own and control the banking industry.

Now I am not saying they are bad people (or good people for that matter). As stated earlier in this book, there are two sides to every coin. The object of this book is to point out that on one side of the bargaining table there are people who make the rules and on the other side of the table sit the people who are required to follow the rules, these people make.

I am writing this book to give you a choice as to which track you want to operate on, and which of the three Golden Rules you want to follow. I made my choice in 1974, when rich dad pointed out

to me that there were investments for the rich, on the Fast Track, and investments for everyone else, those found in the Rat Race. I wanted out of the Rat Race so I chose to operate according to the rules of the rich as well as personally follow the first two Golden Rules. I definitely did not want to follow Golden Rule #3.

Why *Teach To Be Rich* Works: In very simple terms, I did not want my money and me to work for the rich. I wanted to my money and me to work for me… so I could become rich. In order to do that, I needed to learn as well as teach.

One of the reasons teaching was such an important part of my development process was because each time I taught someone what my rich dad taught me, I better understood my rich dad's lesson. In other words, by teaching others what rich dad taught me, I got more into rich dad's world and could see his world through his eyes. Even today, when teaching someone else, I suddenly better understand a lesson rich dad was trying to get into my thick head years ago. That is why I recommend you read or reread *Rich Dad Poor Dad,* before or after finishing this book. I believe you will more clearly see a world very few people ever see.

As I got more into rich dad's world, old financial beliefs that used to make sense suddenly made no sense at all. For example, I often wondered why my poor dad always said "Save money" while my rich dad did not believe in saving money. Because I had my poor dad's ideas on saving money, I could not understand my rich dad's point of view. Then one day, while doing my best to explain to a friend why rich dad thought that saving money was foolish, I suddenly made a mental shift, and I saw rich dad's point of view. Today, I do not save money. Today, I understand why rich dad often said, "Savers are losers."

After you play the CASHFLOW game several times and teach a number of people how to play the game, I am pretty certain you will learn why saving money makes no sense for a person with a higher financial IQ. You see, saving is a good idea for most people, but not for those few people who know how to keep their cash flowing. Once I understood my rich dad's point of view on saving money, my mind opened up and caught a glimpse of a world very few people ever see… a world of so much money that saving money made no sense… a world that someone like Bill Gates lives in, a world beyond being financially free. Bill Gates found this world through computer software and I found this world — obviously, not on the same scale as Bill Gates — by teaching myself and others to be rich.

INTRODUCTION TO PART II

The Price Of Advice

In the mid-1970s, when I was working for the Xerox Corporation in Honolulu, Hawaii, the company sent a group of us to a financial planning seminar. We were served the standard hotel banquet lunch, the speaker got up and began talking about the 3-legged stool of financial planning.

The diagram below is the 3-legged stool:

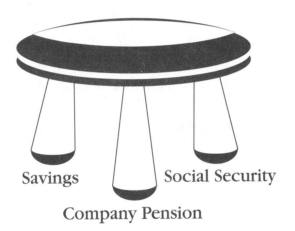

Savings   Social Security

Company Pension

From 3-Legged Stool To Frisbee

As most of us know, the world has changed. The 3-legged stool advice may have been good advice for our parents' generation, but the world has changed. For millions of people today, the 3-legged stool has turned into a Frisbee.

One of the reasons why the 3-legged stool has turned into a Frisbee is because of three economic changes that happened just as this financial planning seminar was taking place.

The Three Changes Are:

1. In 1965, just as we were entering the Vietnam War in full force, President Johnson decided to fight the War on Poverty, so he added Medicare to Social Security. Now we were fighting two wars we could not win. The reason Medicare is the demise of Social Security is because, today, Medicare is a much larger, unfunded liability than Social Security. As of 2004, the bill for Social Security was $10.4 trillion and growing. Now the bill for Medicare is $62 trillion and growing. If not for Medicare, the bill for Social Security might be affordable. Combined, the total bill is not.

2. In 1971, the U.S. dollar stopped being money and was turned into a currency. When money becomes a currency, savers become losers... so why would a person want to save?

3. In 1974, Congress passed ERISA, the Employees Retirement Income Security Act. ERISA eventually led to the formation of the 401(k) plan, a plan that shifted the responsibility of retirement from the corporation to the individual... in most cases an individual without any financial education. Today, there are millions of workers without any retirement plan, even if their company offers one. Even if you have a retirement plan, you will eventually have to pay for those who do not.

Is It Financial Advice... Or A Sales Pitch?

After the financial planning seminar, I went to rich dad and told him what I learned about the 3-legged stool and other bits of financial advice I learned at the seminar.

Instead of being pleased that I attended the seminar, he seemed displeased, often shaking his head. Finally, I asked him, "Why do you shake your head every time you hear about the 3-legged stool or the advice of 'work hard, save money, get out of debt, invest for the long term, and diversify?' Don't you think that the advisor is just trying to help someone else with some sound financial advice?"

Rich dad thought about my question for a while and then said, "In most cases, I believe people are trying to be helpful... but there are still others who are being devious and know they are dispensing old advice that is bad financial advice."

"Why would anyone do that?" I asked.

"Because that advice is not really financial advice... it is really a sales pitch that unsuspecting people think is financial advice. It would be like someone telling you about a great restaurant and not telling you that he owned the restaurant."

"So I think he is being a good guy helping me, but he is really helping himself."

Rich dad nodded, smiled and said, "You got it. In life you need to know the difference between friendly advice and a sales pitch. If you can't tell the difference between advice and a sales pitch, you won't know the difference between Golden Rule #1 and Golden Rule #3.

In Part II of this book you will find out more about why the 3-legged stool became a Frisbee, and why the advice of *work hard, save money, get out of debt, invest for the long term and diversify is really a sales pitch.* And worst of all, you'll find out why it's old advice that, if followed today, can be financially dangerous advice.

Chapter Six

WHY "WORK HARD" IS OBSOLETE ADVICE

In 1943, the Congress of the United States passed the Current Tax Payment Act. The act penalized working people — more specifically, employees. It did this by changing the tax law. This is Golden Rule #2 in action because the law taxed working people, not the rich people who owned the companies or the people who had money working for them.

It is easier to understand when looking at simple diagrams of cashflow patterns.

1. Employees:

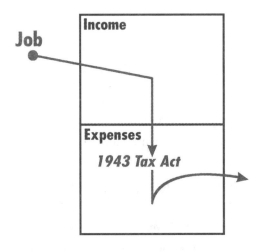

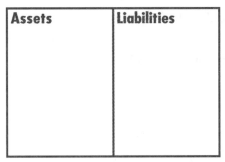

Prior to 1943 there were income taxes, but the government was having a difficult time collecting the taxes. So the Current Tax Payment Act was passed, which meant the government had the right to get paid its taxes at the same time the employee got paid. This was the beginning of employers withholding employees' income taxes before they were paid, and then the employer was required to send the withheld taxes to the government. In other words, the age-old saying of "Pay yourself first" was no longer possible for employees because the government now got paid first.

2. Business Owners:

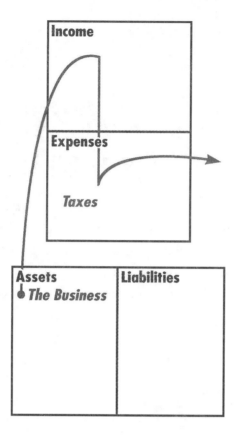

Following the cash flow arrow, you may notice that a business owner is allowed to pay their expenses *before* they pay their taxes. According to rich dad, this massive tax loophole is one of the reasons why the rich get richer. They get richer because they *spend before they pay taxes.* Employees *pay their taxes before they can spend.*

Looking at the diagram on the next page, you may understand why rich dad said this loophole is such a massive loophole.

The same tax advantages hold true for rich investors… but these tax advantages are not available to those with 401(k) or similar plans, which is one reason why Kim and I do not have retirement plans. For one thing, we are already retired, without a retirement plan, but we also do not like the tax rules for most retirement plans. There are better tax rules for people who know how to invest on the Fast Track and I will go into some of them in a later chapter.

Three Types Of Income

Those of you who have read the other *Rich Dad* books already know there are three different types of income and three different types of taxes. They are:

     1. Earned — taxed as high as 50%

     2. Portfolio — taxed as high as 20%

     3. Passive — may avoid taxes altogether

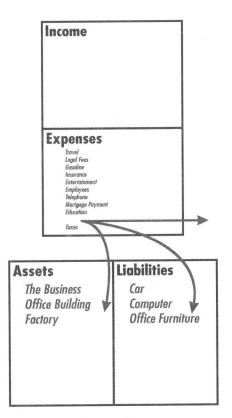

The 1943 Current Tax Payment Act taxed earned income — in most cases, income that people work for. As you can tell, one of the problems with working hard for earned income is that the harder you work, the more you pay in taxes...the highest of taxes. On top of that, the government collects its share before you get paid. This is just one of the reasons why rich dad said that working hard for money was an obsolete and a bad idea. It became an obsolete idea after 1943.

In the Information Age, a person with better, more up-to-date information will do better financially than a person with obsolete financial information. As you can tell by the three types of income, the financially intelligent thing to do is learn how to work for *passive income* first, which is most often rental income from real estate or *portfolio income*, which is capital gains income from stocks, bonds, and mutual funds.

Now I can hear some of you say, "Isn't *portfolio income* what I am saving for in my 401(k) plan retirement plan?" The answer in most cases is "No." When you retire with a 401(k) plan, the money you withdraw is taxed at the ***earned income*** tax rate, not the *passive* or *portfolio* income tax rate. (Many people do not realize this until they start withdrawing from their plan.)

A 401(k) Plan Is For People Who Plan On Being Poor

Today you hear many people saying, "When I retire my income will go down." In other words, when they retire they plan on being poorer than they are today. For people planning on being poorer at retirement, a 401(k) plan might be a good idea. The reason a 401(k) plan may work for a person who is planning on being poorer at retirement is because the money they withdraw from their 401(k) plan will be taxed at a lower tax rate, since their income will be low. That is also why so many financial planners say, "You will be able to withdraw your money at a lower tax rate because your income will be lower." One of the reasons Kim and I do not have a 401(k) plan today is simply because we have no plans to be poorer when we are older. Besides, since most of our income is *passive income*, we operate at a lower tax rate even though we have very high incomes.

Financial Advice Or A Sales Pitch

Many financial advisors recommend you maximize your 401(k) plan or similar plans. They say they recommend this course of action because the employer often contributes money to your retirement, and your money grows tax-free until you need it for retirement. To a person with limited financial education, this sounds like sound financial advice. Yet, if you have a higher financial IQ, you may realize that this advice is really a sales pitch designed to make the financial planner and the fund companies richer. While it is not a lie, it is hardly the truth or the whole picture of the real world of investing. In other words, there are investments with better tax advantages that are safer and less risky. These will be covered later in this book.

The reason most financial planners and mutual fund companies will not recommend these other investments is simply because they are not paid a commission to sell those investments to you. The point is, a true advisor should give you the whole picture and let you choose what is best for you, rather than what is best for the financial advisor. If they give you the whole picture, then that is financial advice. If they give you only the options that will make them richer, it is a sales pitch.

A friend of mine who left the financial planning industry said to me, "At work, we used to say, for an investment to be a good investment, it had to be good for our company, good for us, as the advisor, and good for the client… Oh well, two out of three isn't bad."

The Worst Kind Of Hard Work

As you can tell by the tax laws, because of Golden Rules #2 and #3, most of the poor and middle class are working hard for the wrong kind of money and are saving for retirement with the wrong kind of money. If you had a better financial education, you would know better than to work all your life for *earned income* and then have your retirement savings taxed as *earned income*. That is not financially smart, yet millions of people think it is the financially smart thing to do. That is the problem with not knowing the difference between a sales pitch and true financial advice.

Author's Note: I realize that many of my readers live in different countries with different types of retirement plans and different laws. While it's not practical to list every country's plan, it is safe to say this: If the government has a retirement plan it is promoting, that plan is probably for the poor and the middle class. I would bet there probably are better plans for people who invest in their financial education before they invest their hard earned money. So, if you live in a country other than the U.S., the best thing to do is find an accountant, attorney, or financial advisor to the rich and ask them what the rich are doing with their retirement savings. If this person tells you the rich are doing the same things the poor and middle class are, you might want to find another advisor, one who advises the rich.

Why *Teach To Be Rich* Works: One of the educational points I designed into the CASHFLOW board game is the difference between the three different types of income. As you now know, our schools teach us to work for *earned income* and our financial advisors have many of us trained to save for *portfolio income*. As I said, to me this is not the best financial advice and is primarily a sales pitch. People who are stuck in the Rat Race are working for *earned income* and saving for

portfolio income. The way out of the Rat Race is to learn how to invest for *portfolio income* and *passive income*, versus save money.

In the Information Age, it is obvious that hard work is not the way to become financially free, simply because there are too many people throughout the world willing to work for less and our own tax laws punish people who work hard for money. The reason why using the CASHFLOW board game to teach yourself and others to grow rich is because you are teaching yourself and others to have money work hard for you and not for someone else.

Always remember these three points:

1. Employees are *taxed first* and spend second. Business owners are allowed to *spend first* and are taxed on what is left, if there is anything left.

2. People who work hard for money are taxed the hardest because they work hard for the most heavily-taxed income... *earned income.* People who save money and invest in a 401(k) are also working for income that is taxed at higher rates.

3. When your money truly works for you, you earn *passive income*... income that is taxed the least, if taxed at all.

Teaching yourself and others to be rich works... if you teach the whole picture on the world of money. Remember, if you offer the big picture and let the person choose, you are providing financial advice and financial education. If people are told only about investments that profit the advisor and the investment company, then it is a sales pitch, disguised as financial advice.

Chapter Seven

WHY "SAVE MONEY" IS OBSOLETE ADVICE

In 1971, President Richard Nixon changed the rules of money. After 1971, the idea of saving money became an obsolete and financially dangerous idea. In 1971, the U.S. dollar ceased being *money* and became a currency. That change has been one of the biggest changes in modern history. The problem is, few people understand what that change meant and how the change has impacted our lives in the past, present, and in the future.

In 1971, the U.S. dollar was real money, simply because it was backed by actual gold and silver. Until 1971, the U.S. dollar was known as a silver certificate. After 1971, the U.S. dollar became a Federal Reserve Note... an IOU from the U.S. Government. As rich dad said, "In 1971, the U.S. dollar stopped being an asset and became a liability."

A Dollar Saved Is Not A Dollar Earned

My poor dad, who believed in saving money, often said, "A dollar saved is a dollar earned." The problem was, he did not pay attention to the changes in money. All his life he saved his money, not realizing that after 1971, his dollar was no longer money but fiat currency, a piece of paper backed by the government... so his dollar saved was no longer a dollar earned.

If my poor dad had purchased more real estate in Hawaii after 1971, instead of trying to save money, he would have been a very rich man when he passed away. Instead he had a savings account sitting in the bank, growing less and less valuable with each passing day.

Buy A Gold Mine

My rich dad was very aware of the impact of the changes in 1971. While I was in Vietnam, in 1972 and 1973, he wrote me letters advising me to watch the price of gold. In one letter he wrote, "The dollar is falling. If you can find a gold mine, buy it." At the time, I did not know what he meant. I did go looking for gold and gold mines in Vietnam and found both for sale, but not at fair prices. Even behind enemy lines in Vietnam, people knew that the value of gold was on the rise, so gold or gold mines were not cheap. As you may know, the price of gold hit approximately $800 an ounce by 1980, before heading back down. In 1996, with gold at an all time low (somewhere around $275 an ounce) my partners and I bought a gold mine in China — at bargain basement prices — and took it public through the Canadian Stock Exchange. As I write today, in 2005, gold is passing $500 an ounce.

Knowing these historical trends can help in making investment decisions. In 1996, even though the financial experts were saying "gold is a dog" or it's "an ancient relic," my partners and I moved forward when pessimism against gold was at an all-time high and prices were approaching a 20-year

low. In 1996, not only was gold at a low, so were gold mines and sentiment for China. In the year 2000, that sentiment changed.

A Golden Education

In my early 20s as a pilot in Vietnam, I really did not understand the relationship between gold and the dollar. Although I did not know much about gold, my search for gold in Vietnam was the beginning of my golden education — an education that has made me millions of dollars, not just in gold, but more in understanding how the relationship between gold and money works. As the years went on, I picked up bits and pieces of information about this ancient relationship between gold and money.

Returning from Vietnam, I spent more time with rich dad who explained why he was both excited and concerned about the 1971 change from money to a currency. To better explain, he drew a graph that looked like this.

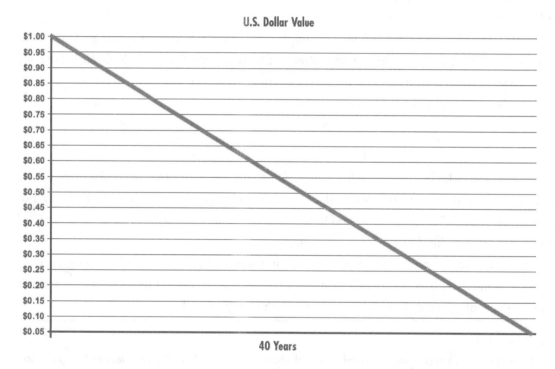

Shocked, I asked rich dad, "You mean a dollar goes down in value over 40 years?"

"Sometimes faster," replied rich dad. "Throughout history, no fiat money or currency has survived the test of time as money. Currencies come and currencies go, but real money is always money."

"Fiat money?" I asked. "What is fiat money?"

"Look it up," said rich dad, handing me his dictionary.

After a few minutes of leafing through his large dictionary, I came across the definition of fiat money.

Webster states:

> ***Fiat money: money (as paper money) not convertible into coin or specie of equivalent value.***

"Not convertible to coin?" I mumbled. Looking up at rich dad I said, "I still do not understand what this definition means."

"Well, look up the word 'fiat,'" said rich dad patiently.

I found the following definition for 'fiat':

> *Fiat: a command or act of will that creates something without or as if without further effort.*

"Not convertible into coin?" I mumbled to myself. "A command or act that creates without further effort?"

Looking up at rich dad I asked, "Does this mean fiat money is something that is created out of thin air?"

Nodding, rich dad said, "It can mean that."

Thinking for a long while, I did my best to expand my mind so it could comprehend what this all meant.

Finally, rich dad mercifully said, "Don't worry. Most people don't understand it… even smart people." Pointing to his graph with the dollar declining in value over 40 years, rich dad said, "Just remember this graph." Then, pointing to the dictionary, he said, "And just remember that fiat money can be created out of thin air and is not convertible into coin or equivalent value. Just remember those two things and you'll be a smarter investor."

My head hurt thinking about all this. Taking my wallet out of my pocket, and pulling out singles and fives in cash, I said to rich dad, "You mean this is not real."

"Well, I am not quite saying that," said rich dad. "It is real as long as you and I think it is real. That green stuff in your hands is real as long as people are willing to work for it, and people are willing to accept it as payment. But the moment we all stop thinking it is real, the passing of the buck stops. The game of musical chairs is over and, hopefully, you have a chair to sit on."

"Why is money not real?" I asked. "Why did they change it from money to a fiat currency?"

"Let me explain by starting with the Bretton Woods system," said rich dad.

"Bretton Woods system?" I moaned. "What is the Bretton Woods system?"

"During the final months of World War II," began rich dad slowly, "The Bretton Woods system was created to help stabilize the world's money."

"Was the world's money in trouble?" I asked.

"In many ways, money was the cause of World War II," said rich dad. "When I was your age, I was fighting the Germans, not the Vietnamese. One reason I was fighting the Germans was because the collapse of the German monetary system gave rise to a man named Hitler."

"How did that happen?" I asked.

"Well, after WWI, the West forced Germany to pay for the damages that the War caused. Money flowed into the U.S., which led to the roaring 20s because our economy boomed. The problem was, Germany's government got poorer and poorer because money kept flowing out of the country. When I was about your age, I began reading about the German government's printing of money. Soon money was cheaper than wallpaper. Shoes that sold for 13 marks, the German currency in 1913, were selling for 32 trillion marks by 1923."

I gasped. "From 13 to 32 trillion marks in just 10 years? How did people survive?"

Rich dad shrugged and said, "I remember a news photo of a German citizen lighting his cigar with a million mark bill. That is how bad it got. People were burning money because everyday it became more and more worthless. There were stories of housewives going to the bakery with a wheelbarrow full of money just to buy a loaf of bread. When one housewife stepped inside to buy the bread, someone stole her wheelbarrow and left the money behind."

"That is what happens when the government can create money out of thin air?" I asked.

"Exactly," said rich dad. "That's why I wrote you in Vietnam once I understood the same thing was going on again. If you are going to be financially savvy, you must understand the relationship between gold, assets, and currencies."

"So keep an eye on the government's printing presses?"

"Absolutely," smiled rich dad. "You see, hyper-inflation wiped out the savings of the middle class in Germany."

"Because their savings went down in value?"

Rich dad nodded, and in a more somber tone said, "And it was the anger of the middle class, not the poor, that gave power to Adolf Hitler, who became Chancellor of Germany in 1933."

"And Hitler not only caused the war but also murdered millions of Jews."

Rich dad nodded.

"But wasn't America entering the Great Depression in 1933?" I asked.

"Yes, but just before the Depression, America was in an economic boom. While Europe was rebuilding after WWI, America was the land of milk and honey. The stock market was on fire. A new technology, radio, was the hot technology of the day. I remember RCA stock starting at $1.50 a share and getting up to almost $600 a share, just before the crash in 1929."

"So our economy crashed, the German economy went down, and by 1939, we were in World War II."

"Which is why, in the final months of WWII, the Bretton Woods system was adopted," replied rich dad. "We all knew that a stable monetary system needed to be in place, if we expected stable economic growth and world peace. You see, money does make the world go around."

"So in 1971, the Bretton Woods system was gone?"

Rich dad nodded and said, "And that is why I wrote to you and advised you to start looking for gold."

"What was the Bretton Woods system?" I asked.

"It was a close substitute for the gold standard," said rich dad. "Instead of using gold as money, the Bretton Woods system fixed the price of gold at $35 an ounce."

"And what does that mean?" I asked.

"It meant that if the United States had 1 million ounces of gold in reserve, the U.S. could print $35 million in paper money. If the U.S. or any government wanted to print more money, it had to have more gold on hand."

"Oh," I replied, still very confused. "Why did they do that?"

"Don't worry about that right now. For now, all I want you to understand is that, for a while, things were calm because the U.S. dollar and other currencies throughout the world were stable, because they were backed by gold. With paper money backed by gold, savers could save their money safely. Before 1971, a dollar saved was truly a dollar earned."

"So what changed?" I asked.

"Well, some 20 years after the Bretton Woods system, sometime in the mid-1960s, the U.S. began importing more than it was exporting. You may remember that is when low-cost Japanese cars, TV sets, and appliances began entering the country. Also, from Germany came the VW Beetle and other high-quality German products."

"Yes, I remember that," I replied. "Suddenly instead of an American-made TV set, our family purchased a Japanese-made TV set. Also, in the 1960s, our family owned a Volkswagen, not a Ford. Today, I own Porsches and Mercedes."

"So every time your family purchased something from Germany or Japan and paid for it with a U.S. dollar, it gave the Germans and Japanese the right to change that dollar into gold. As more and more Americans began buying foreign products, the U.S. gold reserves went down."

"What is wrong with that?" I asked.

"Well, when our gold reserves go down, our economy shrinks and jobs are lost. Money was leaving the country and our wealth was going down. It's the same as a person who spends more than they earn. Back then, if a country or a person spent more than it earned, it went bankrupt. Today, only people go bankrupt. Today, countries just keep printing more money… so the value of money goes down."

"Oh," I said softly.

"Because the U.S. was struggling, importing more and exporting less, in 1971 President Nixon junked the Bretton Woods agreement and the U.S. dollar became fiat money… money created out of nothing… representing nothing more than an IOU. Since the U.S. was so strong and most countries wanted to do business with us, the other countries went along with the change. In 1971, instead of gold being the money of the world, the U.S. dollar became the reserve currency of the world. Never in the history of the world has one country's fiat currency been the standard of the world. Up until 1971, precious metals such as gold and silver were the standard that made the world go round."

"So what does that mean?" I asked.

"Well, it means a lot… much more than I can explain in an hour," said rich dad. "For now, just remember that in 1971 savers became losers because the dollar was no longer money. Also, for the first time in history, the world accepted an I.O.U. instead of gold as money."

"OK," I said. "But why did savers become losers?"

Smiling rich dad said, "I was afraid you were going to ask me that. Look, let me explain it as simply as possible. After 1971, let's say you buy a Japanese car. Your money is sent to Japan and you get the car. The Japanese company now has your U.S. dollars… tons of them. They cannot spend U.S. dollars in Japan. So they come to the U.S. to buy our assets. When they buy our assets, our assets go up in price."

"Isn't that good?" I asked.

"Yes, for some people… but not for all people."

"For which people is this *not* good for?" I asked.

"For hard-working people who save money and try to stay out of debt," said rich dad.

"What?" I asked in astonishment. "Why do you say that?"

"For many reasons," said rich dad patiently. "One reason is because the cost of their house goes up. So a person needs to work harder just to afford a home. Look at my home. I purchased it for $45,000 in 1968 and today in 1974, it's worth $750,000. The Japanese came to town with tons of our money to buy houses in Hawaii. With the average person in Hawaii earning less than $30,000 a year,

how do they afford to buy a home?"

"So we buy a cheaper Japanese-made car or stereo… or any consumer goods, but then we have to pay more for real assets."

Nodding, rich dad said, "When the Japanese, or German, or Canadian company receives your dollar, they return to the U.S. to buy real estate, businesses, stocks, and bonds. This drives asset prices up which makes it harder for the average working person to acquire assets."

"But they get a cheaper car?" I asked.

"Yes," said rich dad. "Let me repeat because it is important you understand this. After 1971, consumer prices started coming down because we could import more high quality products at lower prices… which meant our factories moved overseas. So wages went down, consumer prices went down, but assets prices went up. Suddenly, the price of owning a home went up. Look at how much your father's home has jumped in price. Can you afford to buy your father's house today?"

"No," I said softly.

"When the Japanese, Germans, and others send their U.S. dollars back to the U.S. to buy bonds, it makes our interest rates lower."

"And what does that mean?" I asked.

"Well, lower interest rates make homes more expensive… and, once again, savers are losers because the interest they receive is less because there are so many foreign countries investing in our bonds. With so much money going into bonds, the cost of borrowing money becomes cheaper… so borrowers win and savers lose.

"And because credit is cheap, and asset prices are high, many people get into debt buying cheap consumer goods instead of assets."

"Correct," said rich dad. "Remember the root of the word of consumer is 'consume.' We tend to buy things that we consume, instead of assets. And it gets worse and worse. After 1971, the U.S. was allowed to buy more than we produced, and pay for what we bought with funny money… something it can only do as long as the world is willing to accept the U.S. dollar as money. When that stops — and it will someday — chaos will break out."

"So the foreign countries do not spend U.S. dollars in their country?"

"No," said rich dad. "If they bought their money with the U.S. dollar it would make their money too expensive. If their money became too expensive, they could not ship us low cost products… so instead of buying their money with our money, they come to the U.S. to buy our assets."

"So we buy their cheap junk and they buy our assets."

"That's it," smiled rich dad. "That is all you need to understand for now. As you watch the world economy, you will learn more and more about this relationship between gold, currencies, and the games countries play."

With my brain overloaded, I asked, "Is there more?"

"A lot more," smiled rich dad. "But you have learned a lot today. As the years go on you will understand more and more about how the system of funny money works."

"Isn't it terrible that most people do not know about this 1971 change?"

"Well," said rich dad, "Remember that this change has done a lot of good as well as a lot of bad. We have achieved a higher standard of living and people do have many nice, more affordable things in their lives. The problem is consumer prices have come down and asset prices have gone up, which is one big reason why the rich have gotten so much richer."

"And the poor and middle class work harder, save money, and try to get out of debt."

Nodding again rich dad said, "Savers are losers and debtors are winners… as long as their debt is for assets, not consumer goods."

Gresham's Law

Gresham's Law states that *"Bad money drives good money out of circulation."* In the mid-1960s, when U.S. coins were switched from silver to a cheap alloy, real coins went into hiding.

As a coin collector in grade school through high school, I suddenly noticed that my dimes and quarters had a copper tinge around the edge. That meant our coins were no longer a precious metal. Immediately, real silver coins went into hiding. That is an example of Gresham's Law in action.

Today, I suspect people know, either consciously or subconsciously, that their money is not real money… which may explain why the savings rate of the U.S. is near zero. People may not be financially educated but they are not stupid. Instead of saving fake money, many would rather go into debt and buy consumers goods, even if those goods do come from China, Japan, or Germany. Could it be that people know that their cheap consumer goods are worth more than their money, as Gresham's Law states?

Effect On Today And Tomorrow

Prior to the year 2000, in fear of the Y2K fiasco, the government printed billions of dollars to keep the economy a float. After 9/11, the government printed billions of dollars to keep the economy afloat. After we invaded Afghanistan and Iraq, once again the U.S. government printed billions of dollars to keep the economy afloat. At the same time, China entered the World Trade Organization and became the biggest creditor in the world and; the U.S. became the biggest debtor. In a few years, the $74 trillion bill for Social Security and Medicare will start coming due as the baby-boom generation retires. This means the government will have to print more and more money, making your savings worth less and less.

Why There Is No Inflation

Today in 2005, we are in the biggest financial boom in history. Real estate prices, gold, and oil prices have gone through the roof. In spite of housing prices doubling and tripling… and oil going from $10 a barrel to $60 a barrel, the economists continue to say that there is no inflation. The reason economists say this is because economists watch the CPI, the Consumer Price Index, and not the price of assets. In overly-simplified terms, consumers are concerned about the CPI, while investors are concerned about asset prices. That is why so many people believe there is no inflation… because most people are consumers, not investors. This is also why the rich are getting richer and the poor and middle class are shopping at the discount stores, looking for bargains from China, hoping to save some money. Meanwhile, the price of their house and gasoline go through the roof while our jobs migrate overseas.

I believe this is in large part due to not having financial education in school. We have a nation of consumers who are getting poorer and poorer, while the rich get richer.

Where I Am Investing My Fake Money

What concerns me is that all booms bust, and since the world's economy now floats on the U.S.

dollar, which is declining in value, who knows how big the next bust will be. That is why I am hanging on to my gold, silver, and oil, even though they are expensive and I could make a lot of money selling them today. In the near future, there will be either hyper-inflation or hyper-deflation if the U.S. does not put its financial house into order… which I doubt it will. Either way, regardless if it is hyper-inflation or hyper-deflation, the results will be tragic for the unprepared and uneducated. Since I do not know which way it will go, I need to have strategies that can handle either situation. Again, that is why I am in oil, gas, real estate, and precious metals. For the next few years, *I want to have my fake money invested in real money*. And once again, before investing your money, get educated.

Authors Note: There are many books that explain the 1971 change in the U.S. dollar. One of the better books I have read is *The Dollar Crisis* by Richard Duncan.

Why Savers Are Losers

In conclusion, this one snap shot may better explain why savers are losers… especially today.

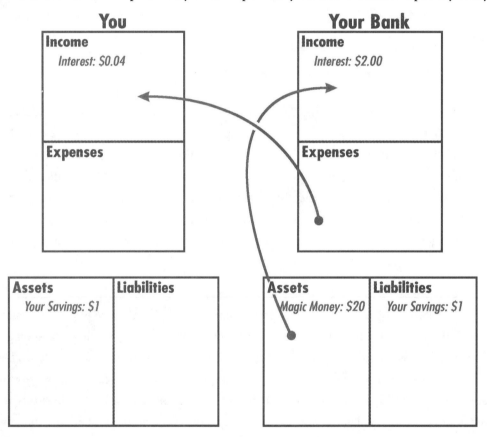

Your dollar is your asset on your financial statement. Your dollar is a liability on the bank's financial statement. This is how the system allows money to be created out of thin air. Like magic, your dollar is now worth $20 to the bank to lend out. This is because the law requires the bank to hold only a percentage of its deposits on hand as a reserve (in this case 5%). The bank pays you 1% interest and charges borrowers, especially on consumer credit, at least 10% interest on the $20.

The net effect: you get paid $.01 per year on your dollar and the bank makes $2 a year on your dollar. So the savers lose because the value of their dollar goes down, and the bank has created 20 more dollars from their one dollar.

As Webster's definition states:

> ***Fiat: a command or act of will that creates something without or as if without further effort.***

Like magic, since 1971, when you deposit your dollar into the bank, the system allows your bank to create at least another $20 right out of thin air, without further effort. To me, this is a prime example of Golden Rules #2 and #3.

Why *Teach To Be Rich* Works: Rich dad often said, "If you want to be rich, you have to know what the word *value* means." He also said, "A rich person buys on value and a poor person buys on *price*."

One of Webster's definitions for the word *value* is "*relative worth, utility, or importance.*"

Between the years 2000 and 2005, the value of the dollar dropped, not only against the world currencies such as the Euro, but also within value in the U.S. as interest rates plummeted. In other words, if a bank paid you 7% interest one year and then only 1% the next year, the value of your money went down. In spite of the drop in value of the dollar, nationally and internationally, financial advisors kept advising people to "save money." To me, this was unsophisticated and obsolete financial advice, especially when oil went from $10 to over $60 a barrel and gold went from $275 to $475 an ounce during approximately the same period of time, because the relative value of your money went down in value when compared to gold and oil as well as real estate.

Value: What Will Someone Else Pay Me For It

When I invest in anything, I know its value is not what I pay for it, but what someone else will pay for it. One of the reasons why I love real estate is simply because I have a good idea what someone will pay me to rent it. The more rent I can collect, the more valuable the property. It's pretty clear.

When playing the CASHFLOW game, players are taught to look for value. For example, say they draw the following Small Deal card:

House For Sale — 3Br/2Ba

Nice 3/2 rental house suddenly available due to estate closing. Well-maintained older property with existing tenant.

Use this yourself or sell to another player.

38% ROI, may sell for $65,000 to $135,000.

Cost: $65,000	Mortgage: $60,000
DownPay: $5,000	Cash Flow: +$160

On this card, while all the information is important, the primary bits of information that measure the value of this property are the last two lines… the down payment of $5,000 and the positive cash flow of $160. In other words, what I will pay relative to what my tenant will pay me. That is how I quickly establish value. Obviously, in real life, I would have to do a lot more due diligence to establish further value.

Now, if I had put that $5,000 in the bank at 1% interest, I would have received $50 a year in pre-tax interest, or approximately $4 a month. Again, compare that $4 a month value to $160 a month in value for the same $5,000 in cash investment. In this comparison, which asset is more valuable? Cash in savings or real estate?

Then consider the possibility of the price of this property increasing in value to $135,000 from $65,000; compare that to the value of your dollars in savings declining just because the government allows banks to create money out of thin air.

Only A Game

I realize this is only a game. Yet, designed into the game are hundreds of mental challenges such as this example, the challenge of evaluating values. If you play this game at least 10 times and teach the game to at least 10 people, I know you will be better able to evaluate values in the real world.

How Close To Real Life Is The Game?

Many times I am asked, "How close to real life is the game?" or "I have never seen investments presented the way the game presents the investments." The reason most people do not see deals presented in the same way the game presents them is because most people are not investors, but consumers. For example, many amateur investors invest from nice brochures, pictures of the property, tours of the condo project, or the sales model. If they invest in a stock, they may look at the glossy annual reports with pictures of the company headquarters or the toothy grin of the CEO. A true investor only needs the bare bones numbers. In fact, a true investor becomes suspicious if too much hype and too many glossy pictures are used to sell the investment.

Why a true investor wants only the bare bone numbers is because he or she has to look at hundreds to thousands of deals a year. The photos of the property, the corporate brochures, or the CEO may be nice… but not at this stage of the investment process. At this stage of the process… just the numbers please.

"I feel as though I am the most fortunate person in Canada when it comes to being "part" of the Rich Dad Team. I took action a few years ago after reading Rich Dad Poor Dad and became a Facilitator of CASHFLOW 101 and 202 games. I host events across Canada and have met thousands of people, many of whom are now good friends and a few more who are now business partners. The likemindedness of the Rich Dad Community is second to none. I really mean this. The people who gather to play the Rich Dad games are such special people, full of giving and openminded to the fact that we can all escape the Rat Race.

I have been out of the Rat Race since reading Rich Dad Poor Dad and now I can share this experience while teaching CASHFLOW 101. Lesson number one: Take ACTION and start building your financial formula."

See you at the Top!
Darren Weeks – Edmonton, Alberta

The following is a real life example of a fact sheet a broker sent me. He sent me over 150 of such sheets to look at. Out of 150 possible investments, I narrowed my search down to three in less than an hour. This is one of the three:

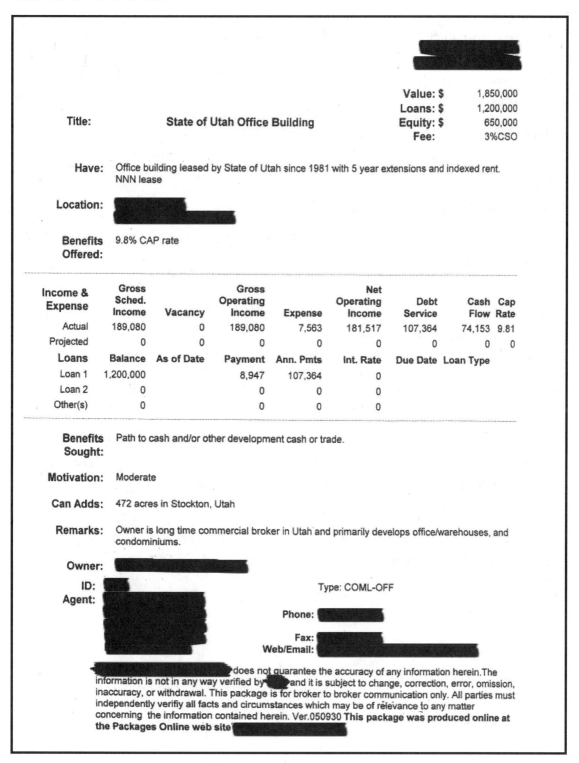

				Value: $	1,850,000
				Loans: $	1,200,000
Title:	**State of Utah Office Building**			Equity: $	650,000
				Fee:	3%CSO

Have: Office building leased by State of Utah since 1981 with 5 year extensions and indexed rent. NNN lease

Location: ▓▓▓▓▓▓▓▓▓▓

Benefits Offered: 9.8% CAP rate

Income & Expense	Gross Sched. Income	Vacancy	Gross Operating Income	Expense	Net Operating Income	Debt Service	Cash Flow	Cap Rate
Actual	189,080	0	189,080	7,563	181,517	107,364	74,153	9.81
Projected	0	0	0	0	0	0	0	0

Loans	Balance	As of Date	Payment	Ann. Pmts	Int. Rate	Due Date	Loan Type
Loan 1	1,200,000		8,947	107,364	0		
Loan 2	0		0	0	0		
Other(s)	0		0	0	0		

Benefits Sought: Path to cash and/or other development cash or trade.

Motivation: Moderate

Can Adds: 472 acres in Stockton, Utah

Remarks: Owner is long time commercial broker in Utah and primarily develops office/warehouses, and condominiums.

Owner: ▓▓▓▓▓▓▓▓▓▓

ID: ▓▓▓▓

Agent: ▓▓▓▓▓▓▓▓▓ Type: COML-OFF

Phone: ▓▓▓▓▓▓

Fax: ▓▓▓▓▓▓▓
Web/Email:

▓▓▓▓▓▓▓▓▓▓ does not guarantee the accuracy of any information herein. The information is not in any way verified by ▓▓▓ and it is subject to change, correction, error, omission, inaccuracy, or withdrawal. This package is for broker to broker communication only. All parties must independently verifiy all facts and circumstances which may be of relevance to any matter concerning the information contained herein. Ver.050930 **This package was produced online at the Packages Online web site** ▓▓▓▓▓▓▓▓▓▓

You may notice that it is very similar to the Small Deal and Big Deal cards found in the CASHFLOW board game. The reason I made the game cards similar is because I created the game for investors, not consumers… consumers who invest from glossy brochures. There is a difference in values between investors and consumers.

Park Your Money

When financial experts say to you, "Save money and invest for the long term" what they want you to do is park your money with them. If you invest the time to improve your financial intelligence, instead of parking your money, you will be able to move your money and gain even higher returns on your capital.

In the book *Rich Dad's Who Took My Money?* I cite an example of parking your money versus moving your money.

Quote:

"Suppose you have $20,000 to invest. The following are three choices you have.

Choice 1:

Invest $20,000 in a mutual fund that earns 5% per year.

After seven years: Your $20,000 should have grown to $28,142 assuming no market fluctuations.

Choice 2:

Invest $20,000 and borrow $180,000 from the bank for a $200,000 rental property and let your equity compound. Assume rental income only breaks even with expenses and the property appreciates at a rate of 5 percent a year.

After seven years: the property will be worth $281,000 and your equity is now $101,420, assuming no market fluctuations.

Choice 3:

Invest $20,000 and borrow $180,000 from the bank for a $200,000 rental property. Rather than letting the equity compound, you borrow against the appreciation every two years and invest in a new property at 10 percent down.

After seven years: the total value of your properties will be worth $2,022,218 and your net equity is $273,198 assuming no market fluctuations.

Summary Of A $20,000 Investment

Net Equity	Average Annual Return On $20,000 Investment
Choice 1: $28,142	5.8%
Choice 2: $101, 420	58.2%
Choice 3: $273, 198	180.9%

So the question is, which return do you want on your $20,000?"

Catch-22

The problem is, most people cannot achieve such returns unless they have the proper financial education and market experience. That is why teaching to be rich works.

The issue is this: Many people, including many financial experts, will say such returns are impossible… while in my experience, such returns are not only possible but achievable — and the example on the previous page is really a conservative return that is easy to achieve. So the Catch-22 is: If you or your advisor thinks such returns are impossible, then they are for you… it's just a matter of values.

A Final Word On Savings

At the risk of sounding like a politician and speaking from both sides of my mouth, I will say that your savings are important. Kim and I have some money in savings. The difference is we hold our savings in gold and silver in a safe deposit box at our bank. We also purchased the gold and silver when prices were much lower, so in many ways our savings have gone up, even though we have not saved any more fiat currency.

If you do not care for gold or silver, then I suggest you keep at least a year's expenses in savings in your local bank. For example, if your family's annual expenses are $50,000 a year, you should have at least $50,000 in savings before you invest in any other assets. Since we all make mistakes, it's good to have a year's supply of money as a cushion.

Chapter Eight

WHY "GET OUT OF DEBT" IS OBSOLETE ADVICE

The Banking Act of 1933, known as the Glass-Steagall Act, was passed by the United States Congress and prevented retail banks from selling securities such as stocks and bonds to the bank's customers. The reason the Act was created was because too many people were buying shares of stock on credit... i.e. debt. Many lawmakers at the time felt that one of the causes of the 1929 stock market crash was too many so-called investors speculating in stocks with debt, not cash. As you may know, debt tends to drive prices higher.

In 1999, the Glass-Steagall Act was repealed and today banks in America are allowed to sell paper assets, especially mutual funds, to their customers.

The point is, even after 1933, the banks continued to loan money on real estate. Even after 1999, banks continue to *not* make loans on paper assets, especially mutual funds.

Playing Monopoly

As a young boy, rich dad taught me about investing by playing the board game *Monopoly*. He would repeatedly say, "The formula for great wealth is found in this game. The formula is four green houses... one red hotel." He would then take his son and me to see his 'green houses' that someday would become his 'red hotel.' By 1968, a year before I graduated from the military academy in New York, he owned his red hotel on Waikiki Beach. In other words, he went from a poor man to a rich man, a very rich man, in about 10 years.

When he was interviewed in our local newspaper, he was asked what the secret of his success was. He simply said, "I play *Monopoly* in real life and I use my banker's money to get rich." As expected, the press criticized him for his risky investment strategy, for not being educated in finance, and implied that his success was just luck. The journalist also hinted that the bank would eventually foreclose on the hotel. Well, a few years later, rich dad sold the hotel to a large insurance company for millions of dollars. The insurance company tore the hotel down and today a massive new hotel sits on Waikiki Beach, where rich dad's red hotel once sat. Although rich dad sold the hotel, he kept the rights to the ground the new hotel was built on and for years, he and his family have received a sizeable lease payment for the land, not the red hotel.

Two Kinds Of Debt

Around the same time, in 1967, my poor dad's career was taking off. He was appointed to the top position in state education, becoming the Superintendent of Education for the state of Hawaii. This required him to move from the town of Hilo on The Big Island of Hawaii to Honolulu. I remember my mom writing letters to me in New York, telling me how expensive houses in Honolulu were.

Finally, after months of searching, she wrote to say they had finally found a home in a prestigious neighborhood, but she was hesitant to tell me how much they were paying. "I can't believe how expensive the house is," she wrote. "The owner was asking $54,000 but we got it for $51,000. I've never been in so much debt in my life. I made Dad promise that we would scrimp and save to pay off that debt as soon as possible. I can't sleep because I'm so worried about how much debt we are in." Today, the house is worth about $1.5 million.

In 1968, rich dad paid $1.2 million dollars for his red hotel, which back then was a lot of money... a lot of debt. Today, even through the red hotel is gone, I doubt if you could buy the land, a city block, for less than $500 million.

In both cases, both men used debt to increase their wealth. The difference is, one dad saw debt as bad and worked hard to get out of debt. My rich dad saw debt as good, and worked hard to acquire more debt. While there are many factors as to why one grew richer and one grew poorer, I believe it was their attitude towards debt — one seeing debt as bad and the other seeing debt as good — that made a significant difference in their wealth.

There is another difference. My poor dad's house, which is still in the family, may be worth $1.5 million but it generates no income. It would be tough to sell the house and move to a new home because houses in the same area are now worth $3 to $5 million. My brother, who occupies the house, has three children. His concern is how do five people, he and his wife and three children, use the financial value of the house appropriately? His primary concern is how his children will be able to afford to buy homes when they are old enough to leave home.

A reminder: One of the reasons why homes have gone up in price so dramatically is because the value of the dollar is coming down. The average person cannot work hard enough or save fast enough to stay ahead of the government's printing presses.

Even though there is no longer a red hotel, the rent from the land and other investments provide a substantial monthly income for rich dad's entire family.

Growth Via Debt

In 1971, when President Nixon took us off the gold standard, the U.S. economy grew rapidly because it could expand debt at will. If you look at who has won financially since 1971, it is those who know how to use debt, while those who were trying to save money and get out of debt lost.

In other words, my poor dad had an obsolete idea regarding debt. He still thought he was borrowing *money*, even after 1971. Instead of borrowing *money*, after 1971, he was borrowing a *currency*... a piece of paper with government ink on it. Instead of borrowing as fast as the government could print it, my poor dad tried to go the other direction and pay off his debt by scrimping, saving, and working harder and harder.

Standing In Line To Get Poorer

Even after the repeal of the Glass-Steagall Act in 1999, which once again allows banks to sell paper assets such as mutual funds to their customers, banks still do not loan money (currency) to invest in paper assets. Even though banks do not sell mutual funds on credit, many savers continue to invest in them (now available through their banks) thinking it is the smart thing to do. They continue to use their money, instead of the bank's money, to acquire wealth quicker. This is because many people still have the old idea that *debt is bad* and *getting out of debt is good*. Hence, millions of people line up to

save their money (currency) and invest in paper assets such as mutual funds, an asset class the bank will not lend money on. Hence, they miss out on borrowing money to invest in real estate — the one asset banks have continually and aggressively loaned money on, even through the Depression. In other words, most people go to the bank to get poorer rather than to get richer.

Looking at a chart printed in *Rich Dad's Who Took My Money?*, you can see the difference in gains between those who used *debt* to finance real estate and those that used their own money (currency) to invest in stocks and mutual funds. Actually, the graph for investing only in mutual funds would be even worse.

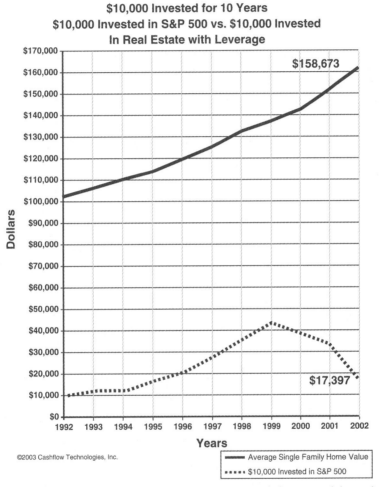

$10,000 Invested for 10 Years
$10,000 Invested in S&P 500 vs. $10,000 Invested
In Real Estate with Leverage

$158,673

$17,397

©2003 Cashflow Technologies, Inc.

— Average Single Family Home Value
····· $10,000 Invested in S&P 500

In other words, debtors who invested in real estate won… and the more debt or leverage they used, the more they won.

Good Debt vs Bad Debt

One of the earliest lessons from my rich dad was that there were two kinds of debt… good debt and bad debt. In simple terms he explained to his son and me that good debt made you rich and bad debt made you poor. He said, "One of the most important life skills you can learn is how to use debt to make you rich. Most people only use debt to make them poor."

Bankers Want Smart Debtors As Customers, Not Savers

Since a bank can take your dollar and magically create 20 or more dollars out of it, depending upon the reserve limit, the bank has a high need for customers who want to borrow money. Why?

Because that is how the bank makes its money. Banks do not make money from savers. Banks make money from debtors.

Why Bad Debt Is Easier To Get Than Good Debt

Have you ever noticed that it is very easy to get a lot of bad debt? I am constantly offered credit cards. Even students without jobs are offered credit cards. One night while watching the evening news, a reporter interviewed a dog owner whose dog was given a credit card through the mail. Watching television, I constantly see advertisements saying, "No credit, bad credit, no problem. Just come in, show us a pay stub and a cancelled rent check and you can drive out with a new car in less than an hour." Or, "Come in and buy the living room furniture of your dreams. Don't worry about payments. We won't bill you for one whole year."

Yet if you want to borrow money to start a business, buy a home, or acquire a piece of investment real estate, the bank will scrutinize you, make the loan process long and hard, take the loan through a committee process, and make you sign your life away through a mountain of paperwork.

Making *bad debt easy to get and good debt hard to get* has always puzzled me. So I asked a friend, a former banker, why bad debt was easier to get than good debt. His reply was, "There are many reasons this happens. Banking is a very complex subject. But in very simple terms, there are two main reasons why bad debt is easier to get than good debt."

To summarize the two reasons:

1. **Different classes of customers.** The reason a bank takes a credit application is to be able to assign different clients to different classes of credit risk. Obviously, the higher the credit risk, the higher the interest rates. As my friend the banker said, "Banks know they are going to lose money from a certain percentage of people who borrow and cannot pay back the money. So those losses are passed on to customers who are more responsible, by charging them the same higher interest rates." He also said, "Ninety percent of all customers only deal with a retail bank that is convenient to them. They use a bank that is close to home and is easily accessible. The bank could have a drive through window, easy parking, or be on their bus line. Ten percent of our customers, who are financially smarter, will not only shop for loans from many lending sources, they will also demand more favorable interest rates. Since these financially smarter customers tend to borrow more money, the banks tend to work harder to get their business, because banks want borrowers, not savers. People who can borrow a lot of money are the kind of customers the bank wants. The more debt you can handle, the more the bank wants you as a customer."

2. **Different assets.** My friend said, "Banks know that if a customer cannot pay the money back, the bank will have to take the property back. For instance, if you cannot pay your car loan, they come and take your car. So most of the documents you sign are legal documents stating how they will repossess your car, furniture, or house. In very simple terms, the more valuable the asset, the more paperwork. In other words, a loan to buy furniture has less paperwork than a loan for a multi-million dollar office building. The reason there is less paperwork is because the bank will not spend much time or money going after your furniture. It often costs them more money to go after the furniture than the furniture is worth. Now a multi-million dollar

office building is worth going after, so they have more paperwork spelling out (in excruciating detail) just how they plan to take the building back."

To summarize, what the banker said to me was, "The average person chooses a bank for convenience. They do not go from bank to bank. The more financially astute investors will shop for loans. They will demand lower interest rates or go to another bank in their city, across the country, or internationally."

Banks will negotiate on interest rates if the loan is a big loan and if the loan is secured by something of real value, such as real estate or a viable business. In other words, since banks have to lend money in order to be profitable, banks like big loans rather than small loans. One reason why banks compete for home loans so vigorously is because they would rather lend $200,000 on a house, which is a more secure asset, rather than $20,000 on living room furniture. Because they compete for the bigger more secure loans, they will often lower their interest rate, the cost of their money.

Since the interest rate may be lower, and the bank's profit margin smaller, the bank needs to make sure the asset is worth the risk and they can afford to take it back, via repossession or foreclosure. These are just some of the reasons why there is much more paperwork for good debt. In other words, most of the paperwork is not about the money… most of the paperwork is about how and why a bank can legally take back your home (the asset) if you fail to pay them. Since their profit margins are smaller on loans for homes, they need to be sure they can take back the property as efficiently as possible. And that is why good debt is harder to get, in overly-simplified terms.

Most people are not financially savvy. They tend only to deal with a local retail bank, consumer credit loan services, short-term loan outlets and pawn shops. The rich tend to deal with investment banks, mortgage banks, or other lenders that do not deal with the public. Ninety percent of people do not buy assets of much value. For most of them, their home is their biggest investment. Because 90% of the people think debt is bad, their loans are small. They also tend to buy assets the bank does not really want and so they end up paying a higher interest on their loans. Since the bank does not really want to take back the asset the person is buying on credit, the paperwork is less. Rather than study the individual and the asset in depth, the bank lumps smaller borrowers into classes, with the higher-risk people paying the highest rates. They play the percentages that a certain percent will default on their loans, and build the default costs into the cost of their money. That is reflected in the interest rate they charge. This is why poor people pay higher interest rates than rich people, even if they are honest, hard-working people who will pay back the loan. It's not personal, it's just percentages. And that is why bad debt is easier to get than good debt, in overly-simplified terms.

Using Debt To Get Rich

My rich dad said, "I love real estate because my banker is my partner."

The point rich dad was making was that a smart investor learns to use debt, your banker's money, to get rich. He said, "My banker is the best partner I have ever had. He lends me the money and I get

to keep all the profits."

The following is an example of what rich dad meant by that statement.

Let's say you buy an investment property for $100,000 and let's say the banker gives you an 80% loan, which means you will need to put up $20,000. The bank is now your partner, yet all your partner, the banker, wants back is his interest payment on the $80,000… You earn money every month from income, you receive tax breaks, and even if you sell the building for $200,000 three years later, all your partner, the bank, wants back is its $80,000 with interest.

The partnership agreement looks like this:

	You	Your Banker
Money contributed	20%	80%
Income from rent	100%	0%
Tax breaks from government	100%	0%
Capital gains from sale	100%	0%

I wish all my partners and investors were so generous. The bank puts up 80% of the money and you get 100% of the upside. The risk is that you also are responsible for 100% of the downside, and how to minimize that risk that will be covered in the next section.

Ask Your Banker For Money To Invest In Mutual Funds

One day, when I returned home to Hawaii on vacation from the military academy I attended in New York, I told rich dad that I had invested in some mutual funds. Although he did not say much, I could tell he did not approve. When I pushed him as to why he was so silent, instead of answering, he set up an appointment for me with his banker.

On the day of the appointment, I sat in front of his banker and rich dad had me ask the banker if he would lend me money to invest in mutual funds. When the banker chuckled, I got my answer. Today, after the 1999 repeal of the Glass-Steagall Act, I find it interesting that banks are allowed to sell mutual funds, but banks will still not lend money to invest in mutual funds. In other words, they don't want to be your partner if you want to buy mutual funds. They'd rather lend you money to buy your living room furniture.

Why *Teach To Be Rich* Works: When designing the CASHFLOW game, one of the skills I wanted people to learn was the ability to use debt as an instrument to become rich. I also wanted people to know, first-hand, how bad debt, via buying Doodads, makes people poor.

Since most people are terrified of debt, I increased the terror by making the interest rate 120% per annum in the game. By making the interest rate so high, buying a Doodad on credit is financially punishing. Yet even though the interest rate is so high, when the player comes across a good investment, he can evaluate if the cost of borrowed money (the interest rate) makes sense, before investing. What many players find out is that even if the interest rate is excessive, they can still make money if, and only if, they can identify a good investment.

What happens in the game is that people who have the thought "Debt is bad" tend to lose the game to people who know that "Debt is good," since the latter know how to use it for a good

investment. After a person, who thinks debt is bad plays the game several times and loses to a person who knows how to use good debt, the old thoughts in his brain begin to loosen their grip and his mind opens to the possibility that there might also be *good debt* in the real world. Once his old mindset gets that message, new information can come in to create a new mindset. When new information comes in, a whole new world of financial possibilities open to the CASHFLOW game player. And that is what education is supposed to do: open the mind, not close it.

Example From The Game

Pictured on the next page is a financial statement (the <u>real</u> game board) from the CASHFLOW game. The numbers written by human hands are the scores of the player. The player has only $375 in cash (paper play money) and has an opportunity to buy a 3-bedroom/2-bath house described on the *Small Deal Opportunity card* the player has just drawn.

House For Sale — 3Br/2Ba

Not lived in for 6 months, this bank-fore-closed house just reduced. Loan includes estimated repair costs.

Use this yourself or sell to another player.

??% ROI, may sell for $65,000 to $135,000.

Cost: $50,000   Mortgage: $50,000

DownPay: $0   Cash Flow: +$100

The question is, can this player buy this property and is it a good deal or a bad deal?

Answer:

Yes, the player can buy this property because it requires no money down. The acquisition price is totally funded by debt. After all expenses are paid on the property, it still provides $100 positive cash flow each month. It may also provide an opportunity to sell the property for $65,000 to $135,000. Since your cost is only $50,000 it could provide a good capital gain opportunity. In the meantime it provides positive cash flow to you every month. It is a good deal.

Suppose the property had a $100 negative cash flow each month with no money down. Is it still a good deal? The answer is "it depends." Since the card also says the property may sell for $65,000 to $135,000 it may be worth the negative cash flow if your plan is to invest for capital gains. Is it a good deal for cash flow? No. Is it a good deal for capital gain? Yes, but only if you find a willing buyer (or a lucky card) in the future. It will mean your net monthly cash flow will decrease by $100. You must decide if this would be a good deal for you.

In summary, debt is a tool, just as a hammer is a tool, a tool that can be used to build a house or tear it down. In the Information Age it is important that people be taught to use debt as a tool to build a strong financial house, rather than tear it down.

Profession	Nurse		Player	Sue

Goal: To get out of the Rat Race and onto the Fast Track by building up your Passive Income to be greater than your Total Expenses

Income Statement

Income	
Description	Cash Flow
Salary:	$3,100
Interest:	
Dividends:	
Real Estate:	
Businesses:	

Auditor	Nina

Person on your right

Passive Income= _____
(Cash Flows from Interest +
Dividends + Real Estate + Businesses)

Total Income: $3,100

Expenses	
Taxes:	$600
Home Mortgage:	$400
School Loan Payment:	$30
Car Payment:	$100
Credit Card Payment:	$90
Retail Payment:	$50
Other Expenses:	$710
Child Expenses:	
Bank Loan Payment:	

Number of Children: _____
(Begin game with 0 Children)

Per Child Expense: $170

Total Expenses: $1,980

Monthly Cash Flow: $1,120
(Pay Check)

Balance Sheet

Assets			Liabilities	
~~Savings:~~ CASH		$375	Home Mortgage:	$47,000
Stocks/Mutual's/CDs	No. of Shares:	Cost/Share:	School Loans:	$6,000
			Car Loans:	$5,000
			Credit Cards:	$3,00
Real Estate:	Down Pay:	Cost:	Retail Debt:	$1,000
			RE Mortgage:	
Business:	Down Pay:	Cost:	Liability: (Business)	
			Bank Loan:	

©1996-2002 CASHFLOW® Technologies, Inc. All rights reserved. CASHFLOW® games are covered by one or more of the following US Patents; 5,826,878; 6,032,957 and 6,106,300. RichDad®, CASHFLOW® and Investing 101® are registered trademarks of CASHFLOW® Technologies, Inc.   G101CTI7

Most people think debt is bad simply because they have not been trained by our school system to use debt properly. Without much financial education, the advice, "Get out of debt" is a great idea. For those who invest the time to learn how to use debt, knowing that there is good debt as well as bad debt is a useful idea.

In the Information Age, now that money is not money but more accurately a currency, learning to use debt to acquire wealth is a very important educational life skill. That is why teaching yourself and others to use debt — rather than avoid debt — is a worthwhile endeavor. It definitely supports Golden Rule #1.

Chapter Nine

WHY "INVEST FOR THE LONG TERM" IS OBSOLETE ADVICE

In 1974, Congress passed an act known as ERISA. ERISA stands for Employee Retirement Income Security Act. Why was this act passed? It definitely was not in line with Golden Rule #1.

The Act was passed because businesses needed to change the rules... Golden Rule #2. Employees were living longer and taking care of them was costing the companies more and more money. In other words, the company's money was working for the employee and not for the employer... hence, Golden Rule #3 was activated. The rich, those who make the rules, wanted to reduce long-term financial obligations as well as tap into the huge pool of employee retirement savings and have that money work for them, not the employees. So in 1974 they changed the rules.

In the Industrial Age, one of the rules for employment was that the company you worked for would take care of you for life even after your working days were over. That is why so many large companies and organizations had professional money managers to efficiently manage the retirement savings of their workers. The worker did not have to know much about money or investing since Industrial Age companies did that for them.

Prior to 1974, most workers had what is known as a *Defined Benefit* or DB retirement plan. After 1974, the plan shifted to a *Defined Contribution* or DC plan. While the changes are significant, most workers are not really aware of the consequences of those changes and that is what concerns me. It is why I write and create educational products such as my board games.

At first many people were not aware of how the 1974 change threatened their retirement security as well as the retirement security of millions of workers throughout the world. They are now becoming aware, which is why the greatest fear in America today is not terrorism, but running out of money during retirement.

Running Out Of Money

The first challenge is that a company is no longer responsible for the employee for life. The shift from DB (defined benefit) to DC (defined contribution) means just that. In the old days, the retirement plans defined the benefits employees would get for life... as long as they lived. The problem is, those benefits became too expensive as workers lived longer. As mentioned previously, General Motors, which still has a DB pension plan, will soon have more retirees to care for than men and women in their workforce. The U.S. Social Security system is in the same predicament. That is why the year 1974 is a significant year. It marked the shift from DB to DC plans, which means the *contribution* is defined, not the *benefits*.

Employers like DC plans because of the limited, well-defined liability. Even though a DC plan is

not as good as a DB plan, many employees like the DC plans because they like seeing their retirement nest egg grow, but they also panic when they see their nest egg shrink, which does happen when the stock market goes down. When the market declined from 2000 to 2003, it was a wake-up call for many retirees and future retirees. Many realized that markets don't always go up, that the people managing their accounts could not protect them, and that they might not have enough money to retire on.

In America, some businesses have a *matching funds* program, which means that for every dollar the employee puts in, the employer matches it, up to a limit. Yet since the 401(k) program is voluntary, many employees do not put much, if any, money into their plan, even if the employer matches their contribution. At least in countries such as Australia, employers are required to contribute to the plan and so are the employees.

In America, many employers provide a 401(k) plan but do not match the employee's contribution. And still more companies do not provide any retirement program at all.

In America, many employees decline to participate even if a plan is provided. In 2001, the Federal Reserve Survey of Consumer Finances found that more than one out of four workers chose not to participate in the plan, even if one was provided. Also, when employees quit their jobs, they often spend what they have accumulated, even though they are running out of time, the time required to accumulate enough of a nest egg for retirement.

The big difference between a DB plan and a DC plan is: Once the employee leaves the company, regardless of whether they are an American, Japanese, or Australian worker, the employee is on their own. If they mismanage their money and spend it too quickly, or a fast-talking con artist talks them into a phony investment scheme, or their kids take the money, or a market crash wipes out their nest egg, or the money simply runs out… they're out of luck. Let's say, at age 86, the person is out of money but has another 10 years to live. That is no longer the company's problem. The employee will be on his or her own.

Now I have heard people say, "I'll just keep working." To me, that shows a lack of foresight. All a person needs to do is go to an assisted living center and count the number of people employers would hire. Then ask the assisted living center manager how much each person is paying per month to stay at the nursing home. In many cases, the cost per month to stay in the nursing home is more than the person earned per month when they were younger and working.

The Numbers Do Not Work

While many people are aware of the possibility of running out of money during retirement, the second challenge many people are not aware of is that the numbers do not work and could never work. In very simple terms, there are not enough shares of company stock to support all the retirees.

Few people know that the top 1% of the richest American, own 50% of all outstanding shares of stocks. The next richest group, the top 9% of the richest Americans, own another 35% of all stock. So the richest 10% of all Americans own 85% of all the shares of stock. That means 90% of the people are supposed to survive on 15% of the remaining shares. This is a classic case of Golden Rules #2 and #3 in action.

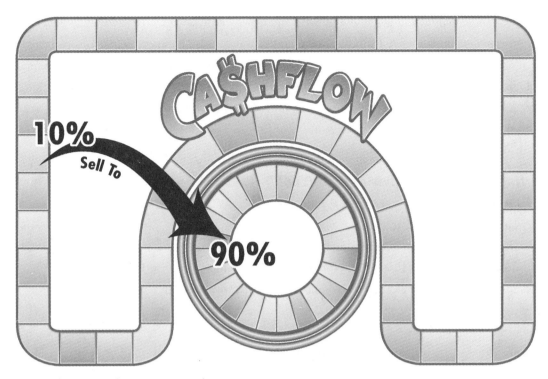

How The Rich Get Richer

How is it possible that a few individuals can own so many shares of stock? Once again, the answer is displayed on the CASHFLOW game board pictured above.

The 10% of people who own 85% of the shares of company stock invest on the Fast Track. For example, the Fast Track investors will form a company owning 100% of the stock. When they take a company public, generally through an Initial Public Offering (IPO), they sell 10% to rich friends and to large financial institutions at an insider's price before the company goes public. Then they sell more — another 10, 20 or 30% (or whatever they choose and the market will bear) — via an IPO to those investors in the Rat Race. The individual investor can then purchase shares of stock or shares of a mutual fund that has purchased the stock.

The owners of the company, the 1%, and their friends, the 9%, obviously want the price of the company's shares on the open market, the Rat Race, to go up because it drives the value of their stock up. One of the ways to control the price of stock is to control the number of shares in the open market place, the Rat Race. It is simply a case of supply and demand.

One Big Scandal

During the Enron scandal, it was revealed that the owners of the company told their employees and shareholders to buy more stock. Analysts on Wall Street also told employees and shareholders to buy more stock... and they did. The problem was: The 10% who knew the truth about the company, the owners and those on Wall Street, were selling shares, not buying shares. While this is an extreme example of stock fraud and manipulation, it is not that far from the standard operating and legal procedures of most publicly-traded companies.

Why The Rich Get Richer

After retirement plans shifted from DB to DC plans, the number of mutual fund companies exploded, the number of financial planners exploded, and the demand for shares of stocks exploded.

One of the reasons why stocks are so over-priced and expensive today, relative to value, is simply because there is so much money from fund companies, and people chasing so few shares of available stock. It's simply Economics 101, the manipulation of supply and demand. Again, this is an example of Golden Rules #2 and #3 in effect and a major reason why the rich — the 10% who own 80% of the shares of stock — are getting richer. It is also another reason why there have been so many scandals in the stock market. While most of us have heard of Enron, Tyco, WorldCom, and others, there are far more insiders who did naughty things and are still doing business today.

Why They Want You To Invest For The Long Term

The increase in the number of mutual fund companies also led to a third abuse. There is one word that says it all when it comes to the sales pitch, "invest for the long-term" and that word is *fees*. In other words, regardless of whether you make or lose money or if the stock market is up or down, the mutual fund company makes money via the fees it collects, and collects for the long-term.

There is a conflict of interest between mutual fund investors and their mutual fund manager. Agency issues arise when fee-collecting mutual fund managers profit at the expense of return-seeking mutual fund investors.

By not issuing financial statements, as any public company is required to do, they do not have to disclose operating expenses. To me, this proves that people who invest in mutual funds are naïve. Why anyone would invest in a venture that is not required to be *transparent* to the investor baffles me. Yet, since most people are not taught in school about financial statements, who can blame people for being a little naïve in the stock market? Ask any banker or any professional investor what they ask for before lending money or investing in a business or a piece of real estate. The answer is the financial statements. Yet, mutual fund companies are not required to issue clear and audited financial statements to their investors. This is how they get away with not talking about true returns and not disclosing their expenses.

Two Kinds Of Mutual Funds

Many people think that there are two kinds of mutual funds — load funds and no-load funds. In reality, there is only one kind of fund: load funds. In the stock market and in real life, there is no such thing as a free lunch and this is true of mutual funds. Because sales commissions, front loads as high as 8.5%, caused a drag on investor returns and investors complained, a marketing strategy — so-called no-load funds — were introduced. To counter this loss in sales commissions and loads, in 1979 the mutual fund industry introduced the 12b-1, which allowed the funds to charge an *annual* marketing fee. Notice the key word in there, the word 'annual.' In other words, they do not charge you a sales commission up front… they now charge you a sales commission *forever* and tell you it is a no-load fund. It is like taking a skunk and painting the white stripe black and calling it a cat. And that is one reason why they advise you to "invest for the long-term." In the long run, long-term investors end up worse off as annual fees accumulate year in and year out, imposing a larger burden than the one-time only, up front fee. On top of that, as your nest egg increases, so do the dollar amounts paid in fees. One of the reasons why mutual fund companies like to brag about their billions of dollars under management is because they are making a lot of money from the fees from investors, even if their investors are not making any money.

Short-Term Investors

Another trick they came up with, hidden in no-load funds, is this: Short-term investors are charged a *departure fee*. In other words, they get you coming and going. They make sure they get their pound of flesh and their sales commission, whether or not the investor makes anything. Once again, this is Golden Rules #2 and #3 in action.

Mutual fund companies do not have to issue audited financial statements. First of all, they do not want the investor to know what their true expenses are, because the funds expenses eat into the investor's profits; and secondly, they know that most investors in mutual funds are not savvy enough to ask for a financial statement in the first place.

Because most people, even many 'A' students, are financially illiterate, the mutual fund companies know that most of their investors think a no-load mutual fund means there is no sales commission, when in reality, a no-load mutual fund means annual sales commissions for the long-term. And that is why they say investing for the long-term is the smart thing to do. This is not investment advice... it is their sales pitch.

Paying High Commissions

I have no problem paying commissions. Everyone needs to earn money in some way, and sales people often earn their money via commissions. So it is not commissions I am upset about... it is deception and ignorance caused by our school systems.

In reality, I like to pay commissions. In fact, I pay very high commissions. For example, the last real estate transaction I was in, I paid a 35% commission to my real estate broker. Why did I pay so much when the standard commission is 6%?

There are two reasons:

1. **I am lazy and busy.**

    I do not have the time to sift through hundreds of real estate deals looking for that great investment.

2. **The best investments a broker has will come to me first.**

    The following is an example of one transaction we did between 2004 and 2005. A broker, a friend Kim and I have known for years, brought us this investment.

    *   A 390 unit apartment complex was being turned into condominiums, in Scottsdale, Arizona.

    *   As investors, we put up the money (approximately $500,000 in cash plus a bank loan) to purchase 10 of the units that were going to be used as models.

    *   The 10 units were purchased at a discounted price.

    *   The owner-developer would pay us a 25% return (approximately $125,000 a year) for the use of those sales models for up to three years, or as long as it took to sell the project out.

    *   Once the project was sold out, or the three years were up, we could sell the 10 units at market price.

Obviously, we said "Yes" to this deal. The broker was to receive 35% of the profits and we received 65%. This was not a "flip" in the traditional sense, because we were receiving income, a positive cash flow, which is very important to us. A true flip is when the buyer does a "buy, hold, and pray," intending to buy low and sell high. If they sell the property fast enough, they make money. If they ask too much and the property sits there for a long time, they may lose money, having to make the monthly payments and discounting their price. That is why Kim and I do not like flips. We like cash flow and *buying* at a discounted price… not *selling* at a discounted price.

The entire condominium project came on line in late 2004, and the buying was frenzied. The entire project was sold out by May of 2005, including our units. Instead of making offers, trying to get us to lower our asking price, people were lining up and bidding up our asking price. For example, a condo we were asking $350,000 for, sold for $425,000. When the dust finally settled, in one year Kim and I got our initial $500,000 back, some cash flow from rent and a little over $1 million in capital gains… and this is *after* the broker was paid his 35% of the profits.

Reinvesting Without Paying Taxes

We then took our $1.5 million (our initial $500,000 investment plus our $1 million in capital gains) and invested in a 288-unit apartment house in Tucson, Arizona, via a 1031 tax-deferred exchange. That means we were able to invest our $1 million in gains, without paying 20% to the state and federal government, legally. Try doing that with stocks, bonds, or mutual funds. So the numbers of the second transaction are:

- 288 units

- Purchased in partnership with Ken McElroy, friend, Rich Dad's Advisor, and author of *The ABCs of Real Estate Investing*.

- After a year of renovations, we expect to earn a 16% return on our $1.5 million or $240,000 a year, $20,000 a month in income, adjustable for inflation.

Now I can hear some of you saying, "But I don't have $500,000 to invest." I want to remind you that Kim and I at one time, not too long ago, had nothing to invest. In fact, in 1985, we had no place to live and lived out of a car. We made our money by *not* following the tried and true advice of "work hard, save money, get out of debt, invest for the long-term and diversify." And instead of missing the biggest economic boom between 1995 and 2005, as many mutual fund investors did, we rode with the boom in the real estate market and became even richer. We got richer because this 10-unit deal is only one of many investments we made during this period.

The point of me mentioning this one investment is not to tout our success. Personally, I am a very private person when it comes to my investments and would rather not disclose anything. The reason I point out this transaction is simply to use a real life investment and compare it to other investments. For example:

- Saving my money. Keeping my $500,000 in the bank at 5% interest = $25,000 taxed at earned income rates… which at my tax bracket would mean I would pay approximately 50% in taxes, leaving me a net of $12,500 in interest income. On top of that, my $500,000 would have gone down in value because the price of gold kept going up during this period, which means the value of the dollar went down.

- Investing in a mutual fund. Who knows what would have happened because my gain or loss would depend upon which mutual fund I invested in.

- Investing in the S&P 500 Index resulted in a 6% increase between June 2004 and June 2005.

To me — taking my $500,000 and receiving a 200% return even after paying a 35% commission, then leveraging my original $500,000 principle and $1 million dollar capital gains without paying taxes, legally, into another investment that is expected to pay $240,000 annually or $20,000 monthly in passive income cash flow, which means we pay less in taxes on that income, for as long as we want the cash flow — was more intelligent. To me, this makes more sense than leaving the money in the bank earning a net $12,500 on our money after taxes. On top of all this, the probability is that after renovating the 288 units, the value of the property will go up in value while dollars sitting in the bank are going down in value.

> **Author's Note:** Once again, I want to remind you that this is not a book about investing in real estate. It is about the value of a financial education. I use this personal real estate investment example only to illustrate some of the differences between different investment vehicles and different investment advisors. In Part III of this book, I believe you will better understand why there are even better investments, with low risk, available to you — if you are willing to first invest in your financial education. If you are not willing to first invest in your financial education, then you can see from the above example, how expensive not being financially educated can be. *If you are not willing to invest in your financial education, then I strongly recommend you follow the advice of 'work hard, save money, get out of debt, invest for the long term, and diversify.'*

There Are No Bad Investments

In the next chapter on diversification, I will go into other types of investments. One of the reasons I use real estate as an example is because it is my investment of choice, my example is a real example, and I feel most comfortable with real estate. That said, there are other investments that do provide excellent returns with a higher degree of safety. The key is not the investment but the financial savvy of the investor. An investor could possibly make more than 200% returns tax-free in mutual funds on a regular basis, as well as more than a 50% cash-on-cash (in my example, $20,000 in monthly income from an initial $500,000 investment a year earlier) return. This person probably owns the mutual fund company. As rich dad often said, "There are no bad investments… only bad investors."

"When managers want to get across the facts of the business to you, it can be done within the rules of accounting.

"Unfortunately, when they want to play games, at least in some industries, it can also be done within the rules of accounting.

"If you can't recognize the differences, you shouldn't be in the equity picking business."

—Warren Buffett

200% Return On Our Money And Of Your Money

As you can tell from that last investment example, sometimes we invest for the long term (the 288-unit apartment house) and sometimes for the short-term (the 10-unit apartment to condominium conversion). We also sometimes invest for *capital gains* (the 10 units); but primarily,

we invest for long-term *cash flow* (the 288 unit apartment house returning us $240,000 annually). Also, we like to make sure we get a return of our investment (the initial $500,000) more than a return on our gains (the $1 million).

An Eight Percent Return

I have a friend who loves his retirement plan. Since he is self-employed, he has an IRA (Individual Retirement Account) instead of a 401(k). It makes him feel like a mini-Warren Buffett. The other day, in a bragging tone, he told me that the mutual fund he is most invested in has returned him an 8% return in 2004. Whenever he talks to me about his stellar returns, I have to bite my tongue. Instead of saying what I want to say, or telling what I know about the mutual fund industry, I simply say "Congratulations."

What I want to ask him are questions such as:

- How much of that 8% has made it to your pocket as real money?

- How do you know that it is really 8%?

- Has the company sent you its annual financial statements?"

- What are the tax consequences of withdrawing that 8%?

- What are the transaction costs to withdraw that 8%?

- How much in fees does the mutual fund company take?

- How do you know what their fees are?

- What is your exit strategy?

- Do you exit with earned, portfolio, or passive income?

- What will you reinvest that 8% in?

- Or will you spend it?

- What happens if the market crashes?

- Will your 8% still be there?

What makes matters even worse is that this friend is a real estate agent who does not invest in real estate. He is a residential real estate broker who deals with homebuyers, not a broker who deals with investors. That may be why he has yet to bring me a deal that warrants a 35% commission.

Why Investing For the Long Term Does Not Work

Personally, I would not be writing this book if that 8% or whatever percent they claim to receive was a real return... but it isn't. It's a fictitious paper return. It isn't real money in their pockets. On top of that, the 8% is often a *short-term* fictitious return... not a real *long-term* return.

David F. Swenson, Chief Investment Officer of Yale University and the best selling author of *Pioneering Portfolio Management* and his latest book, *Unconventional Success*, states and I quote:

Rich Dad

"Mutual-fund complexes employ a variety of subterfuges to mask poor performance, ranging from the extreme of merging poorly performing funds out of existence to more subtle manipulative techniques. When large mutual-fund companies highlight a handful of funds, the firms invariably choose the best-performing, leaving poor-performing nowhere to be seen. If a fund boasts an excellent five-year and a mediocre ten-year record, the company trumpets the strong numbers in dramatic advertising campaigns and buries the weak in the small type of an offering prospectus. Selective presentation of data enhances the superficial appeal of mutual fund offerings, providing an unrealistic picture to the unsophisticated investor." (page 176)

A Two-Decade Study

In his book, *Unconventional Success*, on page 213, Mr. Swenson reviews what he calls a well-executed study by Robert Arnott, Andrew Berkin, and Jia Ye, which examined mutual fund returns over two decades ending in 1998. The results showed that over the course of 20 years, the average mutual fund under-performed the Vanguard 500 Index Fund. In other words, most of the high-salaried fund managers did not beat the index, a mechanical market-mimicking fund. In other words, you don't need a fund manager and you don't need to pay those hidden fees.

In their study, Arnott, Berkin, and Ye found that over a period of 15 years, and when tax consequences are factored in, only 4% of all mutual funds beat the Vanguard 500 Index and beat it only by 0.6%, while the average margin of defeat for the losing mutual funds was –4.8%. This is why I say the advice of *invest for the long term*," especially if you invest in mutual funds, does not make sense. If the winning margin was just 0.6%, why pay all those fees? And if your fund manager cannot beat the Vanguard 500 Index fund, losing –4.8% on average, again why pay all those fees? I don't mind paying my brokers 35% if they make me 200% in real, tax-deferred money in a year. But I resent paying anything for advice that at best beats the Vanguard 500 Index fund by a mere 0.6%.

In simple terms, I believe Mr. Swenson is saying that mutual fund companies are not teaching people to fish and they are definitely not giving people fish. They are in the business of selling fish and, given the fees they collect for so little in return, it makes them selfish.

High fees for the long term and low returns are the result of our school system not teaching people about money, causing people to say, "I have some money, what should I do with it?" When people wander around asking that question, they often turn their money over to people who sell fish but do not teach people to fish.

You may also have noticed that the study stopped in 1998, two years before one of the biggest stock market crashes in history, a crash the market has still not recovered from in 2005. I wonder what Arnott, Berkin, and Ye would find if they extended their study seven more years and included the stock market crash as compared to the real estate market boom? Even though many mutual fund investors lost money, barely made money, or failed to make money, a lot of money, in the biggest real estate boom in history, the mutual fund owners made money from fees because millions of people did as they were told… and invested for the long term.

Why *Teach To Be Rich* Works: The subject of investing is a very large subject. Just in this chapter, Why 'Invest For the Long Term is Obsolete Advice,' there are multiple lessons that are important, lessons that could fill volumes of books. For now, I will only focus on five lessons from this chapter.

Lesson #1: Expand your reality. When I mentioned a 200% return on my money in one year, did you think that kind of return is possible or impossible? Did you say to yourself, "He can do that, but I can't." Or "He can do that in Arizona, but you can't do that where I live?" Or "He's lying. No one can earn 200% on their money in a year." Or "I don't have $500,000 to invest. That's why I can't earn 200% on my money." Or "It's easy for him, he's rich and he has rich friends."

If you had comments such as these, then you experienced a challenge of realities... one reality saying 200% or more is possible and the other reality saying it's not possible. One of the lessons I built into the board game CASHFLOW was the challenge of expanding one's reality... to open your mind to what is possible, rather than think something is impossible. You see, if you think something is not possible, the probability is it isn't possible... even if it is. For example, if I say, "I can't afford to go to college," I probably can't... even though I could. Or if you say, "I'll never have $500,000 to invest," then you probably won't. Henry Ford said, "If you think you can, you can; if you think you can't, you can't. Either way you're right."

There have been too many times in the classes I was teaching when a person would stand up and say, "You can't do that," or "You can do that in Arizona, but can't do that here in California, or New York, or Sydney, or Tokyo, or London, or Cape Town, and even Phoenix." No matter where I am teaching, there are always people who will say "You can't do that here." Or "That's impossible." Or "You're lying to us." Comments such as those mean I have said something outside of their reality... or mental context... outside their view of the world.

One Finger Points Forward And Three Point Back

When I hear such comments, I know the problem is not in what I am saying but in the reality of the person challenging me. As I have stated in other books, whenever someone points their finger at me and says to me "You can't do this or that," I remind them that there is one finger pointing at me and three fingers pointing back at them.

When designing my board game, I took into account all the times people stood up and pointed their finger at me, telling me I could not do what I was doing. That is why I designed into the game the ability to expand one's reality, or experience what I call a *change of context.*

As I studied education and how people learned, I came to realize that a poor person could never become rich, unless there was a change in their context... from the context of a poor person to a context of a rich person. The reason so many lottery winners eventually return to being poor is simply because the amount of money in their hands changed but the money capacity of their brain, their *mental context about money*, did not change.

I've Played Your Game Once

Often people come up to me and say, "I've played your game once."
In response, I may say, "Only once?"
To which they may reply, "Yes. I got out of Rat Race so I know the game."
Every time I hear a person say such things, I know they have missed an important aspect of the

game, the possibility of expanding their context.

Looking at the two financial statements pictured on the next two pages, you will notice each have different numbers on the Passive Income line.

Profession	**Teacher**	Player	**John**

Goal: To get out of the Rat Race and onto the Fast Track by building up your Passive Income to be greater than your Total Expenses

Income Statement

Auditor	**Ryan**

Person on your right

Income

Description	Cash Flow
Salary:	$3,300
Interest:	
Dividends:	
2BIG Power	$130,000
Real Estate:	
3/2 House	$300
4-Plex	$600
16U Apartment	$2,550
Businesses:	
Auto Wash	$1800

Passive Income= **$135,250**
(Cash Flows from Interest + Dividends + Real Estate + Businesses)

Total Income: $138,550

Expenses

Taxes:	$630
Home Mortgage:	$500
School Loan Payment:	$60
Car Payment:	$200
Credit Card Payment:	$90
Retail Payment:	$50
Other Expenses:	$760
Child Expenses:	
Bank Loan Payment:	$200

Number of Children: _____
(Begin game with 0 Children)

Per Child Expense: _$180_

Total Expenses: $2,390

Monthly Cash Flow: $136,160
(Pay Check)

Balance Sheet

Assets

	No. of Shares:	Cost/Share:
Savings:		
Stocks/Mutual's/CDs		
OK4U	600	$20
2BIG	13,000	$1,200
Real Estate:	Down Pay:	Cost:
3/2 House	$5,000	$95,000
4-Plex	$15,000	$125.000
16Apt	$50,000	$500,000
Business:	Down Pay:	Cost:
Auto Wash	$50,000	$350,000

Liabilities

Home Mortgage:	$50,000
School Loans:	$12,000
Car Loans:	$5,000
Credit Cards:	$3,00
Retail Debt:	$1,000
RE Mortgage:	
3/2 House	$90,000
4-Plex	$110,000
16Apt	$450,000
Liability: (Business)	
Auto Wash	$300,000
Bank Loan:	

©1996-2002 CASHFLOW® Technologies, Inc. All rights reserved. CASHFLOW® games are covered by one or more of the following US Patents; 5,826,878; 6,032,957 and 6,106,300. RichDad®, CASHFLOW® and Investing 101® are registered trademarks of CASHFLOW® Technologies, Inc.

G101CT17

One player completed the game with $135,250 in passive income.

Profession	**Janitor**	Player	**Shannon**

Goal: To get out of the Rat Race and onto the Fast Track by building up your Passive Income to be greater than your Total Expenses

Income Statement

Income

Description	Cash Flow
Salary:	$1,600
Interest:	
Dividends:	
Real Estate:	
2/1 House	$315
Businesses:	

Auditor	**Linda**

Person on your right

Passive Income= $315
(Cash Flows from Interest +
Dividends + Real Estate + Businesses)

Total
Income: $1,915

Expenses

Taxes:	$280
Home Mortgage:	$200
School Loan Payment:	
Car Payment:	$60
Credit Card Payment:	$60
Retail Payment:	$50
Other Expenses:	$300
Child Expenses:	
Bank Loan Payment:	$200

Number of
Children: _____
(Begin game with 0 Children)
Per Child
Expense: $70

Total
Expenses: $950

Monthly
Cash Flow: $965
(Pay Check)

Balance Sheet

Assets

Savings:		
Stocks/Mutual's/CDs	No. of Shares:	Cost/Share:
Real Estate:	Down Pay:	Cost:
2/1 House	$2,000	$52,000
Business:	Down Pay:	Cost:

Liabilities

Home Mortgage:	$20,000
School Loans:	
Car Loans:	$4,000
Credit Cards:	$2,000
Retail Debt:	$1,000
RE Mortgage:	
2/1 House	$50,000
Liability: (Business)	
Bank Loan:	

©1996-2002 CASHFLOW® Technologies, Inc. All rights reserved. CASHFLOW® games are covered by one or more of the following US Patents; 5,826,878; 6,032,957 and 6,106,300. RichDad®, CASHFLOW® and Investing 101® are registered trademarks of CASHFLOW® Technologies, Inc.

G101CTI7

Another player completed the game with only $315 in passive income.

Notice that scores are vastly different, even though it is the same game, same time, and same rules. Just as in real life, many people start the game of life with nothing, but some wind up with a much more abundant life. One reason why is the difference in realities… different contexts.

One of the reasons for playing the game as many times as possible is to expand your context. As you expand your context, you will notice that your scores will gradually increase. When you teach others to play the game, you will find your context expanding again. This is Golden Rule #1 in action.

When people's contexts expand during game, many of them report being able to see greater opportunities in the real world. When reading *Rich Dad's Success Stories*, you will find many of the people found financial opportunities all around them, after playing the CASHFLOW game a number of times. One of the reasons they could see more opportunities that were right in front of them was because their context was expanded and their eyes were opened to greater possibilities.

My 'personal best' playing the game has been a little over $30 million a month in passive income. To achieve that mark I had to really push my context. I have heard of people gaining over $1 billion a month playing the game… the same game… same rules. Just as Tiger Woods and I both play golf… same game… same rules… but his scores are consistently better than mine since he plays the game from a different context. In Part IV of this book, I will go into the power of context and its impact upon financial possibilities in more depth.

When it comes to the subject of context, always remember Henry Ford's words of wisdom which are, "If you think you can, you can; if you think you can't, you can't. Either way, you're right."

Lesson #2: Increasing your mental speed. One of the reasons the game seems to take so long at first is simply because the person playing the game is learning to process multiple bits of information. This takes time to learn. For example, let's say the player draws the following card from the game:

Stock — OK4U Drug Co.

Booming market raises share price of this long time maker of medicines.

<u>Only you may buy</u> as many shares as you want at this price.

<u>Everyone may sell</u> at this price.

Symbol OK4U   **Today's price: $50**

No dividend (Yield or ROI= 0%)

Trading Range: $5 to $40

The player then begins to process the information on the card, analyzing it, then comparing it to their current financial position on their financial statement on the next diagram.

| Profession | | Player | |

Goal: To get out of the Rat Race and onto the Fast Track by building up your Passive Income to be greater than your Total Expenses

Income Statement

Income

Description	Cash Flow
Salary:	
Interest:	
Dividends:	
Real Estate:	
Businesses:	

Auditor

Person on your right

Passive Income= _____
(Cash Flows from Interest +
Dividends + Real Estate + Businesses)

Total Income: _____

Expenses

Taxes:	
Home Mortgage:	
School Loan Payment:	
Car Payment:	
Credit Card Payment:	
Retail Payment:	
Other Expenses:	
Child Expenses:	
Bank Loan Payment:	

Number of Children: _____
(Begin game with 0 Children)
Per Child Expense: _____

Total Expenses: _____

Monthly Cash Flow: _____
(Pay Check)

Balance Sheet

Assets			Liabilities	
Savings:			Home Mortgage:	
Stocks/Mutual's/CDs	No. of Shares:	Cost/Share:	School Loans:	
			Car Loans:	
			Credit Cards:	
Real Estate:	Down Pay:	Cost:	Retail Debt:	
			RE Mortgage:	
Business:	Down Pay:	Cost:	Liability: (Business)	
			Bank Loan:	

©1996-2002 CASHFLOW® Technologies, Inc. All rights reserved. CASHFLOW® games are covered by one or more of the following US Patents; 5,826,878; 6,032,957 and 6,106,300. RichDad®, CASHFLOW® and Investing 101® are registered trademarks of CASHFLOW® Technologies, Inc.

G101CTI7

The player then needs to determine if the opportunity fits their financial strategy and if it will help them reach their financial goals (which in the case of the game is to get out of the Rat Race) and get on to the Fast Track with enough money and financial intelligence to do well on the Fast Track pictured on the game board on the next page.

When first learning the game, this analytical and strategic planning process takes a while to learn.

In the first example, the stock OK4U, appeared on a Stock Market Opportunity card. There are other Opportunity cards, such as the real estate card, pictured below.

House for Sale — 3 Br/2Ba

Nice 3/2 house available in depressed market due to layoffs. Would make good investment property for right buyer.

Use this yourself or sell to another player.

60% ROI, may sell for $65,000 to $135,000.

Cost: $50,000	**Mortgage: $46,000**
DownPay: $4,000	**Cash Flow: +$200**

Once again, the player who draws this card needs to analyze this investment opportunity and compare it to their current financial position and financial strategy.

Other Opportunity cards feature:

1. **Precious metals**

Rare Gold Coin

You spot an unusual 1500's Royal Spanish New World (Havana Mint Only) "pieces of eight" gold coin in good condition at a swap meet. One only, seller asks $500.

Use this yourself or sell to another player.

0% ROI, may sell for $0 to $4,000.

Cost: $500	Liability: $0
DownPay: $500	Cash Flow: $0

2. **Mutual funds**

Mutual Fund — GRO4US Fund

Lower interest rates drive market and fund to strong showing.

Only you may buy as many units as you want at this price.

Everyone may sell at this price.

Symbol GRO4US   Today's price: $30

No dividend (Yield or ROI = 0%)

Trading Range: $10 to $30

3. **Business card**

Start a Company Part Time

Develop interesting idea for a software program, so you start a company to produce and sell it. No profits during startup, long hours, no extra pay.

Use this yourself or sell to another player.

0% ROI, may sell for ??, if anything.

Cost: $5,000	Liability: $0
DownPay: $5,000	Cash Flow: $0

As I said, one of the reasons the game takes a while to learn is because there is a lot to learn. Between these opportunity cards and other game event cards, such as Doodad cards and Market cards, the novice player must process many bits of financial data while still trying to win the game. This is why I recommend playing the game at least four times, just to learn the game. This is also why I cringe when someone says, "I played your game once."

How Fast Is Your Brain?

In the Information Age, the person that wins is the person who can take many random bits of information and process them. Increasing the speed at which you can process financial information is one of the more important aspects I built into the educational process of the game. The more you play the game, the faster you will find your ability to process random bits of financial data. When you can do that in the real world, you will probably find that your financial success increases.

Slow Drivers

Most of us have experienced the frustration of being stuck behind slow drivers, especially when we're in a hurry. Today, this is how I often feel when I talk to investors who think investing their money for the long term — gaining an 8% highly-taxed, non-transparent, fee- and expense-heavy return in mutual funds — is the smart thing to do. So that is why I designed into the board game the ability to not only increase a person's context but also the ability to process financial information at higher rates of speed… but you have to play the game more than once and be willing to help players who are slower than you are. You can also learn a lot by having faster players teach you how to process information faster.

Lesson #3: Know the difference between short-term and long-term investments. You may notice in my example of starting with $500,000, investing in 10 units for one year, and then converting it, tax-deferred, into a 288-unit apartment house for at least a 10-year holding period, that I was not always investing for the long-term. In the example, I was sometimes investing for capital gains and sometimes investing for cash flow. Sometimes I had a short window and sometimes I had a longer window. In other words, I simply don't hand my money over… to strangers… for the long term.

In many people's world, the idea of blindly turning their money over to experts — most who cannot beat the S&P 500 over the long-term — makes sense to them. To these same people, paying these so-called experts more fees as their nest egg increases, for the long term, also makes sense.

But to me, it does not make sense. To me, it is not financially intelligent. In the real world, at least *my* real world, it makes more sense to know when to go long and when to go short, know what my entry strategies and my exit strategies are before I enter, when to go for *cash flow* and when to go for *capital gains*, and to pay my transaction costs only when I need to. This important aspect of being a professional investor was designed into the game. Many people do not even know they are learning these important investor skills, simply because these skills have been embedded into the game. That means people are learning a lot while they are having a lot of fun.

Lesson #4: Know the difference between relationships and transactions. The one big thing that puzzles me is how people can blindly turn their money — money for their financial future, money for their financial security — over to total strangers. My financial future and financial security is very important to me and that is why I want to know who I invest my money with. That is why it is important to know the difference between a *transaction* and a *relationship*.

The other day, I went into my local supermarket to buy food for dinner. The checkout girl smiled

and said, "Have a nice day," as I left the store. Although we have smiled and been cordial to each other for years, I would call our business together a *transaction*. In other words, if she quit and a new checkout person took her place, we would probably still be cordial during the transaction.

When it comes to investing my money, in most cases I want a relationship. One of the reasons why Kim and I got the 10 apartments to condominium conversion deal was because we have a relationship with the broker. Not only are we long-term friends in business, we are friends in life. We see each other socially and often go to the gym or hike together. I have tremendous respect for him and his wife and I would say they have respect for us.

When we invested our tax-deferred million dollars into the 288-unit apartment house, we invested with two other long-term professional as well as social friends, whom we have invested with in other bigger investments.

When the transaction on the 288-unit apartment house hit a snag, our friend the broker stepped in, on the side of both parties, and helped us make the deal an even better one for all of us, even though he did not receive a commission for his assistance. That's an example of a relationship investment.

Lesson #5: The Importance of Checking the Numbers. Looking at the financial statement from the CASHFLOW game, in the next diagram, notice that I have pointed an arrow to the word Auditor.

In the real world of business and investing, this person — the auditor — is one of the more important people in the long-term operation of the business or investment. That is why I built this role into the play of the game.

Unfortunately, when I observe the game being played, I notice that many players do not fill this line in, nor do they perform the audit. To me, that shows that the person lacks sophistication in their financial life. They obviously do not think the audit or the auditor is important. They probably do not have monthly or weekly financial audits in real life.

Rich dad drummed into his son's head (and mine) the importance of being able to audit numbers and allowing professionals to audit your numbers. In simple terms, it is a matter of checks and balances. That is why it is an important aspect of the game.

By taking the time to check your playing partner's numbers, you learn more about money, finances, numbers, and how others think. By having another player check your numbers, you learn more about how you think and how your fellow player thinks.

When our friend, the broker, stepped in to audit our 288-unit deal, we all learned a lot about how each party thought differently and how we could make a good deal even better. That is the power of an audit in real life and the power of relationship-based business versus transaction-based business… and that is why the auditing function and the auditor role are built into the CASHFLOW game. It's Golden Rule #1.

Profession _____   ## Player _____

Goal: To get out of the Rat Race and onto the Fast Track by building up your Passive Income to be greater than your Total Expenses

Income Statement

Income

Description	Cash Flow
Salary:	
Interest:	
Dividends:	
Real Estate:	
Businesses:	

Expenses

Taxes:
Home Mortgage:
School Loan Payment:
Car Payment:
Credit Card Payment:
Retail Payment:
Other Expenses:
Child Expenses:
Bank Loan Payment:

Auditor _____

Person on your right

Passive Income= _____
(Cash Flows from Interest +
Dividends + Real Estate + Businesses)

Total Income: _____

Number of Children: _____
(Begin game with 0 Children)
Per Child Expense: _____

Total Expenses: _____

Monthly Cash Flow: _____
(Pay Check)

Balance Sheet

Assets

Savings:
Stocks/Mutual's/CDs   No. of Shares: Cost/Share:

Real Estate: Down Pay: Cost:

Business: Down Pay: Cost:

Liabilities

Home Mortgage:
School Loans:
Car Loans:
Credit Cards:
Retail Debt:
RE Mortgage:

Liability: (Business)

Bank Loan:

©1996-2002 CASHFLOW® Technologies, Inc. All rights reserved. CASHFLOW® games are covered by one or more of the following US Patents; 5,826,878; 6,032,957 and 6,106,300. RichDad®, CASHFLOW® and Investing 101® are registered trademarks of CASHFLOW® Technologies, Inc.   G101CTI7

In Summary...

Instead of acting like sheep in a flock, being herded by a salesperson disguised as a shepherd... teaching yourself and others to be rich makes more sense to me.

Author's Note: If you do not believe the magnitude of the problem and how bad mutual funds are as a primary investment for retirement, I suggest you read David F. Swensen, Chief Investment Officer of Yale University's book, *Unconventional Success*: A Fundamental Approach to Personal Finance. While I do not follow his investment strategy, I do appreciate his comments on the mutual fund industry.

Second Author's Note: Rich dad often said "It is easy to get richer if you are smart and rich and have rich and smart friends." So instead of being a *long-term investor* and blindly turning your money over to total strangers, why not teach others to be rich, meet new friends, develop *long-term relationships*, and help each other become rich. That is what I did, and I find helping friends get rich is much more rewarding than having total strangers, who I will probably never meet, become richer. To me, Golden Rule #1 is a much better rule than Golden Rule #3. That is why *Teach to be Rich* works for me.

Chapter Ten

WHY "DIVERSIFY" IS OBSOLETE ADVICE

Warren Buffett, America's richest and best-known investor, has this to say about diversification. He said:

"Diversification is required when investors do not understand what they are doing."

Who Do You Agree With?

If America's richest investor is saying diversification is not required if you know what you are doing, then why do so many so-called experts recommend you diversify? Who do you agree with? Warren Buffett or the other financial experts?

Personally, I agree with Mr. Buffett. I do not diversify, at least not in the way most financial advisors recommend. Yet, if you do not understand what you are doing, then diversify. I am certain that many investment advisors recommend diversification because they themselves do not understand what they are doing. In many ways, recommending that you diversify is their way of protecting you from *their* lack of understanding.

When I asked my rich dad his opinion on diversification he said, "Diversification is like going to the race track and betting on *all* the horses, rather than trying to pick the winner. By betting on the all the horses, you may not lose much money, but you also do not make much money." He also believed a reason why so many financial advisors recommend diversification is simply because they cannot pick a winner… so they play it safe, and try not to have you get angry at them, or expose their lack of ability to pick winners. They recommend you bet on all the horses.

On this subject he also said, "A mutual fund is like a multiple-vitamin. They both contain a variety of elements that are good for you. When you diversify and buy several mutual funds, it is the same as taking three or four vitamins. You spend a lot of money, but do not gain much more value."

When is Diversifying… Not Really Diversifying

When I was in school, my rich dad taught me that there are three basic asset classes. They are:

1. Paper Assets — Assets such as stocks, bonds, mutual funds

2. Real Estate — Assets such as raw land or buildings

3. Businesses — Privately-held and public

Rich dad said, "Of all three assets, the hardest asset to own is a business. Businesses are complex with many moving parts and are people-dependent. Yet, if you are good at business, you can become very, very, rich. In fact, the richest people in the world are entrepreneurs, people who start and build businesses. The next most difficult asset to own is real estate. For many people just buying their home is an ordeal of epic proportion. When they think of buying large apartment houses, retail malls, or office buildings and managing them, most would rather not invest in such a complex asset. Obviously, the easiest of the three asset classes to own is paper assets. You can simply call a brokerage house, open an account and for as little as $100 you're an investor. No mess, no stress, no management, and very little paperwork. That is why more people own paper assets than own real estate or a business." Rich dad also said, "You don't have to be financially smart to do well in paper assets. Simply buy, hold, and pray. But if you want to be successful in real estate or in business, you had better be much smarter than the average investor."

On the subject of diversification, rich dad said, "Many people who own paper assets think they are diversified, but in reality, many aren't diversified." He explained further saying "Some people say they are diversified because they are invested in different shares of stock of different companies; or different countries through a mutual fund, bonds, via a bond fund; or real estate via a REIT (Real Estate Investment Trust); or commodities via a precious metals fund. Even if they are investing in different types of assets, they are technically still invested in only one asset class, paper assets."

That means many people who think they are diversified really are not. Many people are only in one asset class, paper assets. Again, that is because paper assets are the easiest to buy, hold, and sell. They are convenient and easily transportable. Unlike a business or real estate, paper assets require very little management or attention once purchased.

Investing In China, Real Estate, And Business

The other day, I met a friend from our days as pilots in the Marine Corps. After we got out, he got his MBA and went to work for a large computer firm as a district sales manager. As the subject of retirement came up, he began telling me about his investment portfolio. He said, "I am well diversified. I own two large cap mutual funds, a small cap fund, I am investing in China through a fund that specializes in Chinese companies, I invest in real estate through a REIT, I have a bond fund for income, and I own two closed-end funds, one specializing in oil and gas and the other in commodities."

"And how are you doing?" I asked.

"Oh, I'm up about 12%," he said with a smile.

"Over what time period?" I asked.

"Oh, over the last year. The market's been going up you know."

"And how are you doing over the past 10 years?" I asked.

"Well, I'm down a little. You know everyone lost money in the crash after 9/11. But the market's coming back so I'm hanging tight."

"Not everyone lost… " I replied. "In the stock market, for every loser there were winners. But that is another story. My concern is, will you be able to afford to retire soon?"

"I hope so," he said with a smile. "If the market keeps going up, I should be able to retire in ten years."

"And if it goes down?" I asked. "What then?"

"Well, I try not to think about that. You know that pessimists never win," he said.

"And neither do foolish optimists," I said to myself.

He smiled and cheerfully continued, "So I keep a positive attitude, watch the market, and hang tight. I'm well diversified and I'm in for the long term." He paused for a moment, looked at me and asked, "And you, when do you plan on retiring?"

"Oh, about 10 years ago," I replied. "I retired in 1994 at the age of 47."

"How did you do that?" he asked.

"By not diversifying," I replied.

Diversified In One Class

My friend had made a mistake many people make. He thought he was well diversified by investing in different funds. Yet when you step back and look at what he has done, he is invested in only one asset class… paper assets. So on one level he is diversified, but on another he is not. When the stock market crashed, everything he was invested in crashed or failed to grow. And while his paper assets were going down, real estate was hitting all time highs. While he is regaining some of his losses in 2005, he has missed out on one of the biggest financial booms in history because he thought he was diversified… and he wasn't. While it is true that diversification prevented him from massive losses, he still lost instead of gained.

Why A $5 Loss Is Really A $10 Loss

Warren Buffett said, "Rule number one is 'Don't lose money.' Rule number two is 'Always remember rule number one.' "

During one of his interviews on television, Mr. Buffett said, "If you lose $5, it takes $10 to get back to where you were." In other words, after the person lost $5, it takes $5 to make up the loss. If he had not lost the first $5 in the first place, and made another $5, he would have been ahead $10 instead of being at break even. That is why a $5 loss is really a loss of $10.

When I attempted to explain Warren Buffett's point of view on losses to my Marine Corps friend, he became agitated and a little defensive. His comment was "I didn't really lose any money. I didn't sell when the market crashed like everyone else did. You don't lose if you don't sell. It's the people who sold after the market crashed that lost the money. I held on like you're supposed to do. The markets coming back so I haven't lost anything. All I have to do is sit tight, keep diversified, and invest for the long term."

Knowing When To Hold And When To Fold

A very important lesson rich dad repeatedly taught his son and me was the strategy of "cutting your losses." He said, "Every professional investor knows that they will occasionally make a mistake and make a bad investment. So professionals know that cutting your losses, as early as possible, is always a strategic option you keep in your bag of tricks." He went to say, "People who need to be right, or refuse to admit they made a mistake, often hold on to their losses, refusing to let go."

"When do you know when it's time to cut your losses?" his son Mike asked him.

"That's the tricky part," said rich dad. "Some people quit too early. Some quit too late. And some never quit at all."

"You mean some people hang on to losses forever?" I asked.

Nodding, rich dad said, "And knowing when to hold and when to fold is a talent that can only be developed with experience. For example, poker players eventually learn that sometimes it is best to fold your hand, even if it's a good hand. And at other times, they hold on to a bad hand and bluff their way into winning."

"Like the song '*The Gambler*' sung by Kenny Rogers says, 'You got to know when to hold 'em and know when to fold 'em…'"

Rich dad nodded and said, "And that takes experience. Professional investors would rather cut early rather than later… yet even if late, they will cut their losses eventually.

"And what about amateur investors?" I asked.

"Amateurs tend to hold on to losers forever."

"Why?" I asked.

"They don't want to admit they made a mistake."

The Worst Kind Of Liar

One day, when rich dad caught me in a lie (denying I had lost a golf match and pretending that I had won), he said, "A person who cannot admit they lost is the biggest loser of all." He also said, "Everyone loses now and then. Only a real loser pretends he never loses. The moment you admit you lost, that you have made mistakes, then you can begin to make corrections, learn, and grow again. But if you pretend you never lose and never make mistakes, then you never learn; and if you stop learning, you stop winning." After pausing for a moment he said, "The worst kind of liar is a liar who believes his own lies."

Diversification Does Not Protect You

If you are in only one asset class, for example paper assets, diversification will not protect you from losses. When the stock market plunged between 2000 and 2003, it should have been crystal clear that diversification did not protect investors. When the paper asset market went down, almost everything went down, even bonds. In spite of this reality, the financial experts continue to rant, on and on, about the importance of diversifying.

The sad truth is, while the amateur investor — the investor saving for retirement or college education for their kids — was listening to the financial experts, investing for the long term, staying diversified, the professional investors were cutting their losses and running. The more the professionals and semi-pros cut their losses, the more the amateur investor lost, simply because they followed their financial advisors words of wisdom, "Invest for the long-term and diversify."

To me, what is even worse is that, as Warren Buffett points out, a $5 loss costs you $10. So on top of that, between 1995 and 2005 they missed out on far more than a $5 dollar loss, they missed out on a multi-trillion dollar move in the real estate market, all because they were investing for the long-term and diversifying, even though they were not diversified.

Other Markets

When rich dad's son and I were in high school, and trying to figure out what we wanted to do when we left school, rich dad pointed out to us that there were many different markets in the world. He pointed out, "There are many different markets to invest in."

The five biggest markets are:

1. The stock market

2. The bond market

3. The real estate market

4. The currency market

5. The commodities market

Author's Note: I put the word "The" in front of each market intentionally. The reason for the "The" is to indicate that each market is a separate and unique market unto itself. And each market can be broken down into an infinite number of sub-markets. For example, the real estate market can be broken into land, commercial real estate, and residential real estate. And each of these categories of real estate can be infinitely broken down into even more sub-markets. For example, land can be broken down into forest land, ranch land, residential land, farmland, etc.

One of the reasons for becoming an expert in a submarket, such as taking farmland and turning it into residential land, is because that is how a person becomes rich. In other words, instead of turning your money over to people who claim to be experts, why not become an expert? In other words, instead of diversifying, why not become an expert to specialize and focus your time and money? That is what Warren Buffett does and that is what I do and what most professionals do. In other words, professionals specialize and amateurs diversify.

Confused Investors

When an amateur investor buys a mutual fund that specializes in commodities, the investor is buying a product developed by Wall Street and packaged for amateurs. The mutual fund goes to the amateurs and tells them, "We are experts. If you want to invest in commodities such as gold, silver, pork bellies, cotton, or wheat, let us do it for you. All you have to do is give us your money and we will pick the best commodities for you. Of course there will be fees we have to collect for this service." The mutual fund company then hires so-called experts to invest the investors' money in the commodity market and sell it through the stock market.

Mutual fund companies do the same thing with real estate. Instead of selling real estate, they say to investors, "We are experts. Give us your money and let us invest in real estate for you." They form a REIT and go to the real estate market to buy real estate. In other words, the investor buys real estate through the stock market, not the real estate market.

Supermarkets And Stock Markets

Supermarkets do the same thing stock markets do. Supermarkets buy cattle from ranchers, via the commodity market. The supermarket then processes the animal into steaks, roasts, and hamburger, neatly packages and prices the cuts of meat, then sells the meats to retail customers via neighborhood stores. The stock market does the same thing with different investments from different markets.

This packaging of products from different investments in different markets, then selling it through the stock market or financial advisors, causes many amateurs to be confused. Many amateurs think there is only one market, the stock market, and only one kind of asset, paper assets. Many amateur investors see the stock market as their one-stop-shop for all their investment needs. They fail to see the different markets behind the stock markets products.

When you look at the CASHFLOW game board, once again consider the difference between the Fast Track and the Rat Race. The Fast Track is where the real professional investors and the rich investors invest. It is from the Fast Track that the stock markets such as Wall Street, NASDAQ, and other foreign stock exchanges get their supply of fresh new shares of stock to sell into the Rat Race.

Just as a rancher brings cattle to market and sells the animals to supermarkets, entrepreneurs and rich investors bring their products from the Fast Track, and sell them to the investors in the Rat Race via the stock market.

In other words, the real game of investing is to take investments from the Fast Track, sanitize, securitize, and package them into bite sizes pieces, and sell them into the Rat Race.

The problem with this is that the consumer in the Rat Race purchases a paper asset that has already had the lion's share of the profits taken out. The real investors, the investors on the Fast Track, have already made most of the money. That is why, in the Rat Race, the returns are often smaller and the investment is far more risky… which is why your friendly neighborhood so-called financial expert recommends you diversify.

In the next part of this book, you will find out why investments on the Fast Track are less risky than the sanitized, securitized, and packaged investments in the Rat Race.

Moving From Market To Market

Between 1995 and 2000 I began moving out of the stock market and into the commodities market. I began investing in gold and oil. Why did I do that? The answer is because gold and oil were very, very inexpensive. Oil in 1997 was approximately $10 a barrel and gold was less than $275 an

ounce. On top of that, all the financial experts were saying to invest in technology stocks. Today, as I write this, oil is over $60 a barrel and gold is over $500 an ounce.

While this may seem like diversifying, I really wasn't — at least not in the sense your neighborhood financial expert says to diversify. Instead of trying to be in all markets, I was moving out of one market into other markets.

You Can't Time Markets?

During one of my talks to investors, an agitated young man stood up and said, "You got lucky. You know you can't time markets." He was referring to another old bit of financial wisdom that recommends you try not to time the ups and downs of markets. Obviously, this bit of wisdom supports the other old bit of financial wisdom, which is to "*Invest for the long term and diversify... so we can continue to collect our fees.*"

Calmly I said, "I was not timing the markets. I was simply taking my profits and moving my profits to an undervalued market. In other words, I like to sell high and buy low."

Still agitated, he shot back, "But to me that is timing the market."

"Maybe to you, but not to me," I replied. "I simply want more bang for my bucks."

"But how did you know when to buy and when to sell?" he demanded.

"Simple," I replied. "When fools are buying, I sell. And when fools are selling, I like to buy."

Speechless for a moment, the young man glared at me and finally said, "So do you think you're an expert on markets?"

Chuckling I said, "No. At the time, many of the market experts were saying such things as "Gold is dead." and "Oil is plentiful." They were also warning people to stay out of China and invest in the good old U.S.A., especially in Silicon Valley."

"So what did you base your decision on? What are you good at?" he asked.

Thinking his question a fair question, I thought awhile and replied, "I like finding bargains with value. I am pretty good at that. I don't believe in buying something just because it's cheap or low-priced. Cheap junk is still junk. For centuries gold has been valuable and oil is a commodity we burn everyday."

Nearly satisfied, the young man thought for awhile and then asked "And what else are you good at?"

"I believe I am good at judging people," I replied.

"And how does that make you a good investor?" he asked.

"I already told you. When fools and experts say to sell, I buy. And when fools and experts are buying, I tend to sell. It's not about market timing. It's about real value and foolish people."

Why *Teach To Be Rich* Works: Diversification is a *defensive* strategy. If you want to become rich, you need to have better *offensive* strategies.

As Warren Buffett says,

> *"Diversification is required when investors do not understand what they are doing."*

So, if you do not understand what you are doing, then I, too, recommend diversify. As stated earlier, diversification is a crude defensive strategy, not a financially smart strategy. This means that diversification is expensive, slow, and still risky.

As stated earlier, in the Information Age, we all need better information. In the Information Age, there are better mental strategies and financial tools available... tools and strategies that are far more effective, less risky, and potentially more profitable than simply diversifying. Instead of diversifying, those who play CASHFLOW learn to trade in and out of different markets. The players learn how to use stocks in some transactions and real estate in others.

Also, in CASHFLOW 101, the players learn to buy low and sell high. If they sell low and buy high, which many investors do in the real world, they lose the game. As simple as the concept *buy low and sell high* is to grasp mentally, in real life and in the game, sometimes it's not that simple. As an example, look at the card below.

Stock — MYT4U Electronics Co.

Low interest rates lead to substantial share price for this home electronics seller.

<u>Only you may buy</u> as many shares as you want at this price.

<u>Everyone may sell</u> at this price.

Symbol MYT4U   Today's price: $30

No dividend (Yield or ROI = 0%)

Trading Range: $5 to $30

The player drawing this card needs to decide if this is a good buy or a bad buy. In order to come to that decision, the player needs to process different and random bits of information. In other words, he needs to think, he needs to use his brain. Some bits of information the player needs to process are:

1. Their financial position

2. Their cash position

3. Their financial objectives

4. The financial positions of the other players

5. The cash positions of the other players

6. How far ahead or behind the other players are

7. The historical market trends so far in the game

8. How much he can borrow... leverage

9. The intrinsic value of the investment

10. And of course, how lucky they feel

As stated in an earlier chapter, when a player first plays CASHFLOW 101, the game may proceed slowly because the player is training his or her brain to process multiple bits of information. He or she will win or lose the game depending upon how he or she processes many different bits of information

and accurately interprets the information.

As you can tell by the list of ten different bits of information on the previous page, a simple conceptual strategy such as *buy low and sell high* is not that simple in the game or in real life. That is why so many people make foolish decision when markets are very high, very low, and in this example, even when the price is in the middle of the trading range.

Return On Investments

Another important strategy taught in the CASHFLOW game is how to value the return on investment (ROI) of an asset. For example, let's say the player buys shares of stock from the opportunity card pictured below.

Stock — OK4U Drug Co.

Market panic causes crash in the shares of this long time maker of medicines.

<u>Only you may buy</u> as many shares as you want at this price.

<u>Everyone may sell</u> at this price.

Symbol OK4U   **Today's price: $1**

No dividend (Yield or ROI = 0%)

Trading Range: $5 to $40

In other words, the stock has taken a pounding in the market so the price has dropped below the historical support level of $5. Even though other investors have lost confidence in this company and are selling, which drives the price down to the new low, the intrepid player buys 1000 shares at $1 per share.

Five turns later, another player draws a card that reads

Stock — OK4U Drug Co.

Inflation worries cause poor share price of this long time maker of medicines.

<u>Only you may buy</u> as many shares as you want at this price.

<u>Everyone may sell</u> at this price.

Symbol OK4U   **Today's price: $10**

No dividend (Yield or ROI = 0%)

Trading Range: $5 to $40

Only the player can buy, but everyone else can sell

This means the rest of the market has realized the error of its ways, and has begun buying. So the price of the stock is creeping up. The player who purchased the stock at $1 per share, then needs to decide if it is better to sell or to hold. If the player sells, he or she pockets $10,000 ($10 X 1,000 shares). If they wait, and later sell for let's say $40 per share, they could earn $40,000, which is obviously better than $10,000.

Here, as in real life, greed and fear meet head-on. Once again the decision to hold or sell is not that simple. In the game, the player has to process the previous 10 bits of information as well as some of the following bits of information.

1. Am I early or late in the game?

2. Can I afford to wait?

3. How many other players are in the game? (the number of players affect the odds of a better card being drawn.

4. When I exit the Rat Race and get on to the Fast Track, how much money do I want? (Some players who exit out of the Rat Race early and get on to the Fast Track, often find they should have stayed in a little longer and accrued a little more money. This is a very similar problem many retirees face before and after retiring, in real life.)

If you do not understand all of this, do not worry. That is what the game is for and why you may want to play it again and again. One of the reasons you play the game repetitively is because, as in life, each time you play you learn something new. If you had not played previous games and learned what you had learned then, then you would not be ready to see what is revealed in the current game. In other words, our learning builds on learning. If you play the game once and stop, you will not learn anything new. So the more you play the game, and if you push yourself to improve your times and scores, you will begin to see and learn things you would never have learned or understood if you had only played the game once or twice.

As Returns Go Up, Returns Go Down

As your learning increases, you will be able to make more distinctions, distinctions that most investors miss. Let's use the same two Opportunity cards as an example:

Only the player can buy, but everyone else can sell

Stock — OK4U Drug Co.

Market panic causes crash in the shares of this long time maker of medicines.

Only you may buy as many shares as you want at this price.

Everyone may sell at this price.

Symbol OK4U   Today's price: $1

No dividend (Yield or ROI = 0%)

Trading Range: $5 to $40

Stock — OK4U Drug Co.

Inflation worries cause poor share price of this long time maker of medicines.

<u>Only you may buy</u> as many shares as you want at this price.

<u>Everyone may sell</u> at this price.

Symbol OK4U   **Today's price: $10**

No dividend (Yield or ROI = 0%)

Trading Range: $5 to $40

The financial IQ question is: *Why does your percentage return go down as the price goes up?* In other words, you purchased 1000 shares at $1. You have an opportunity to sell at $10... but you want to wait and hold to see if the stock will reach $40. Why does your percentage return decrease at $40? This may seem like a trick question, yet it is a real life question many amateurs miss.

The answer is, your percentage return decreases because your return on equity decreases as the stock prices goes up.

Let me explain. Since you invested only $1 per share, your cash-on-cash return at $10 a share is 1000% return. But let's say you hold and are waiting for the price to get to $40 a share; your return on equity actually goes down if you wait for the price to go up.

Why? The answer is, at $10 a share, your new equity is $10. If you wait to sell at $40, your return on *equity* ($10) will only be 400%. So in this example, the percentage return on equity (not your investment) goes down as the price goes up.

Again, this may seem like a trick or trivial question, yet to a professional investor, it is one way of evaluating the value of investment, and helps in the decision to sell or hold at $10 rather than wait for a possible opportunity to sell at $40. And again, if it does not make much sense to you, don't worry. The more you play the game, and you stack learning upon learning, you will be able to make better decisions as to whether to buy, sell, or hold, and in turn make more money faster, with less risk.

Calculating Return On Investment vs Return On Equity

In the real world, many investors do not make the distinction between *return on investment* and *return on equity*. For example, a person puts $10,000 down to buy a $100,000 home. Five years later the house is valued at $300,000. The investor crows that he has made a $200,000 ($300,000-$100,000) gain on his $10,000 investment, a 2,000% ROI (return on investment). Then they brag at the next cocktail party, "My net worth went up by $200,000." The problem is, they sit there with that $200,000 equity and the equity is not returning anything to them. So their *return on equity* is zero. In other words, that money, the $200,000 equity, is just sitting there not working and the investor remains stuck, working hard in the Rat Race. That is the difference between *return on investment* and *return on equity*.

Deciding To Sell

A number of years ago, Kim and I purchased a 30-unit apartment house for $800,000. We put approximately $150,000 down and we earned about $4,000 per month, or $48,000 a year, net passive income. That meant we were receiving approximately 30% cash on cash return on our $150,000.

About a year ago, we realized that our property was now worth about $2 million dollars and our income from the property had remained the same, approximately $48,000 a year. The reason rents had not gone up was because so many tenants were buying their own homes, now that interest rates were low, the rental market was soft, and rental income stayed the same.

One of the reasons we decided to sell was because prices were going up but our return on equity was going down. At a $2 million valuation, our equity was now approximately $1.4 million (our initial down payment plus appreciation). With our net cash flow income flat at $48,000 a year, that meant our return on equity had gone down as the price went up. When I divided $48,000 income by the new equity value of the property of $1.4 million our return on equity dropped from approximately 30% to approximately 3%. We sold the property and purchased several million dollars' worth of property with our $1.4 million in cash... in effect, we decided to convert non-performing equity into performing equity.

We thought about borrowing out our equity but with rents remaining low, the rents would not support the new debt... so we sold.

That is a real life example of using what we learned in the game to evaluate our investments and decide if we are going to buy, sell, or hold. Kim and I do not simply turn our money over to so-called experts, or blindly invest for the long term and diversify. It's our money and we actively manage it, making sure our money works harder than we do. At a 30% return our money was working hard. At a 3% return, we were working harder than our money.

By reinvesting our equity, tax-deferred, again through a 1031 exchange, the $1.4 million at a minimum 15% cash-on-cash return earns approximately $210,000 per year, or $17,500 a month in passive (taxed at a lower rate than earned income) income. This beats the $48,000 or $4,000 a month income we were receiving. As of the time this writing, we have not yet reinvested the $1.4 million so my numbers are projections. I am confident we can beat a 15% return and definitely beat investing for the long-term in mutual funds and diversifying.

This little distinction, on the difference between *return-on-cash* and *return-on-equity*, is important because millions of investors have a lot of money sitting in their retirement plans or in savings that is not working very hard for them... but I assure you, their money is working hard for the rich who manage the money for them. That is one more reason why the rich are getting richer and the poor and middle class are working hard in the Rat Race.

Again, if you do not fully understand the difference between a *cash-on-cash* return the *return-on-equity*, and why the percentage of return may go down as the value of the asset goes up, do not worry. Those are distinctions I designed into the game that can only be learned by playing, learning, teaching others and challenging yourself to beat your previous scores. The net effect is: The better you are at evaluating investments and the returns, the better you will be at buying, selling, holding and evaluating investments in the real world. You will not want to simply parrot, as most amateur investors do, "Invest for the long term and diversify." You will not be blind to Golden Rule #3 as most people are. You will not simply turn your money over to the rich and let your money make them richer. And that is why teaching yourself and others can make you richer. Again, it is simply Golden Rule #1.

Author's Note: In CASHFLOW 202, you will learn other more advanced strategies that beat diversification hands down. In the real world, professional investors do not diversify. In the real world, professional investors use strategic tools such as *stops, call options* and *put options* to protect the value of their assets against losses. These professional trader tools are really insurance plans, insurance plans not available to mutual fund investors, which is why they diversify.

After you feel you have mastered CASHFLOW 101, then you may want to move on to CASHFLOW 202. Once you have mastered 202, you will know why professional investors do not diversify, why professional investors make more money with less risk, and why they seem to have more fun.

Second Author's Note: As you get smarter, so does the game, which means if you want to be challenged, the game will meet your challenge for more knowledge. And the more financial knowledge you have, the richer you become. That is why I cringe when I hear someone say, "I've played your game once."

In Closing

So the question remains, why does Warren Buffett say, "Diversification is required when investors do not understand what they are doing." The answer will be found in Part III of this book. Part III will explain what Warren Buffett understands.

INTRODUCTION TO PART III:
WHY INVESTING IS NOT RISKY

Is This What Your
Financial Advisor Looks Like?

**Are you taking a financial advice from a
fortune teller or an investor?**

Does Your Financial Advisor Look Like This?

One of the reasons so many people think investing is risky is because they take financial advice from people who have crystal balls and pretend to be able to predict the future.

It is easy to detect the difference between a fortune teller and an investor by the words they use. A fortune teller masquerading as a financial expert will often be heard saying such things as:

1. "The value of your home will be 10% higher by January."

2. "I expect bio-tech stocks to be the place to be next year."

3. "In the third quarter, prices will come down again."

4. "Interest rates will be higher in two years."

5. "Your retirement benefits are guaranteed."

6. "Home values always go up."

7. "Save money and invest for the long term."

8. "You can't lose money investing in gold."

9. "You'll be a millionaire in three years."

10. "The stock market always goes up over time."

A real investor will be heard saying:

1. "My cash-on-cash return is 18% per year after taxes."

2. "I can increase my asset value by spending money on a new garage."

3. "I can increase my income by reducing these expenses."

4. "I can increase the income from my investment by refinancing my debt to a lower interest rate."

5. "My income increased from my investment because I reduced the taxes."

6. "I hired a new manager. The last one was incompetent."

Three Big Differences Between Fortune Tellers And Investors

There are three reasons why most people think investing is risky. They are:

1. **They do not know the difference between financial predictions and financial controls**

   Most financial advisors recommend investments the advisor or the investor has no *control* over — and neither do you. Examples of investments without financial controls are stocks, bonds, and mutual funds.

   Since most financial advisors do not have financial controls, they talk about financial predictions.

Without financial controls, a real investor knows they are playing fortune teller, gazing into a crystal ball, trying to predict the future. To a real investor, that is not investing… that is gambling… that is fortune telling.

2. **No money-back guarantees**

Most fortune tellers do not offer a money back guarantee. They do not have to, because what they are talking about is in the future. As long as they paint a picture of a bright future, you (the client) will tend to leave happy. Twenty years from now, if their predictions do not come true, will they still be there to give you your money back?

3. **Fortune tellers and gamblers invest for capital gains**

Investors invest for financial controls and for cash flow.

People who invest for capital gains invest in tomorrow… the *future*. That is why they count on prices going up. Capital gains can be found in most investment vehicles including stocks, bonds, mutual funds, real estate, and precious metals.

People who invest for cash flow invest in *today*. A person can invest for cash flow using stocks, bonds, mutual funds, real estate, and businesses.

A real investor invests for control over cash flow because they want a guarantee of getting their money back. A dreamer invests for capital gains, because they believe in the predictions of fortune tellers who may or may not be fortune tellers in the future. It is generally people who invest for capital gains who say, "Investing is risky." And for them, it is.

What Makes Part III Different

Part III of this book goes beyond *capital gains* versus *cash flow*. Instead of depending upon fortune tellers, in this book you will learn about how to take control over investments by teaching yourself and others to raise their financial IQ.

Once a person learns how to control an investment, they can control cash flow as well as capital gains. Once they can do that, they become an *investor* rather than a *fortune teller*.

And once you become an *investor*, you will understand *why investing does not have to be risky*.

The reason investing is not risky for a true investor is simply because an investor knows how to control their investment today and tomorrow. They do not have to invest for the long term and diversify in order to be successful today and tomorrow.

Chapter Eleven
WHY INVESTING IS NOT RISKY

One day, when I was about 15 years old, I said to my rich dad, "Investing must really be risky."

Hearing this, rich dad stopped what he was doing and asked, "What makes you say investing is risky? Have I ever said that to you?"

"Well, no," I stammered, trying to back pedal a little. "My dad always says it, though. That is why he always says 'There is nothing safer than money in the bank.'"

Rich dad smirked, shook his head, and said nothing. Even though he spoke no words, I got his message.

"But isn't investing risky?" his son Mike asked.

"No, investing is not risky," rich dad shot back. "How many times do I have to tell you that not having a sound financial education and investing is risky… but investing is not risky. Let me show you." Turning his yellow legal tablet to face him he wrote.

He then said, "The reason so many people say investing is risky is simply because they have no control."

"No control?" I responded in a puzzled tone. "Control of what?"

"What have I been teaching both of you?" asked rich dad in an exasperated tone. "All I've been teaching you is about controls."

Mike and I sat silently, not really knowing what he was talking about. We had not heard the word 'controls' before.

"Have I been wasting my time?" asked rich dad. "Everything I teach you two boys is about how to gain financial control of money, business and your investments. The more control you have, the less risk there is."

Again there was nothing but confused silence from Mike and me, so we just sat there on the other side of his desk and let him carry on.

"So have I been wasting my time?" asked rich dad again. "Have you not understood what I have

been teaching you and why I've been teaching you? All I've been teaching you is about control… control over your money, control over your life… controls very few people have."

Pausing, rich dad took a breath and then turned to me directly and said, "Your father has no financial education, even though he spent years in school. It is this lack of financial education that causes him to have no control over his life and why he says 'Get a safe secure job with a good retirement plan.' Or tells you, 'Investing is risky,' or 'Safe as money in the bank.' He says these things because he has no control over his money and his life."

"Oh," I said quietly, still not sure what rich dad was saying. "Tell me what you are talking about… what you mean by controls? I really don't know."

Pausing for a long moment, rich dad gathered his thoughts and finally said, "Let me answer your question in a different way. A way you can understand. You're learning to drive right now. Is that correct?"

"Yeah," I said nodding, wondering where he was going to go next. "What does driving a car have to do with investing?"

"Well, there is risk in driving a car, but driving a car does not have to be risky. Why is that?" asked rich dad.

"I don't know…" I said. "I'm just now learning to drive."

Rich dad laughed and said, "Good point." He then stood and led his son and me out of his office and into the parking lot where his car was parked. Opening the door of his car he said, "Every car comes with controls. If a car did not have controls, driving a car would be extremely risky. Can you point out some of the controls?"

Thinking for a moment and staring into the car, I took a guess, pointed and said "The steering wheel?"

"Correct. A steering wheel allows you to control your direction while driving. If a car does not have a steering wheel, I would not drive it," said rich dad with a laugh. "What other controls does a car come with?"

"The gas pedal," said Mike, beginning to catch on. "The gas pedal gives you control over the speed of the car."

"And you need the brakes if you have a gas pedal," I said, better understanding what rich dad meant by controls. "If you do not have brakes you are not in control of the car."

"Very good," said rich dad, knowing we understood his lesson. "What other controls are important in driving a car?"

Mike and I looked and thought for a long time. But at 15 years of age, and just learning to drive, we really did not know everything about driving a car.

"What's this?" asked rich dad finally, pointing to the gearshift on the steering column.

"The gear shift?" Mike asked. "That's a control?"

"Of course," said rich dad, patiently. "Why else would they put it here. The gearshift controls the gears, and the gears control the car going forward or backwards. Gears also help us get the car started from a dead stop, climb a hill, go down a hill and go faster on open roads. The gearshift is a very important control."

"Oh," we said in unison.

"What other controls do you need to safely drive a car?" asked rich dad.

Once again there was silence because Mike and I had no idea what other controls there were.

"OK," smiled rich dad. "I'll tell you about two more controls that are important to taking full control of a car. But I'll do that inside so I can write it down on a piece of paper."

At his desk once again, rich dad began writing on his legal tablet the list of controls a car has. He wrote:

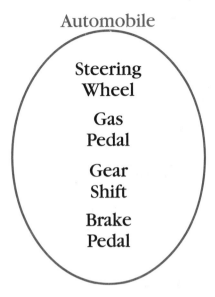

Looking up he asked, "Think of anything else? There are two more very important controls that are necessary to drive a car safely."

For a long silent moment, both Mike and I sat there thinking, but had no answers.

Finally rich dad said, "Driver's education and insurance."

"What?" I asked.

Without replying, rich dad wrote and drew on his legal pad:

"If you do not have control of any one of these six things, driving will be a risky adventure. When learning to drive, you will need to learn how to coordinate all of these six things simultaneously. That is why you need to take a driver's education course."

Investment Controls

Nodding, Mike and I sat there for a long while. Finally I asked, "So what does this have to do with investing and investing not being risky?

"Same lesson," smiled rich dad. "The reason your dad thinks investing is risky is because he has never learned how to control an investment."

"An investment has controls?" Mike asked.

"Absolutely," said rich dad. "If you learn to manage the controls of the investment, you can make a lot of money with very little risk."

"And what are the controls?" I asked.

Rich dad chuckled, "Remember this diagram?" he said, drawing on his legal pad.

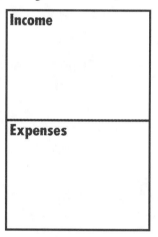

"Yeah… " I replied slowly. "You've been showing us that diagram for years."

"And why do you think I spend so much time with you on this diagram?" asked rich dad.

"We don't really know," said Mike. "We're only 15 years old."

"Because I'm teaching you to take control of your life. People who cannot control these four boxes in their life, have lost control of their life. People who have no control of these four boxes in an investment always think investing is risky."

"You mean like my dad?" I asked.

"Yes, exactly," said rich dad. "Your dad thinks investing is risky because he has not been trained to control these four controls of an investment."

"So if I have control over these four boxes, I would control the investment?" I asked. And rich dad nodded.

"Your dad invests in the stock market? Is that correct?" asked rich dad.

"He used to, until he lost his money."

"So why did he lose his money?" asked rich dad.

"Because he did not have control over these four boxes?" I answered hesitantly and pointing at the Income, Expense, Asset and Liability columns of the financial statement.

Rich dad nodded and added, "He invests in investments he has no control over… that is why he thinks investing is risky."

"And you don't?" asked Mike. "I mean… invest in investments you don't have control of?"

"Of course not," answered rich dad. "Do you think I'm stupid? Do you think I'd buy a car without a steering wheel, gas pedal, or brakes?

"No," I said softly.

"And that is why your dad always talks about job security," rich dad continued. "He thinks job security is important because he has very little control over his job."

"Job security, too?" I asked. "He has no control over his job?"

"He doesn't own his job… does he?" asked rich dad. "He doesn't control how much he makes. He doesn't control the hours he works. If he didn't show up for work, he'd be fired… and that is what motivates most workers… the fear of being fired, losing their job, and not having any income," rich dad said, pointing to the Income column of the financial statement. "If he loses his job his income stops. That is why people like him think security is so important. Security is important because they have no control."

"And do you have control over your income?" I asked.

"Yes, I do. But not from this column," said rich dad pointing to the Income column of the financial statement."

Puzzled once again, Mike and I sat staring at rich dad who was pointing at the Income column. Finally Mike asked, "So which column do you have financial control from?"

Laughing out loud, rich dad said, "I thought you boys understood this," as he pointed to the Asset column. "This is where financial control comes from. This is where financial security comes from… not from a job and not from here," he said, pointing once again to the Income column.

After a long silence, I asked, "I understand the part about the lack of job security. But tell me again why he lost money in the stock market? And explain to me how you can invest with control and he can not."

Realizing that the conversation was a little over our heads, rich dad once again went back to his yellow legal tablet and drew the following diagrams.

"When your dad invests in stocks, his financial statement looks like this."

Poor Dad's Financial Statement

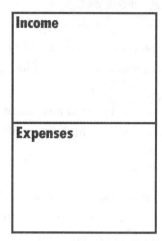

Income	
Expenses	

Assets	Liabilities
Shares of Stock	

Rich Dad's Financial Statement

Income	
Expenses	

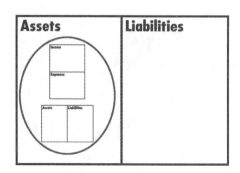

Assets	Liabilities

Pointing to the financial statement of the asset inside the Asset column, rich dad said, "When I buy an asset, I buy the entire asset. I buy control of the entire financial statement."

"So that is why you like buying real estate?" Mike asked. "You buy the control of the asset."

Rich dad nodded. "And if I buy a share of stock or mutual fund, I buy an asset I have no control of. Again, that would be like buying a car without a steering wheel."

"The same is true when you purchase a business," I added. "You buy the business because you have control."

Again rich dad nodded, this time with a smile because he knew we understood his lesson. "One of the reasons the rich get richer is because they have more control over their financial matters."

"So that's why you've been teaching us so much about the financial statement. You want us to learn to have control over the income, expenses, assets, and liabilities of our investments." Mike said.

"Not just over your investments," said rich dad, shaking his head. "I want you boys to grow up having control over your lives. If you cannot control your personal finances, you lose control over your life. That's why your dad struggles financially no matter how many college degrees he has, how hard he works, or how many pay raises he receives. He struggles financially because he has no financial education and very little control over the money in his life."

Turning once again to his yellow legal tablet, rich dad pointed to the Income column of the financial statement and said,

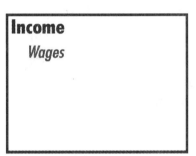

"Your dad has very little control over how much he makes. Even if he works harder, the state has guidelines as to how much a person in his position can make.

Expenses
Taxes
Mortgage Payment
Car Payment
Credit Card Payments
Other Expenses
Child Expenses

"He is definitely out of control here. Even if his income does not go up, I suspect his expenses are getting higher. Your family has four children. Children do not get less expensive as they get older. I'll bet he's worried about how he's going to afford a college education for you and the three other kids."

"He's already told me he is not going to pay for my college education," I added. "He said the day I graduate from high school I am on my own."

"That's good," smiled rich dad. "You'll grow up faster because of that. You'll learn to respect money rather than expect people to give you money."

Getting back to the legal tablet, rich dad pointed to the Liabilities column.

"Because your family is growing," rich dad said pointing to my stomach, "your dad bought a bigger house and a new car, and a station wagon to haul all you growing kids around. Is that correct?"

I just nodded and tried to hide my stomach by pulling my shirt down lower. "I'm playing football. That's why I'm heavier," I said defensively.

"Well, growing kids who eat more, a bigger house and new car are liabilities that add to your family's expenses. So your dad has growing expenses and a fixed income. That's not a good financial position to be in."

Liabilities
Mortgage
School Loans
Car Loans
Credit Cards

"So what can he do?" I asked.

"Well, he tried investing," said rich dad, pointing now to the Asset column.

"Yes, and he lost," I said. "He lost about a $1,000 in the stock market. And for our family, that was a lot of money. In fact, that is all he had in savings… savings he was keeping so he could afford to send us kids to college. Now he says he will never invest again. That is why he says investing is risky. That is why he believes money in the bank is a lot safer."

Assets
Shares of Stock

"I understand," said rich dad sympathetically. "Yet can you see that the cause of the problem is the same?"

"What is the cause of the problem?" I asked. "My dad?"

"Not really," smiled rich dad. "Your dad is a very good man. He is doing the best he can with what he knows."

"So what's the problem?" I asked.

"The lack of controls… dummy," said Mike. "Haven't you learned anything yet? My dad is not attacking your dad… so don't take it so personally. Millions of people are in your dad's shoes. Millions of people are working hard, earning money, but struggling from paycheck to paycheck."

"Millions?" I asked.

"Billions," said rich dad. "If you think your family is struggling, wait until you go to other parts of the world. Compared to other families in other countries, your family has it pretty good."

"But I guess the problem is the same. It's a lack of financial controls," I said softly.

"The problem is a lack of financial education," said rich dad. "You see, lack of financial control is only a symptom of a lack of financial education. So that is why I teach you boys about money, after school, since I know schools do not think a financial education is important. I teach you boys about money because I want you to be in control over your finances… and if you are in control of your finances, you will be in control of your life."

There was a long silence. I better understood how important my financial education was going to be, and how it would affect the rest of my life. I now understood why rich dad went over and over his simple diagram of the financial statement sketched on his yellow legal tablet. It seemed that every time he drew that diagram, I learned something new… something that would change the future of my life for the better. I now understood that the reason the financial statement was so important was because it helped define the areas of my life where I was either in control or out of control.

Finally the silence was broken when Mike asked, "So, let me get this straight… You're trying to tell us that Robert's dad is out of control of his financial life. Because he is out of control, due to a lack of financial education, he has financial problems. The family is always short of money."

"That's correct," said rich dad. "Anytime a family or a business has financial problems, something is out of control. It could be expenses, it could be not enough income, it could be too many liabilities — or investing in bad investments."

"So in my dad's case, he is out of control personally and in an attempt to solve his financial problems, he invests in shares of stocks, an asset he has no control over."

Rich dad nodded, saying, "Many people are in the same boat. They just try to solve the problem in different ways. Your father tried the stock market and he lost. Some people go back to school to get a higher degree. Some work two and three jobs, believing that working harder will solve their problems. Others go to Las Vegas and gamble. And still others buy bigger homes and cars, thinking that a house and car are assets, and thinking that looking good is the way to get rich. They believe in *faking it till they make it*."

Mike and I laughed at that. The tension I was feeling about my dad was disappearing. I realized he was a good man doing the best he could with what he knew. I could now appreciate the lesson from rich dad.

"Please explain to me why investing in stocks is investing in an asset I have no control over. I think I know, but I want the lesson to sink in," I said.

Once again, rich dad turned to his yellow legal tablet and drew a financial statement.

"If you invest in a stock, let's say shares of General Electric, do you have any influence over that company's income?"

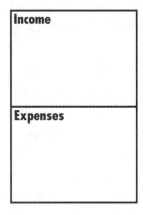

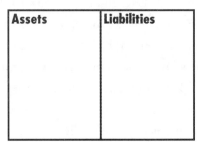

"I don't know," said Mike.

"Well, the answer is you and I don't. Even if we owned ten thousand shares of GM stock, we have no say in how much money they earn."

Pointing to the Expense column, rich dad said, "And I don't have control over how the company spends its money. I can't say, "I'm cutting salaries or selling the private jet. Nor do I have any say in what they borrow money for, or what they invest their money in. The reason I don't like investing in stocks is because I don't like being out of control."

"But you have control over the income of your real estate," I said.

"Yes, and my expenses, and the asset and the liabilities," said rich dad, pointing to each box as he spoke. "But if I buy a paper asset, such as a stock or mutual fund, all I have control over is when I buy or sell and how much I pay. That is why I rarely invest in them."

"But you do invest in them?" I asked.

"Yes, but rarely. Later, when you're older, I will explain to you how I invest in paper assets. There are ways to gain control over paper assets, but that is not the lesson I want you to learn today. Today's lesson is about the importance of controls. Before we continue, let's go get some lunch. I'm hungry."

"Great," I said, patting my stomach. With that, the three of us went to lunch at a restaurant near rich dad's office.

While we waited for lunch, rich dad summarized the day's lesson by comparing driving a car to investing in assets. He drew the diagram on the next page as we waited.

Pointing to the diagram he asked, "If you went to drive a car, and you found out the car did not have a steering wheel, would you drive it?"

"No. Of course not," I replied.

"How about if it was missing a gas pedal?"

"No, of course not," both Mike and I replied. "We may be young, but we're not stupid."

"OK… what if the car had no brakes, or gear shift?"

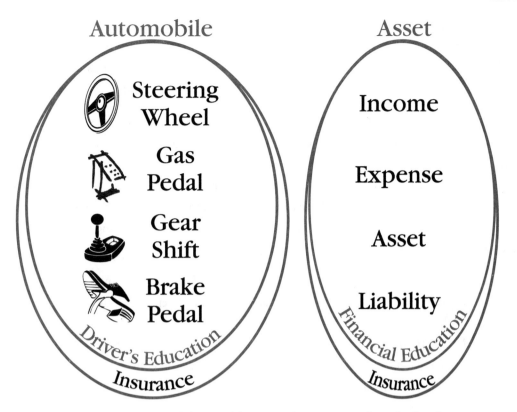

Again we said in unison, "No. Why would anyone drive a car without brakes?"

"And if you had a friend, who had no driver's education and did not know how to drive a car, would you let him drive your car?"

"No," we said out loud, almost shouting. "We wouldn't let him drive — and we wouldn't ride with him."

"And what if the car had no insurance? Would you drive it?"

"No!" we howled.

"That would really be too risky," said Mike. "Even if we could drive and had the other controls, what if we got into an accident, or someone hit us? Driving without insurance is really stupid."

Rich dad was chuckling away like a proud father, knowing we understood his lesson. Finally he said, "Yet when it comes to investing, that is what most people do. They invest in investments they have no control over and then say that investing is risky."

Investment Vehicles

Rich dad went on to explain that investments are often referred to as *investment vehicles*. He said, "The reason they are called vehicles is because they are supposed to take you and your money from one point to another." He also said, "All vehicles, regardless of whether they are vehicles for transportation or for investment, need controls and well-trained management. If a vehicle is missing controls or the management is poorly trained, risk is high."

He explained that the reason he did not like mutual funds was because a mutual fund was like riding a bus filled with people who do not know how to drive, and who do not know they are riding a bus without insurance. He said, "Even if the bus has a good driver, the problem with mutual funds is that they are almost impossible to insure. And if you cannot insure something, banks tend not to lend money for it. If you have no controls, cannot buy insurance, or can't get a bank to be your partner in

the investment, why invest? If all you can do is buy, hold, pray, and diversify… get smart and find better investments."

The key words in that last statement are *get smart*. If you are not willing to get smart, then invest in mutual funds. For people who are not financially smart, mutual funds are the smart investment.

Why *Teach To Be Rich* Works: I believe what Warren Buffett meant when he said, "Diversification is required when investors do not understand what they are doing," is that what he *understands* is how to *control* the investment. In other words, he does not simply buy shares of stock in a company. He either buys the company outright, including control of the management, or he buys enough shares of stock to have *control* of the company. What he understands is the power and importance of *control*. And since most investors do not have or know about *control*, then they need to diversify.

So when you teach yourself and others to be rich, what you are really teaching is the importance of understanding the power of controls — first over yourself, and then over your money.

Feeling Out Of Control

Today, many people report feeling out of control. Many feel out of control of their jobs. Afraid of losing their job or their seniority, many are willing to work for less. They also feel out of control financially, especially in the world of investing. That is because many people are investing in investments in which they have absolutely no control. On top of that, they send their kids to school to learn the same things about life they did: *Get a job and invest in mutual funds for the long term through their retirement plan.* No wonder they feel out of control. No wonder they have been programmed to think investing is risky. Anything is risky if you have no control.

Teacher Of The Year

I believe this is one reason why (as I quoted earlier in this book) John Taylor Gatto said,

"Schools were conceived to service the economy and the social order rather than kids and families — that is why it is compulsory. As a consequence, the school cannot help anybody grow up, because its prime directive is to retard maturity. It does this by teaching that everything is difficult, that other people run our lives"

John Taylor Gatto goes on to quote, Mr. Mort Zukerman, owner of *U.S. News and World Report*, who says, "Workers in America live in constant panic, a panic against being left out, they know that companies owe them nothing, there is no power to appeal to for managements decision. Fear is our secret supercharger, it gives management the flexibility other nations never have." Zukerman says that "Even after six years of economic expansion, American workers including management workers fret they might not survive. In 1996, almost half the employees of large firms feared being laid off. This is double the number fearful of being laid off in 1991 when things were not nearly as good as they are now. This keeps wages under control."

Since many workers are afraid of losing their jobs, they work for less. On top of that, they are told to turn their money over to total strangers and trust them to invest for the long-term, primarily in mutual funds, an investment vehicle they have absolutely no control over. That is why it is also important to understand what David F. Swenson, Chief Investment Officer of Yale University, means

when he states in his book *Unconventional Success*:

> *"Mutual-fund companies employ a variety of subterfuges to mask poor performance, ranging from the extreme of merging poorly-performing funds out of existence to more subtle, manipulative techniques."*

In other words, the average investor cannot tell what their real returns are. As rich dad said, "A mutual fund is like a bus filled with people who do not know how to drive and who do not know that the bus has no insurance."

You may recall from an earlier chapter, Mr. Swenson quotes a study that shows when tax consequences are factored in over the long-term, only 4% of all mutual funds beat the Vanguard 500 Index fund and by less than 1% over a 15-year period. That means 96% of all mutual funds did not beat the S&P 500.

Less Job Security And Financial Security

In the Industrial Age, blue collar workers worried about their jobs being shipped overseas. In the Information Age, white collar workers are worried about their jobs being shipped overseas. Add to this the ups and downs of the stock market, the falling dollar, rising oil prices, housing prices going through the roof, college tuition becoming more and more expensive, government programs such as Social Security and Medicare that are said to be going broke… no wonder so many people feel out of control with their lives. That is why so many people believe that the company or the government should take care of them once their working days are over. Since being taken care of for life has become less and less of a possibility, these uncertainties may be what's fueling the greatest fear in America today: The fear of running out of money during retirement. It is a real fear.

Why Doesn't School Teach Us About Money?

With all these global changes going on, I have often wondered why schools do not teach young people about money. After all, smart or slow, rich or poor, graduate or dropout, we will all use money for the rest of our lives. In my world, knowing about money and how to manage my money are vital life skills. In spite of how obvious this is, in most cases, schools tend to treat money as an evil subject, not worthy of academic investigation.

One reason why schools do not teach students about the subject of money is because many educators feel that the subject of money is a subject below them… in other words, *academic arrogance*. Another reason may be because most educators know very little about money… and I ask, "How can they teach what they do not know?" In other words, *academic ignorance*.

There is another reason that John Taylor Gatto touched on, my father told me about, and Dr. Buckminister Fuller was angry about. And that is the control over education — the hijacking of the educational system by the rich.

All three men, my dad, Dr. Fuller, and John Taylor Gatto, basically said the same thing. In my opinion, if schools taught the subject of money in the same way I wrote about in Part II of this book, the world's bankers would come down hard on the school system. What would happen, if schools taught the subject of money from a historical perspective stating that…

- In 1971, *money became a currency* and savers became losers

- *Bad debt* is easy to get and *good debt* is hard to get

- In 1974, with the passage of ERISA, the rich changed the rules and long-term financial security was gone

- The reason investment bankers say to *"invest for the long term"* is because they want to collect fees for the long term; and the reason they advise you to *diversify*, is because they themselves cannot pick a good investment, they want you to buy more stocks.

- They fail to tell you that they want you to invest in an asset they have no control over and neither do you.

I believe if the school system adopted a policy to teach financial history, the rich, via their representatives in Congress, would find a way to stop such education by cutting off their funding.

What Held Me Back

One of the reasons I have been hesitant to write what I know is out of fear of retribution. Some of you may recall that I came under media attack when I wrote *Rich Dad's Prophecy*, a book on the coming stock market crash caused by the passage of ERISA in 1974. Many of the financial publications, that are owned by investment bankers or whose main advertisers are investment bankers such and mutual fund companies, wrote articles about me which prove the First Amendment, freedom of speech, is alive and well. As we all know, our freedom of speech includes the right to lie. Although still concerned, I talked to my wife, Kim, and my partner, Sharon, and we decided this book is worth writing. So we overcame our concerns and are willing to withstand the attack, if and when it comes.

The Main Reason Why

So those are some of the reasons why I believe our schools do not teach the subject of money. But there is one more reason why I think that schools do not teach about money, and I think it is the main reason. That reason is simply because parents do not request the subject be taught. Many parents are still in the Industrial Age, not realizing that in 1974, with the passage of ERISA, the rules changed and Golden Rule #3 took full control. Many parents still believe all children need is to get a good education, so they can get a good job, and the company and the government will take care of them for the rest of their lives. Again, I believe that parents are the main reason.

Teaching People To Take Control Of Their Lives

Rather than try to change the school system and risk really upsetting the investment bankers of the world, we at Rich Dad decided to write what we know best and create products that support only those who want to learn what my rich dad taught me.

Simply said, what my rich dad taught me was not only to take control over assets… he taught me to take control of my life. He was against turning control of my life over to others, as my poor dad did and which the school system still teaches us to do, in compliance with Golden Rule #3.

Teaching yourself and others to take control of your money means you are teaching yourself and others to take control of your lives. That is why *Teach To Be Rich* works. It's the best part of Golden Rule #1.

Chapter Twelve
TAKING CONTROL OF YOUR MONEY AND YOUR LIFE

In reviewing my rich dad's comparison of controlling a car and controlling assets, you may notice that the key to being a good driver and a good investor is education. To control a car, the key is driver's education. With assets, the key is financial education.

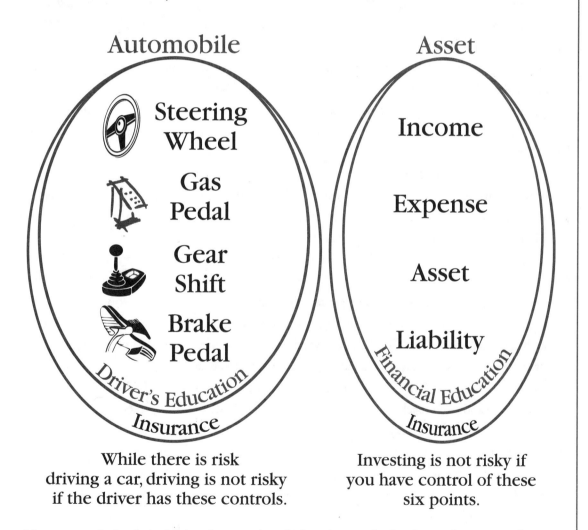

Automobile
- Steering Wheel
- Gas Pedal
- Gear Shift
- Brake Pedal

Driver's Education
Insurance

While there is risk
driving a car, driving is not risky
if the driver has these controls.

Asset
- Income
- Expense
- Asset
- Liability

Financial Education
Insurance

Investing is not risky if
you have control of these
six points.

Most parents insist their children learn to drive before driving the family car alone. Since driving a car is such a big responsibility, posing substantial physical as well as financial risks, many of our schools offer driver's education courses. And governments have strict licensing requirements, including passing grades on written and behind-the-wheel tests, for granting a driver's license. Yet, when it comes to money, there is no financial education, no tests verifying that we are competent to manage our own

money.

Instead of educating young people about money in school, young people today learn about money from credit card companies. Small wonder American citizens are the most indebted people on earth and the U.S. government is the biggest debtor nation in the world. If our kids learn nothing about money in school, how can we expect our political leaders to know much about money? After all, the kids and the political leaders receive their financial education from the same people… the people who issue credit cards.

Why Your Banker Does Not Ask You For Your Report Card

One of the better real life lessons I learned from my rich dad was that bankers do not ask you for your report card. Rich dad said, "My banker has never asked me for my report card or what my grade point average was. My banker has never asked what school I went to, what I majored in, or if I was an 'A' student or a 'C' student. All my banker wants to see is my financial statement. My financial statement is my report card in the real world. My financial statement shows him how smart I am with money. My financial statement shows my banker my financial IQ."

The reason bankers want to see your financial statement or the financial statement of a business is simply to verify how smart or how incompetent a person is financially. A financial statement is a reflection of a person's financial education and their money management skills. The problem is, probably 99% of all high school graduates have no idea what a financial statement is. But they <u>do</u> know what a credit card is.

To be fair, some schools are implementing financial education courses in their curriculum. The problem is, most of those programs are recommending children learn to "work hard, save money, get out of debt, invest for the long term, and diversify." While this is technically 'financial education,' my question is, who really benefits from this education?

One of the reasons bankers do not ask you for your report card, or ask what your grade point average was, is because they do not care about how well you did in school. They do not care if you are a hard-working person, or that you save money. They also do not want you to get out of debt. And they may only want you to invest for the long term and diversify if you buy your mutual funds through their financial advisory services, for which (of course) they receive a commission plus fees.

In reality, bankers are most interested in how much debt you can afford. Bankers are looking for people to lend money to. They are looking for people who are *creditworthy*… which means people who borrow money and pay it back. If your financial statement shows that you can borrow a lot of money and pay it back, the bank loves you. They want your business. You are their best kind of customer. And because they want you as a customer, they offer you their lowest interest rates and most favorable terms. If you are a credit risk, or only want to borrow small amounts of money, or are always trying to get out of debt, the bank has another program for you. It is called a credit card with high interest rates.

That is the primary reason why banks do not ask you for your report card or grade point average. The banks are not interested in how well you did in school. Banks are interested primarily in one thing: How much money can you borrow and at what interest rate? Your report card or grade point average does not tell them that.

Big Deals

4-plex for Sale

Nice, well maintained 4-plex in good neighborhood. Stable tenants, positive cash flow, few problems. Full records.

Use this yourself or sell to another player.

48% ROI, may sell for $100,00 to $140,000.

Cost: $125,000
DownPay: $15,000
Mortgage: $110,000
Cash Flow: +$600

Small Deals

Stock — MYT4U

High inflation leads to poor share pr___ this home electronics seller.

<u>Only you</u> may buy as many shares as you want at this price.

<u>Everyone may sell</u> at this price

Symbol MYT4U

No dividend (Yield or RO___

Trading Range: $5 to $3___

House For Sale

Low down payment to pick up th__ house, owner/seller unexpectedly mo__ out of town. Right person will do well.

Use this yourself or sell to another player.

40% ROI, may sell for $65,000 to $135,000.

Cost: $50,000
$3,000
Mortgage: $47,000
Cash Flow: +$100

___rtment Houses for Sale

2 buildings totaling 24 units for sale. Owner managed with on-site assistant. Retirement prompts sale.

Use this yourself or sell to another player.

54% ROI, may sell for $600,000 to $960,000.

Cost: $575,000
DownPay: $75,000
Mortgage: $500,000
Cash Flow: + $3,400

Automated Business for Sale

Successful 4 bay coin operated auto wash near busy intersection. Seller is moving to retirement community out of state.

Use this yourself or sell to another player.

86% ROI. No other buyers in sight.

Cost: $125,000
DownPay: $25,000
Liability: $100,000
Cash Flow: + $1,800

Tenant Damages Your Property

Tenant fails to pay rent for 2 months and then skips town leaving damage to your rental property.

Insurance covers most damage and costs, but you still are out of pocket $500.

Pay $500 if you own any rental property. (Bank will lend you the money on usual terms.)

Only the person who draws this card pays.

Board spaces: Pay Check, Charity (Use 1 or 2 dice for next 3 turns if you donate 10% of Total Income), Opportunity Big/Small Deal, Doodads, Opportunity Big/Small Deal, The Market, Opportunity Big/Small Deal, Pay Check, Opportunity Big/Small Deal, Downsized, The Market, Opportunity Big/Small Deal, Doodads, Opportunity Big/Small Deal, Baby, Opportunity Big/Small Deal, Doodads

Start Here

Doodad Cards

Your Child Needs Braces

Pay $2000

(if you have a child)

Apartment House Buyer

REIT offers $30,000 per unit for all units in apartment houses of 12 units or more. Has own financing. Buyer has funds from sale of complex in another city.

<u>Everyone</u> may sell at this price.

If you sell, pay off the related mortgage and give up the cash flow you currently receive on this property.

The Market

___ouse Buyer — 3Br/2Ba

__ou are offered $135,000 for a 3/2 rental house. Buyer has own financing.

<u>Everyone may sell</u> at this price.

If you sell, pay off the related mortgage and give up the cash flow you currently receive on this property.

Go to Casino!

Lose $200 at the tables

Buy Big Screen TV

Pay $4000

(Credit cards OK. If you buy on credit add $4000 to credit cards liability and add $120 to your monthly expenses.)

Small Business Improves

The small business you founded has found a major company to distribute its product. Your sales increase 150%.

This brings more problems and requires more time from you, but Monthly Net Income goes up $400.

<u>Everyone</u> who owns a business they started is affected and <u>increases</u> their cash flows by $400 per month on all such businesses.

Dinner with the President
Buy a table for 10 friends to dine with the President at a gala ball for visiting dignitaries from around the world.
$100,000

T-Shirt Stores
(5 outlets)
+$8,000/mo CF
48% CCR
$200,000 down

A Research Center for Cancer & AIDS
Your money brings together top researchers & doctors in one place, dedicated to eliminating these 2 diseases.
$225,000

CA$HFLOW DAY

7 Wonders of the World
Go by plane, boat, bicycle, camel, canoe & limo to the 7 Wonders of the World. First class luxury all the way!
$200,000

Software Co. IPO
Buy 250,000 shares at 10¢/share. If you roll a 6 on one die, shares go to $2/share – get $500,000 cash from Bank. Roll less than 6, get $0.
$25,000 Investment

Russian Oil Deal
+$75,000/mo CF if you roll 4 or higher on one die, or else $0 CF.
$300,000 Investment

Heli-Ski the Swiss Alps
A winter of helicopter skiing by day and playing at the glamorous hot spots at night. A medieval castle is your accommodation.
$150,000

Auto Repair Shop
+$6,000/mo CF
48% CCR
$150,000 down

A Gift of Faith
Your religious organization is growing by leaps & bounds. New buildings are needed. You donate...
$175,000

Beauty Salons
(3 shops)
+$10,000/mo CF
48% CCR
$250,000 down

Run for Mayor
Your financial expertise spurs masses of people to beg you to lead the city. You run and, of course, win. This is the start of your Presidential race. Campaign costs you
$125,000

Chicken Franchise
(2 outlets)
+$10,000/mo CF
40% CCR
$300,000 down

Park Named After You
Tear down abandoned warehouse & build new recreational park. Donate police sub-station for park safety.
$225,000

Tax Audit!
Pay accountants and lawyers **one half** your cash.

Private Fishing Cabin on a Montana Lake
Fish from the dock of this remote cabin. Enjoy 6 months of solitude. Use of float plane included.
$100,000

Buy a Gold Mine
+$25,000/mo CF if you roll 3 or higher on one die, or else $0 CF.
$150,000 Investment

Cannes Film Festival
Party with the stars! Tour France, plus one week in Cannes rubbing elbows with celebrities. You even land a starring role!
$125,000

CA$HFLOW DAY

Truck Parts Maker
+$5,000/mo CF
40% CCR
$150,000 down

Yacht Racing
You & your crew fly to Perth, Australia. Spend one week racing a 12-meter against the fastest boats in the world.
$150,000

Heat & A/C Service
+$10,000/mo CF
60% CCR
$200,000 down

Charity
For $100,000 you may roll 1, 2, or 3 dice on each turn.

The More You Play this Game

CA$H

Opportunity Cards

Big Deal

Choose either a "Small Deal" or a "Big Deal" when you land on "Opportunity". Big Deals take at least $6,000 to get into. (The largest Small Deal requires $5,000).

Place used cards on the bottom of the deck.

Small Deal

Choose either a "Small Deal" or a "Big Deal" when you land on "Opportunity". The largest Small Deal takes $5,000 to get into. (Big Deals start at $6,000).

Place used cards on the bottom of the deck.

The Rat Race Goal:
Move from the Rat Race to the Fast Track

You may move from the Rat Race to the Fast Track at the start of any turn if your PASSIVE INCOME IS GREATER THAN YOUR TOTAL EXPENSES

The Market

Opportunity Big/Small Deal

Pay Check

Opportunity Big/Small Deal

Charity
Use 1 or 2 dice for next 3 turns if you donate 10% of Total Income

Opportunity Big/Small Deal

Doodads

Opportunity Big/Small Deal

The Market

Opportunity Big/Small Deal

Start Here

Pay Check
When passing over or landing on Pay Check, get your Monthly Cash Flow from the Bank. If this amount is negative (minus), pay it to the Bank.

If you forget to ask for your Pay Check, it is lost.

HOW TO GET OU

Some of the gains and returns have been exaggerated to expedite play. Always seek professional advice when making financial investments.

Divorce! Lose all of your cash.

Be a "Jet-Setter". Have your own personal jet available for one year, to whisk you away wherever & whenever your heart desires. $250,000

60 Unit Apartment Building +$8,000/mo CF 32% CCR $300,000 down

Golf Around the World. You take 3 friends on a first class, 5-star resort tour to play the 50 best golf courses in the world. $150,000

Pizza Franchise (2 locations) +$7,000/mo CF 37% CCR $225,000 down

A Kid's Library. Add a wing to your city's library devoted to young writers and artists. Art celebrities visit often to support your work. $175,000

FLOW

the Richer* You Become

*When it comes to money, your greatest asset is your financial knowledge.

200 unit Mini Storage +$6,000/mo CF 36% CCR $200,000 down

South Sea Island Fantasy. Pampered in luxury for two full months. Relax, unwind in warm waters, deserted beaches, and romantic nights. $100,000

Bio-Tech Co. IPO. Buy 500,000 shares at 10¢/share. If you roll a 5 or 6 on one die, shares go to $1/share – get $500,000 cash from Bank. Roll less than 5, get $0. $50,000 Investment

Capitalists' Peace Corps. Set up entrepreneurial business schools in 3rd world nations. Instructors are business people donating their knowledge & time. $200,000

Dry Cleaner (2 stores) +$3,000/mo CF 36% CCR $100,000 down

Cruise the Mediterranean on a Private Yacht. Visit small harbors in Italy, France, and Greece for a month with 12 friends. $100,000

CASHFLOW DAY

The Market

Draw a Market card when you land on "The Market". Read it out loud. You may sell your assets if you choose. (Other Players may sell if the card allows.)

If you sell, remember to adjust your Game Card.

Place used cards on the bottom of the deck.

Doodads

Draw a Doodads card when you land on "Doodads". You must follow the instructions.

You may borrow (see rules) to pay Doodads items.

Place used cards on the bottom of the deck.

The Fast Track Goals:
1) Buy your Dream.
2) Buy businesses to increase your Monthly Cash Flow.

Fast Track

Quick Food Marts (3 stores) +$5,000/mo CF 50% CCR $120,000 down

Ancient Asian Cities. A private plane & private guide take you & 5 friends to the most remote spots of Asia... where no tourists have gone before. $150,000

Burger Franchise +$9,500/mo CF 38% CCR $300,000 down

Pro Team Box Seats. License a 12 person private skybox booth with food and beverage service at your favorite team's stadium. $200,000

Family Restaurant Chain +$14,000/mo CF 56% CCR $300,000 down

Buy a Forest. Stop the loss of ancient trees. Donate 1,000 acres of forest and create a nature walk for all to enjoy. $250,000

Opportunity Big/Small Deal

Baby. Congratulations! Add all your child expenses per player.

Opportunity Big/Small Deal

Pay Check

Opportunity Big/Small Deal

The Market

Opportunity Big/Small Deal

Doodads

Opportunity Big/Small Deal

Downsized. Lose pay for... Lose 2 turns

Enter Here

This Game was created in 1996, the Chinese year of the Rat.

Lawsuit! Pay one half your cash to defend yourself.

African Photo Safari. Take 6 friends on a wild safari, photographing the most exotic animals in the world. Enjoy 5-star luxury in your tent. $100,000

Cookware Infomercial +$50,000/mo CF if you roll 4 or higher on one die, or else $0 CF. $225,000 Investment

A Mini-Farm in the City. Create a hands-on farm eco-system for city kids to learn and care for animals & plants. $150,000

OF THE RAT RACE

©1996, 1997 CASHFLOW Technologies, Inc.
Patent Pending. All rights reserved.

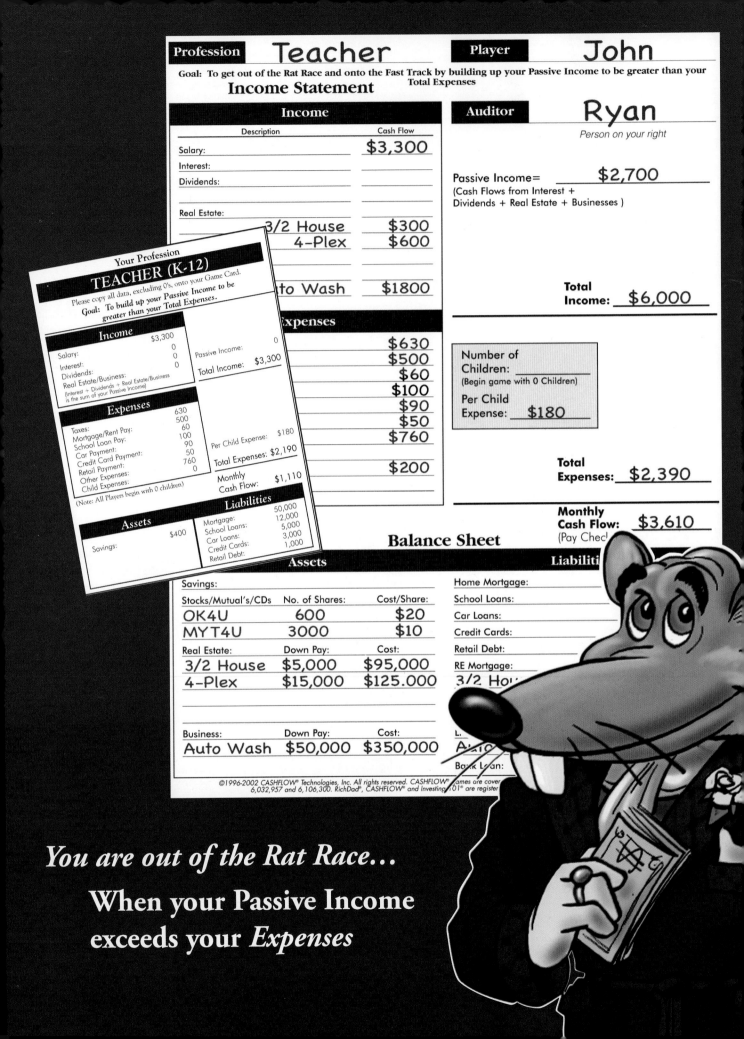

Does Your Banker Love You?

Rich dad loved his bankers. My poor dad hated bankers. He often saw the banks and bankers as enemies, exploiters of the poor. And rich dad's bankers loved rich dad. They often invited him to have lunch at the bank's exclusive, private restaurant on top of the bank. They wanted to play golf with rich dad or take him to sporting events. Poor dad's bankers ignored him. Rich dad's bankers always wanted to lend him more money. My poor dad's bankers always wanted to know when they would get their money back.

Having two dads allowed me to see the differences between my two dads' attitudes towards banks and bankers. Also, I noticed the banks and bankers attitudes towards my two dads. Early in my life, I learned that I needed to decide what kind of relationship I wanted with my banks and bankers. Did I want the kind of relationship my rich dad had with his bankers or did I want the relationship my poor dad had with his? Obviously, I chose my rich dad's relationship. Today, some of my best friends are my bankers... *mortgage bankers* for my real estate investments like the Big Deal cards found on the CASHFLOW board game. And for my investments on the Fast Track, my *investment bankers* are important when taking a small company public, through an IPO (Initial Public Offering). That is why I love my bankers. We have a great relationship because we need each other to get richer. And because we are friends and look out for one another, we are constantly advising and learning from one another.

Author's Note: One of my friends who is a banker, Scott McPherson, has been generous enough to record an audio CD with me as an educational product. The CD is titled *"How to Get Your Banker to Say 'Yes.'"* This CD is important for anyone who wants their banker to be their friend rather than their enemy. It is available through our website, www.richdad.com

How Good Is Your Financial Report Card?

Looking at the controls again, on the next page, you can see the important role education plays in both processes. If you are a poor driver, you will most likely have a poor driving record... a record filled with accidents, tickets, and other violations. If you have a poor driving record, that means you will probably pay more for repairs, tickets, and car insurance.

The same is true with your financial education and your financial records. If you have a poor financial education, instead of traffic tickets, your financial history will reflect a person who pays financial penalties such late fees, service charges and higher interest rates. Similar to of moving and speeding violations on your driving record, your credit history will reflect financial violations known as bankruptcies, foreclosures, evictions, liens, and lawsuits. Worst of all, if you have a low financial IQ, you may unwittingly invest in investments without insurance... investments such as mutual funds, which are uninsurable.

So when a banker looks at your financial report card (also known as your financial statement and pictured on the next page), the banker is looking for your financial IQ, which will tell your banker how creditworthy you are and what kind of insurance or assurances the bank will need in order to lend you money. Obviously, if you have very low income, there is very little a bank can do other than issue you a credit card at a high interest rate. The high interest rate is the bank's insurance policy. And if you have high expenses, all the bank can do is issue you a credit card at higher interest rates. The same is true for too many liabilities. Also, when a banker checks your liabilities they want to know if you have good liabilities or bad liabilities. Good liabilities may be a mortgage for your home. Bad liabilities are

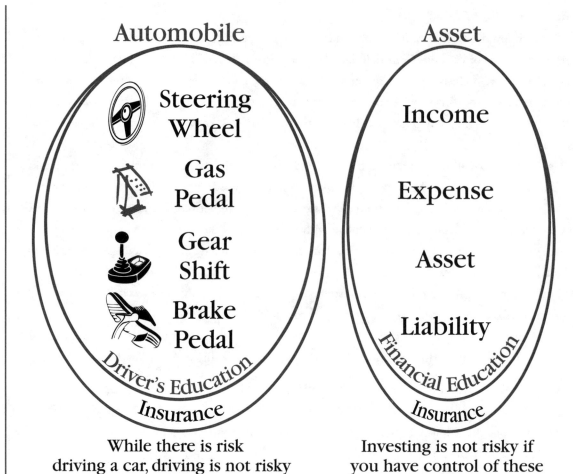

Automobile

Steering Wheel

Gas Pedal

Gear Shift

Brake Pedal

Driver's Education

Insurance

While there is risk
driving a car, driving is not risky
if the driver has these controls.

Asset

Income

Expense

Asset

Liability

Financial Education

Insurance

Investing is not risky if
you have control of these
six points.

Income	
Expenses	

Assets	Liabilities

consumer loans and credit card debt. Again, you are rewarded or penalized appropriately for good liabilities or bad liabilities via the interest percentage rate.

When it comes to assets, one thing a banker looks at is how much insurance your assets have. When your banker is a partner in your real estate investment, your banker wants you to pay for all sorts of different types of insurance. Some examples of insurance coverage bankers require are mortgage, fire, and flood insurance. Bankers also require pest insurance, requesting inspections for termites as well as special type of pest insurance known as liability insurance, which offers some protection against law suits from human termites.

A good financial record also affects your insurance rates when it comes to loans, just as auto insurance companies adjust rates for good drivers and bad drivers. For example, if you have a bad financial report card, many banks require you take a recourse loan, which means if you fail to pay the loan back, the bank can come after your other assets. A *recourse* loan is a form of banking insurance. If you or the asset you are purchasing reflects a high financial IQ, banks do not require *recourse* financing… and will offer you *non-recourse* financing instead. Any professional investor will tell you that *non-recourse* financing is much better than recourse financing. If you have a poor financial record and a low financial IQ, all you can expect to be offered is recourse financing or high interest rates.

Is Your Investment Insured?

Worst of all, if you have a low financial IQ, you may not know that the investment vehicle you are investing in is uninsurable. Any smart driver knows not to drive a car without insurance. Yet very few investors know that their primary investment vehicle, mutual funds, are uninsurable. That is why banks don't lend money to buy mutual funds like they do with real estate. Ask your insurance agent if they will insure your home or your car or your real estate investments? In most cases, they will be happy to see if they can provide you the insurance coverage you desire. Then ask your insurance broker if he or she will insure your mutual funds against market crashes? In most cases, I am sure the insurance agent will ask you to look for another insurance agent. Why do they not want to insure mutual funds against losses? I believe you already know the answer. Once you begin to understand the relationship between education, risk and insurance, your financial IQ will go up and your risks will be minimized.

These are a few examples of how driver's education and financial education can affect both a person's driving record and financial records — as well as his or her life. You can also see how a good driving record and good financial record can mean lower costs, fewer penalties, better relationships, less stress, lower risks, greater pleasure from life, and more favorable insurance and interest rates.

Just as driver's education teaches you to take control over a car, true financial education teaches you to take control over your money and your life. In the following chapters, I will go into each of the controls in more detail, controls such as income and expenses, and explain how to raise your financial IQ in each area. You will see that the higher your financial IQ, relative to each control, the higher your returns will be with fewer penalties, lower risks, and the ability to have more fun out of life. It's simply a matter of taking control of your money and your life.

Why *Teach To Be Rich* Works: When a person follows the advice of "work hard, save money, get out of debt, invest for the long term, and diversify," the biggest problem is that he or she does not learn very much. In the Information Age, we need more information if we are to survive and succeed in life. Looking at the financial statement here, it is easy to see what the education system is focused on — and what it is *not* focused on.

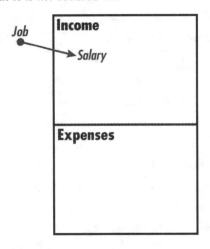

Learning About Income

All schools are focused on is teaching you to get a job so you can earn a salary. That is about as far as the system goes. The school system does not teach children anything about the different types of income. Hence, they teach kids to work for the worst kind of income, earned income, the most highly-taxed of all three income types.

Learning About Expenses

Schools spend no time on expenses, except to say reduce expenses, save money, and live below your means. They do not get into the reality that there are good expenses and bad expenses. In other words, good expenses can make you rich and bad expenses make you poor. To know the difference between good expenses and bad expenses would require a higher form of financial IQ, one that is not available in our school system or in most homes.

Learning About Liabilities

When it comes to the liability column, most schools teach kids that their house is an asset, when it is really a liability. If you have read *Rich Dad Poor Dad*, you may know that one of the biggest mistakes people make is to call liabilities assets. Instead of teaching kids that *bad debt makes you poor and good debt makes you rich*, many parents and teachers simply lump all debt into one category... bad debt. One of the clearest indicators of a high financial IQ is a person's ability to use debt to make them richer. If

you know how to do that, your banker will truly be your friend. People with a low financial IQ only know how to use debt to make them poorer. If all you know is how to take debt and create more debt, you will be one of those people who see bankers as your enemy and may even see bankers as the enemy of humanity. You will fail to see that the real enemy is the lack of financial education.

Learning About Assets

One of the reasons why so many people wind up poor at the end of their working lives is simply because they failed to acquire many real assets. For those of you who have read *Rich Dad Poor Dad*, you already know rich dad's different definitions of assets and liabilities. Simply stated, "Assets put money in your pocket and liabilities take money from your pocket." The reality that most people think their house is an asset proves most people do not know the difference between their assets and a hole in the ground. It also reflects how poor financial education in our schools is.

To make matters worse, if a person truly understood the relationship between expenses, assets and liabilities, that person would know that their retirement plan is really a liability, not an asset. All a person needs to do is look at where the cash is flowing. In most cases with people saving for retirement, the cash is flowing out of their pocket, not into their pocket. In true financial terms, people who are feeding their retirement plan are really feeding an *under-funded liability*. If and when that retirement plan begins to put money into the person's pocket, then and only then does that liability become an asset.

Turning Liabilities Into Assets

Another indicator of a person's financial IQ is if they know how to take a liability and turn it into an asset. If they know how to do that, they will be rich for the rest of their lives.

Many people struggle financially because they spend their lives turning assets into liabilities. For example, many people take their cash, an asset, and get further in debt. Or they take a good piece of real estate, or a business, and let the real estate fall into disrepair or cause the business to lose money.

Yet one of the best investment opportunities is to look for a run-down piece of real estate or a mismanaged business, and turn the liability into an asset. In other words, what many smart investors do is look for a bad investor, take control of that person's liabilities, acquire them, and turn the liabilities into assets.

Your Financial Report Card

True financial education means teaching a person about all components of a financial statement. Looking at the financial statement from the CASHFLOW game, it is easy to see why so many people struggle financially all their lives. They struggle financially simply because the educational system has only focused on the salary line of the income statement.

The school system omits any form of meaningful education on the other aspects of the financial statement. No wonder so many people are paying so many financial penalties for financial violations, violations they do not even know they are causing. Instead of being financially educated, earning more money, paying less in taxes, working less, and lowering their risk exposure, most people spend their lives working hard and being heavily penalized financially. They are penalized by paying higher taxes, higher interest rates, late fees, service charges, hidden charges, accepting recourse financing, and worst of all, investing in investment vehicles for their retirement that are uninsurable.

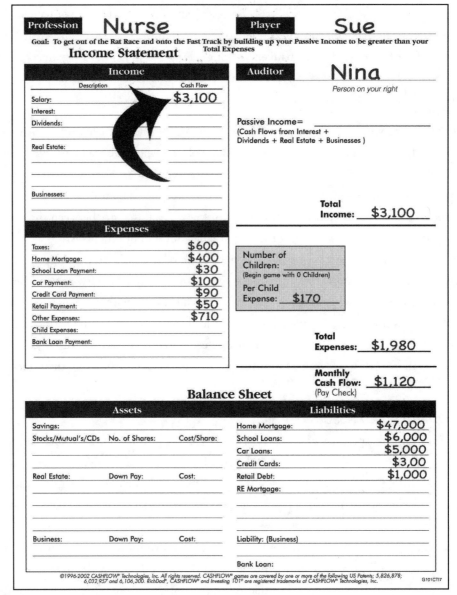

Profession	Nurse		Player	Sue

Goal: To get out of the Rat Race and onto the Fast Track by building up your Passive Income to be greater than your Total Expenses

Income Statement

Income

Description	Cash Flow
Salary:	$3,100
Interest:	
Dividends:	
Real Estate:	
Businesses:	

Auditor	Nina

Person on your right

Passive Income= _____
(Cash Flows from Interest +
Dividends + Real Estate + Businesses)

Total Income:	$3,100

Expenses

Taxes:	$600
Home Mortgage:	$400
School Loan Payment:	$30
Car Payment:	$100
Credit Card Payment:	$90
Retail Payment:	$50
Other Expenses:	$710
Child Expenses:	
Bank Loan Payment:	

Number of Children: _____
(Begin game with 0 Children)

Per Child Expense: $170

Total Expenses:	$1,980

Monthly Cash Flow: (Pay Check)	$1,120

Balance Sheet

Assets

Savings:		
Stocks/Mutual's/CDs	No. of Shares:	Cost/Share:
Real Estate:	Down Pay:	Cost:
Business:	Down Pay:	Cost:

Liabilities

Home Mortgage:	$47,000
School Loans:	$6,000
Car Loans:	$5,000
Credit Cards:	$3,00
Retail Debt:	$1,000
RE Mortgage:	
Liability: (Business)	
Bank Loan:	

©1996-2002 CASHFLOW® Technologies, Inc. All rights reserved. CASHFLOW® games are covered by one or more of the following US Patents; 5,826,878; 6,032,957 and 6,106,300. RichDad®, CASHFLOW® and Investing 101® are registered trademarks of CASHFLOW® Technologies, Inc.

G101CT17

How Do You Measure Financial IQ?

My poor dad sincerely believed a high-paying job was the most important thing on a financial statement. That is why he thought a high salary was indicative of a high IQ, as shown above.

Obviously my rich dad didn't agree with my poor dad. My rich dad did not want a high salary. He thought a high salary was a sign of financial failure, of a low financial IQ. Why did he think that? He thought that simply because a high salary is the most highly-penalized of all income types. Just as we are penalized for driving 60 miles an hour in a 15 mile per hour school zone, people who earn a high salary are penalized. The faster you go with your car the higher your fine. The more you earn, in the form of a salary, the higher your tax 'fine.'

Higher Financial IQ = Lower Fines

Again, looking at the financial statement from the CASHFLOW game, on the diagram below, you will clearly see what my rich dad thought was the true indicator of a high financial IQ.

In my rich dad's mind, the amount of passive income a person earned was the true measure of how high a person's financial IQ was. As he said, "Anyone can work hard for money. It takes a person with a high financial IQ to have their money work hard for them."

The arrow pointing to the *passive income* amount on the financial statement because that measures the player's financial IQ. Passive income that involves the least physical work, delivers the highest of returns, and is the least penalized of all incomes.

In conclusion, just as driver's education can reduce costs, penalties, risks, and increase returns, the same is true of true financial education. That is why teaching yourself and others to be rich works. It works because you are teaching yourself and others to take control of your money and your lives. It is Golden Rule #1.

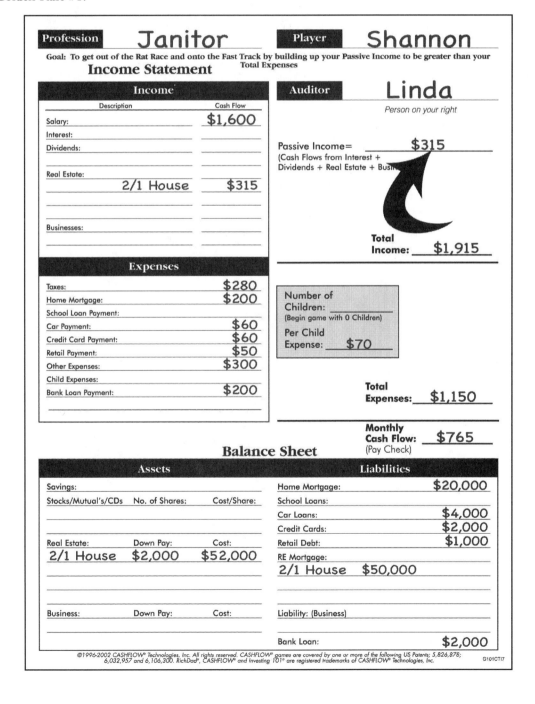

Chapter Thirteen

WHAT KIND OF MONEY ARE YOU WORKING FOR? – OR – TAKING CONTROL OF YOUR MONEY

Most people want more money. That is why, when people think about money, they think about the Income column. And when it comes to more money from income, the primary form of income most people think of is income earned by working for money. That is why most parents say to their kids, "Go to school so you can get a high-paying job."

Looking at the financial statement from the CASHFLOW game, it is easy to see what kind of income most parents are talking about.

Income Statement

Income		
	Description	Cash Flow
Salary:		$3,100
Interest:		
Dividends:		
Real Estate:		
Businesses:		

This is the same kind of income my poor dad thought was important. In fact, I believe it was the only form of income he knew about.

As a young person, my rich dad taught me to value other forms of income, the income indicated by the diagram on the next page.

Three Types Of Income

The lesson here is that there are *three basic* types of income. There are more, but for now, let's focus on the basic three:

   1. Earned income

   2. Portfolio income

   3. Passive income

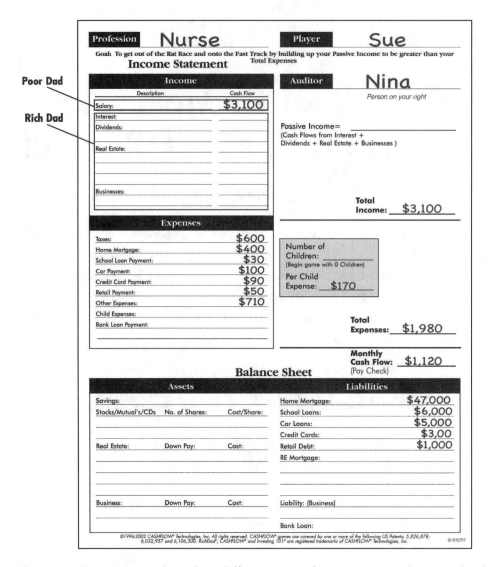

As I have stated many times, these three different types of income are taxed, or penalized, differently. Because the tax laws, subject to Golden Rule #2, tax different incomes differently, the accounting profession must label these incomes differently... hence the three different classifications. In different countries, these names might be different so be sure to check with a local accountant or tax specialist to get the appropriate names for the different classifications. Now I can hear some people saying, "Not in my country. In my country we all work for the same kind of income." In most cases, that kind of thinking demonstrates a lower financial IQ. The fact is, in most countries throughout the world, there are different classifications for different types of income and taxes... income and taxes for the rich and income and taxes for the poor and middle class.

Currently, the combined state and federal taxes in the U.S. run in the following approximate percentages, including Social Security taxes.

1. Earned income – as high as 50%

2. Portfolio income – as low as 20%

3. Passive income – as low as 0%

This is an overly-simplified example of the three basic types of income and applicable taxes.

Why Poor People Don't Get Ahead

One of the reasons poor people and hard-working people do not get ahead financially is simply because they are working hard for the wrong kind of income. I have met people who are working at three different jobs… two jobs during the weekday and one job on the weekend. I have also met working couples who do the same thing, only multiplied by two. Their hard work and increased income only pushes them into higher income tax brackets. In other words, just as a driver is penalized for driving a car at 55 mph in a school zone where the speed limit is 15 mph, a hard worker is penalized via our tax system for working hard, trying to get ahead — because he working hard for the wrong kind of income. In other words he is penalized for trying to go fast in the slow lane. This illustrates the financial and physical penalty for having a weak financial education.

Investing For The Wrong Type Of Income

Looking at the income statement pictured below, it is important to know which kind of income you want below your salary line.

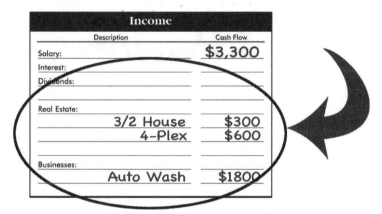

The reason knowing what kind of income to work for and what kind of income to invest for is important becomes apparent when you look at the Expense column.

Income Statement

Income		
Description		Cash Flow
Salary:		$3,100
Interest:		
Dividends:		
Real Estate:		
	3/2 House	$300
	4-Plex	$600
Businesses:		
	Auto Wash	$1800

Expenses	
Taxes:	$600
Home Mortgage:	$400
School Loan Payment:	$30
Car Payment:	$100
Credit Card Payment:	$90
Retail Payment:	$50
Other Expenses:	$710
Child Expenses:	
Bank Loan Payment:	

Taxes Are Your Largest Expense

Rich dad said, "It is important to know that there are different types of income. The reason it is important to know the different types of income is because there are different types of taxes." He went on to say, "When you think of income, you must also think of taxes. Taxes are your largest expense."

When looking at the Income column from the CASHFLOW game, it is important to know that each form of income has a different tax rate.

Income Statement

Income	
Description	Cash Flow
Salary:	$3,300
Interest:	
Dividends:	
Real Estate:	
3/2 House	$300
4-Plex	$600
Businesses:	
Auto Wash	$1800

Expenses	
Taxes:	$630
Home Mortgage:	$500
School Loan Payment:	$60
Car Payment:	$100
Credit Card Payment:	$90
Retail Payment:	$50
Other Expenses:	$760
Child Expenses:	
Bank Loan Payment:	$200

In other words, the financially intelligent thing to do, whenever you think of income, is to also think about taxes. Repeating what I wrote earlier, *different incomes have different tax rates.*

You Working For Money

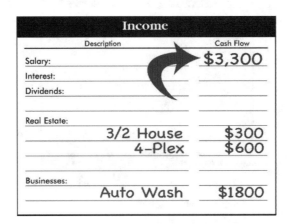

Income	
Description	Cash Flow
Salary:	$3,300
Interest:	
Dividends:	
Real Estate:	
3/2 House	$300
4-Plex	$600
Businesses:	
Auto Wash	$1800

Your Money Working For You

Income	
Description	Cash Flow
Salary:	$3,300
Interest:	
Dividends:	
Real Estate:	
3/2 House	$300
4-Plex	$600
Businesses:	
Auto Wash	$1800

Investing For The Best income And The Best Taxes

One of the problems with having a job is that you work for the worst kind of income, earned income, the most heavily taxed of all incomes. That may be why entrepreneurs such as Steven Jobs of Apple Computers and Sergey Brin of Google only have salaries of $1 a year. Even Warren Buffett, one of the richest investors in the world and founder of Berkshire Hathaway, one of the most expensive and successful funds, has a salary of less than $100,000 a year. I believe one of the reasons why so many mutual fund managers are not as successful as Warren Buffett is because they are highly-paid employees, and not investors or entrepreneurs.

Rich dad said, "Good investments provide income with good tax rates. Bad investments provide income with bad tax rates."

In other words, *before* you invest, you need to know what kind of income you are investing for and the tax consequences.

Bad Tax Rates

1. You working for money (salary, commissions, bonuses)

2. Income from savings

3. Income from 401(k) retirement plans.

Good Tax Rates

1. Tax-free income, often from government bonds

2. Income from real estate (offset by depreciation, resulting in lower or no current taxes)

3. Tax-deferred capital gains from the sale of real estate

4. Income from oil and gas ventures

Working And Investing For The Wrong Income

As stated earlier in this chapter, in addition to working for the wrong kind of income, earned income, most employees invest for the wrong type of income. If they put their retirement savings into a

401(k), their income taxes may be deferred, but when that income is withdrawn, the original savings plus the gains will be taxed at the then-current earned income rate. That is why I stated earlier that *a 401(k) plan only works for people who plan on being poorer at retirement.*

Yet, even if they are poorer at retirement, they may still be taxed excessively. For example, let's say a person puts $10,000 into his or her 401(k) plan at age 25. They are given a temporary tax break on that $10,000 in income. Let's says it's a 50% tax savings, or $5,000 they do not have to pay in taxes. They leave that money in the account, as they are told to do, and in 40 years, when they are 65, that $10,000 has grown to $100,000. When they begin to withdraw that money, they now have to pay the taxes, not only on the $10,000 but on the $90,000 gain as well.

"So what is the big deal?" you may ask. "You knew you were going to pay taxes someday."

Yes, you will pay taxes, but a sophisticated investor would ask… "At what tax rate?" before investing. In other words, a sophisticated investor has an entry and an exit strategy, before investing, and the tax consequences are part of that strategy.

In this example, let's say the person with the $100,000 at age 65 has other investments that provide them income and they are in the highest income bracket.

On top of that, if a person breaks the cardinal rule of *invest for the long term* and begins withdrawing the money from their 401(k) plan early, once again they are severely penalized. Why are they penalized? Is it because the government really wants investors to save for their retirement? Or could it be because the mutual fund companies stop getting their fees if the person withdraws their money early?

Flippers Are Not Investors

During the boom in real estate between 2000 and 2005, a popular way of making money in real estate was by *flipping* properties. In simple terms, a real estate flipper is someone who buys low and sells high, without any intention of holding or managing the property for the long term. For example, a flipper may buy a house for $150,000, maybe fix it up, and then put it back on the market for $250,000. If a greater fool comes long and pays the flipper's asking price, the flipper may put the $100,000 in capital gains, or portfolio income, in his pocket.

If the flipper holds the property for over a year, however, that again will become a long-term capital gain and the tax rate will drop to the lower capital gains rates, around 15% to over 20% depending upon state tax laws.

But, if a flipper flips too many properties too many times, let's say six properties in a year, the IRS may take the position that this is the flipper's profession and therefore treat the income as ordinary earned income. Not only would the flipper lose the benefit of the one-year holding period, but he could also be subject to employment taxes as well.

> *"I am a better investor because I am a businessman, and a better businessman because I am an investor."*
>
> –Warren Buffett

Employment taxes include:

1. FICA or Social security taxes

2. Medicare taxes

3. FUTA, federal unemployment tax

4. State and local employment taxes

It is imperative to structure your business entities properly and to consider the tax implications as well. The lessons here are to understand the tax rates applicable to the income that you are working for, and to recognize that it is most advantageous to work for income that is taxed at the lowest rate possible.

Why Some Teachers Make More Than Others

One of the reasons I did not want to become a teacher was because I always thought that teachers did not make much money. I knew my father and his friends were not as rich as my rich dad and his friends. Once I made my decision to teach, I realized that how much money I made as a teacher was more dependent upon what quadrant I earned my income from, and had nothing to do with the profession of teaching.

The diagram below is the CASHFLOW Quadrant. It is also the title of book number two in the Rich Dad series of books. The quadrant has been one of my guiding beacons as I navigated the twists and turns my life.

E Stands for employee
S Stands for self-employed or small business owner
B Stands for business owner (defined as 500 employees or more)
I Stands for investor

If I were a teacher from the 'E' quadrant, which most teachers are, I knew I would not earn much money. A teacher's role is an important role, yet if the teacher is teaching only 30 students, it is hard to justify a high salary. Although I love teaching, I did not want to teach within the traditional educational system as an employee. More than my issues with the pay, I did not want to put up with the bureaucracy. I saw my dad put up with it for most of his life, and I wanted no part of it.

If I were to be a teacher from the 'S' quadrant, I could earn more money. And I did earn my money in this quadrant for about 10 years. Teaching business and investing to adults, outside the school system, allowed me to determine my class sizes and how much I charged. We had two events a year where we had approximately 500 attendees paying $5,000 each for a week-long class. Needless to

say, those events were profitable. At one point, Kim and I had grown our business education company to eleven offices world wide, before selling the business.

In 1994, Kim and I retired. She was 37 and I was 47. We retired because we were investors in the I quadrant. We were able to retire, without a pension or 401(k) or mutual funds, because we practiced what we taught.

Can A Public School Teacher Be Rich?

Is it possible for a public school teacher in the 'E' quadrant, a person who may not make much money, to become rich? The answer is "Yes." Many have. Again, how much income a person earns is not dictated by the profession or the pay scale of the profession. How much income a person earns depends solely on the quadrant or number of quadrants this person draws income from. For example, a school teacher in the 'E' quadrant, earning let's say $30,000 a year could still become a millionaire if they built a part-time business in the 'B' quadrant or invested in the 'I' quadrant.

Over the years, I have met several schoolteachers who became millionaires by starting a part-time network marketing business, a 'B' quadrant business. Several of this group became very rich by investing their earnings from their 'B' quadrant into real estate investments in the 'I' quadrant. Between 2000 and 2005, when the real estate boom hit, several became multi-multi-millionaires. As far as I know, they are still teaching in the 'E' quadrant. Why? The answer is they love their work as teachers. They love teaching young people. As rich dad said, "How much money you earn is not so much a function of your profession, but which of the quadrants you operate from."

My skill as a teacher comes from my skill as an investor and my skill as an investor comes from my skill as a businessman. Warren Buffett once said. "I am a better investor because I am a businessman, and a better businessman because I am an investor."

Millionaire Garbage Collector

While in school in New York, a friend of mine wanted me to meet a friend of his girlfriend's, so he fixed me up on a blind date. Driving up to her house, in an exclusive neighborhood on Long Island, I was impressed by the size of her home. In hopes of breaking the ice and starting a conversation, I asked her what her father did. She smiled and said, "He's a garbage collector."

After stammering around a bit, shocked by her answer, I asked, "How can a garbage collector live in such an exclusive neighborhood?"

She smiled and said, "He owns one of the largest fleets of garbage trucks on Long Island. He started out as one of the guys hanging on the back of the truck, but now he owns his own company. He has the contracts to pick up the garbage all over the Island. That's how we can afford to live in this neighborhood." Once again, it's not the profession... it's the quadrant. That is why so many people say the second Rich Dad book, *Rich Dad's CASHFLOW Quadrant*, is the most important book for anyone who wants to become rich.

Best-Selling Author

After retiring in 1994, I took a year off and contemplated the rest of my life. One of the best things about money is that, if invested wisely, it can buy a person time... time to do whatever they want to do. In my case, I took a year off and began working on my board game CASHFLOW and my book *Rich Dad Poor Dad*.

In April of 1997, on my fiftieth birthday, the book, the board game, and a 'B' quadrant business

was launched. Although Kim and I were financially well off in 1994, by 2004 we were richer than our wildest dreams. Instead of teaching Kim and I as an 'E' or 'S' quadrant teacher, by transferring the lessons my rich dad taught me into books and games, we entered the 'B' quadrant in 1997 with Sharon as our partner. Repeating what rich dad said, "How much money you earn is not so much a function of your profession, but which of the quadrants you operate from."

In the year 2000, I walked on the set of Oprah Winfrey's TV show and my life changed. I was on her show because I had become a *New York Times* best-selling author… quite a feat for a person who flunked out of high school twice because I could not write.

Not only was her show beamed to approximately 20 million households in the U.S., Oprah was syndicated to over one hundred countries throughout the world. Today, *Rich Dad Poor Dad* and my CASHFLOW game are read and played throughout the world.

Sometimes, when things are calm and quiet, I reflect to that day on the beach in 1979, when I heard the words, "You will not be rich until you teach others to be rich." In those quiet moments, I sit, give thanks, and realize that becoming rich is simply a function of enriching other people's lives. That day in 1979 was a turning point because I stopped thinking only about making myself rich and started thinking about how to make others rich. As rich dad often said, "The secret of success is to always put the welfare of others before your own."

Taking Control Of The Income Column

Unfortunately, most people leave school knowing only about one kind of income and one kind of investment… in my opinion, the worst kind. This lack of financial information often handicaps them their entire working lives.

One aspect of raising a person's financial IQ is learning how to take control of the Income Column. This means knowing how to increase one's income at will, as well as knowing the tax consequences associated with that income. In other words, if you need more money, how fast can you increase your income as well as know how much of that income will be taken by the government?

Former Beatle John Lennon once said, "If I need a swimming pool, I write a song." A few months ago, I wanted a new car. When I talked to Kim about it, she simply said, "Write a book." For large sums of money, I may go to the stock market and raise capital, or I may simply find a new customer and sell more products to them. Now I am not saying you need to learn to write songs or to write books. The point I am making is that rich dad trained his son and me to learn how to raise capital or make more money rapidly. It wasn't easy, like going out to get a part-time job, but in the long run, learning how to create more income quickly is a skill that has proven to be invaluable.

The Most Important Business Skill

One of the most important skills in increasing income is the ability to sell. Whenever I meet someone who complains about not having enough money, it is often because *they have little to sell or cannot sell.*

Rich dad said over and over again to his son and me, "Sales equals income." That is why he insisted I take formal sales training classes and work as a salesman, knocking on doors to get real world experience. When I left the Marine Corps, instead of going to fly for the airlines as many of my fellow pilots did, I went to work for the Xerox Corporation, not for the money, but for the education,

training, and real world experience with selling.

If you are serious about increasing your income, you may want to consider taking a sales training course, or working for a company in sales. While not everyone can get a job with Xerox, a company with a great sales training program, everyone can sign up with a network marketing or direct sales company that will be more than happy to give you some of the best real-life sales training in the world, if you want to learn.

Another option is to look at buying a franchise that trains you to sell. One of my best friends, Blair Singer, a great educator, Rich Dad's Advisor, and author of SalesDogs, launched a franchise company, Sales Partners. Sales Partners trains people to be sales trainers, who then go to businesses and work with the owners to improve the companies' sales… because *sales equals income*. Since most businesses always want more sales, that is a pretty easy sale to make. If you are interested in owning your own Sales Partners franchise business, learning professional sales skills, teaching others to sell, move from the 'E' or 'S' quadrant to the 'B' and 'T' quadrants, be trained by one of the best educators I know, Blair Singer is the person to learn from.

My point in mentioning my friend Blair Singer's program is not necessarily to promote only him. My point is there are many ways a person can learn to increase their income… if they want to learn. So the real question is, do you want to learn how to take control over the Income column? If you are willing, then the next question is, "How bad do you want it? Are you willing to do whatever it takes?" If your desire is not strong enough, then go back to school, get a good job, save money, get out of debt, invest for the long term, and diversify. Unfortunately, if you go to school, you will learn how to work for the worst kind of income and invest in the worst kind of assets. School is where a person is guided by Golden Rule #3.

Why *Teach To Be Rich* Works: One of the more important money lessons rich dad taught me was how to turn *earned income* into *portfolio income* or *passive income*. Again, the reason this is important is because each type of income is taxed at a different percentage rate. As this chapter explains, it is financially wise to not only know what kind of income you work for, but also the tax consequences associated with that income.

Whenever I hear someone say, "I found a good job with a 401(k) plan," I cringe. As you know by now, having a job and a 401(k) plan is working for the worst kind of income,when tax consequences are factored in.

Now I am not against paying taxes. In reality, Kim and I personally pay millions in taxes every year. Indirectly, we also pay millions more in taxes via our companies and our employees. Taxes are the cost of living in a civilized society. Without taxes, there would be no schools, roads, fire or police departments, airports, libraries, etc. etc. etc. Every time I hear someone say they are not paying their taxes, I want to say to them, "I hope your home doesn't catch on fire or you don't ever need a police officer when someone breaks into your home." The government, in spite of all its inefficiencies and waste, performs functions essential for our communities and world to function. That is why I pay my taxes. So although I pay millions in taxes, the amount I pay is a lower percentage of my income simply because I know what kind of income to work for and which quadrants to work from.

One of the more important lessons in the CASHFLOW game is how to turn earned income into

lower-tax portfolio or passive income. In other words, how to turn income from the 'E' quadrant into income from the 'I' quadrant.

Look at the two Opportunity cards from the board game below, and see if you know which card turns *earned income* into *portfolio income* and which card turns *earned income* into *passive income*.

Stock — MYT4U Electronics Co.
Fast growing seller of home electronics headed by 32 year old Harvard grad.
<u>Only you may buy</u> as many shares as you want at this price.
<u>Everyone may sell</u> at this price.
Symbol MYT4U   Today's price: $20
No dividend (Yield or ROI = 0%)
Trading Range: $5 to $30

House For Sale — 3Br/2Ba
Low down payment to pick up this 3/2 house, owner/seller unexpectedly moving out of town. Right person will do well.
Use this yourself or sell to another player.
40% ROI, may sell for $65,000 to $135,000.
Cost: $50,000   Mortgage: $47,000
DownPay: $3,000   Cash Flow: +$100

If you know the difference… congratulations. If you do not know the difference, then investing the time to learn the difference will open your mind to a whole new world of money, a world very few people ever see… even though it is right in front of their eyes. And that is why *Rich Dad's Teach To Be Rich*, works. After all, it is Golden Rule #1.

A Final Thought

When I left school many of my friends were making more income than I was as doctors, lawyers, accountants and airline pilots. But today, I earn much more than most of them, even though I was a 'C' student. Instead of taking a high-paying job, I followed my rich dad's advice and took the time to learn the following:

1. The different incomes

2. The different tax rates

3. How to sell

4. How to have money work for me

5. How to raise money quickly if I need it

6. How to have people work for me

7. How to convert earned income into portfolio or passive income

This is what I invested my time in learning. I wanted to learn these subjects in order to increase my financial IQ and take control of the Income column. None are that hard to learn, if you want to learn. In fact, you already know a lot of what you need to learn. On top of that, you already know more than most people who get paid to dish out financial advice… which is frightening when you think about it.

I recommend you play the CASHFLOW game after reading this book, paying closer attention to the different forms of income… and how to convert bad income into good income. If you pay closer

attention, you will begin to see things you have never seen before. The game is designed to open your eyes so you can find out what you need to learn next.

Another point: Once you begin to see what most people do not see, then invest some time learning more about the Income column. Much of what you will need to learn, the real life experiences, can be learned through on-the-job training, or working on weekends, or joining groups of like-minded people. It's easy to learn… if you want to learn.

As I wrote in *Rich Dad Poor Dad*, don't work to earn… instead work to learn. That is why, instead of going for a high-paying job, as most of my classmates did, I set out to gain the financial education, skills, and real world experience that would teach me to earn much more money than most jobs could ever pay me, pay a lower percentage in taxes, and earn that money without having to work for it day in and day out.

In summary, the problem with most people who go to school is that they go to school to learn how to work for money… the wrong kind of money. Working for the wrong kind of money and investing for the wrong kind of money means they have lost control over the Income column. If you plan on being rich, you need to know more about money than simply how to work for it.

Chapter Fourteen

WHY CHEAP PEOPLE DON'T GET RICH – OR – TAKING CONTROL OF THE EXPENSE COLUMN

How many times have you heard someone say, "Cut expenses. We need to save money." My poor dad said these words a lot. The sad thing is, cutting expenses and saving money did not make my poor dad rich.

My rich dad said "If you want to be rich, you need to know how to spend money… not save money." As you already know, the U.S. dollar became a currency in 1971. After 1971, savers began losing because they were saving a currency that, by design, goes down in value. That is why after 1971, it became more important to know how to spend money, not save money.

The Most Important Column

Rich dad said, "Of the four columns (Income, Expense, Assets and Liabilities) that make up a financial statement, the Expense column is the most important." He also said, "To me, looking at the Expense column is like looking into a crystal ball. Through the Expense column I can see a person's past, present, and future. I can also tell if they are smart, cheap, foolish, or a coward with money."

Posted below is a picture of the Expense column from the CASHFLOW game.

Expenses
Taxes:
Home Mortgage:
School Loan Payment:
Car Payment:
Credit Card Payment:
Retail Payment:
Other Expenses:
Child Expenses:
Bank Loan Payment:

You may notice that the expenses are pretty standard. That means whether we are rich, poor, or middle class, we all have the same types of expenses. The difference is the dollar amounts after the categories of expenses and which expenses we consider important.

For example, my poor dad thought his house was his biggest investment, so his biggest expense was his home mortgage. My rich dad wanted to be rich, so his biggest expense was the last category, Bank Loan Payment. The more you play the CASHFLOW game, the more you will learn how a person's life is impacted by what expenses he thinks are important and which expenses he thinks are bad. The difference is an indicator of financial IQ and different values in life.

Starting The Game

To begin the game, one of the first things a player does is randomly draw a profession card. Professions run the gamut from janitor, truck driver, lawyer and nurse to engineer, teacher, police officer and medical doctor. The incomes were calibrated to represent the relative income, expenses, assets and liabilities of each profession. In other words, the higher your income, the more your lifestyle costs.

For example, pictured below is the profession card of a medical doctor.

Notice the income and the corresponding expenses. While the doctor has the highest income of all the professions in the game, an income of $13,200, the doctor also has the highest expenses at $9,650. Most first-time players who draw the doctor's card cheer when they look at the high income just as

people do in real life. Later on, as the game progresses, they discover that the doctor's expenses are a drag on the game.

The next card is the janitor's card, the lowest paid of all profession cards.

Your Profession

JANITOR

Please copy all data, excluding 0's, onto your Game Card.

Goal: To build up your Passive Income to be greater than your Total Expenses.

Income

Salary:	$1,600
Interest:	0
Dividends:	0
Real Estate/Business:	0

(Interest + Dividends + Real Estate/Business is the sum of your Passive Income)

Passive Income:	0
Total Income:	$1,600

Expenses

Taxes:	280
Mortgage/Rent Pay:	200
School Loan Pay:	0
Car Payment:	60
Credit Card Payment:	60
Retail Payment:	50
Other Expenses:	300
Child Expenses:	0

(Note: All Players begin with 0 children)

Per Child Expense:	$70
Total Expenses:	$950
Monthly Cash Flow:	$650

Assets

Savings:	$560

Liabilities

Mortgage:	20,000
School Loans:	0
Car Loans:	4,000
Credit Cards:	2,000
Retail Debt:	1,000

Notice the income and the corresponding expenses. The janitor's income is $1,600 and total expenses are $950. Many first time players moan when drawing this card. They think a janitor's low income handicaps them. They do not yet realize the impact of expenses on the game. Then after they have played a few games, they often cheer when they draw the janitor's profession card instead of moaning.

Let's look at one more profession... a more middle-of-the-road profession, a K-12 teacher. The teacher's profession card is pictured below.

<table>
<tr><td colspan="2" align="center">**Your Profession**</td></tr>
<tr><td colspan="2" align="center">## TEACHER (K-12)</td></tr>
<tr><td colspan="2" align="center">Please copy all data, excluding 0's, onto your Game Card.</td></tr>
<tr><td colspan="2" align="center">**Goal: To build up your Passive Income to be greater than your Total Expenses.**</td></tr>
</table>

Income

Salary:	$3,300
Interest:	0
Dividends:	0
Real Estate/Business:	0

(Interest + Dividends + Real Estate/Business is the sum of your Passive Income)

Passive Income:	0
Total Income:	$3,300

Expenses

Taxes:	630
Mortgage/Rent Pay:	500
School Loan Pay:	60
Car Payment:	100
Credit Card Payment:	90
Retail Payment:	50
Other Expenses:	760
Child Expenses:	0

Per Child Expense:	$180
Total Expenses:	$2,190

(Note: All Players begin with 0 children)

Monthly Cash Flow:	$1,110

Assets

Savings:	$400

Liabilities

Mortgage:	50,000
School Loans:	12,000
Car Loans:	5,000
Credit Cards:	3,000
Retail Debt:	1,000

To start the game, the person drawing this card begins transferring the teacher's numbers to his or her game financial statement. After transferring all the numbers, the player's financial statement will look like this.

Profession	Teacher		Player	John

Goal: To get out of the Rat Race and onto the Fast Track by building up your Passive Income to be greater than your Total Expenses

Income Statement

Income

Description	Cash Flow
Salary:	$3,300
Interest:	
Dividends:	
Real Estate:	
Businesses:	

Auditor	Ryan

Person on your right

Passive Income= _____
(Cash Flows from Interest +
Dividends + Real Estate + Businesses)

Total Income: $3,300

Expenses

Taxes:	$630
Home Mortgage:	$500
School Loan Payment:	$60
Car Payment:	$100
Credit Card Payment:	$90
Retail Payment:	$50
Other Expenses:	$760
Child Expenses:	
Bank Loan Payment:	

Number of Children: _____
(Begin game with 0 Children)

Per Child Expense: $180

Total Expenses: $2,190

Monthly Cash Flow: $1,110
(Pay Check)

Balance Sheet

Assets

Savings:		$400
Stocks/Mutual's/CDs	No. of Shares:	Cost/Share:
Real Estate:	Down Pay:	Cost:
Business:	Down Pay:	Cost:

Liabilities

Home Mortgage:	$50,000
School Loans:	$12,000
Car Loans:	$5,000
Credit Cards:	$3,00
Retail Debt:	$1,000
RE Mortgage:	
Liability: (Business)	
Bank Loan:	

©1996-2002 CASHFLOW® Technologies, Inc. All rights reserved. CASHFLOW® games are covered by one or more of the following US Patents; 5,826,878; 6,032,957 and 6,106,300. RichDad®, CASHFLOW® and Investing 101® are registered trademarks of CASHFLOW® Technologies, Inc.

G101CTI7

Ideally, a game will have four to six players, all with different professions and starting financial positions. Now the game is about ready to begin.

But before beginning, I would like to look at just the teacher's starting Expense column, pictured below.

Expenses	
Taxes:	$630
Home Mortgage:	$500
School Loan Payment:	$60
Car Payment:	$100
Credit Card Payment:	$90
Retail Payment:	$50
Other Expenses:	$760
Child Expenses:	
Bank Loan Payment:	

If the Expense column really is like a crystal ball, these are some of the questions I would ask:

1. What do these expenses say about this player's past, present, and future?

2. What will happen to this player if they do not change their expenses?

3. What will happen if this player just cuts expenses?

4. How will saving money affect this player's future?

When designing this game, I designed each profession's expenses to reflect a financial statement that was stuck in the past. You may want to look at the entire financial statement and see if you understand why these expenses reflect the past.

The answer to question #2 is that if this person does not change their expenses, they will not have a very abundant financial future.

And the answers to questions #3 and #4 are, even if they cut their expenses and begins saving money, this person's future will probably not change. Their future will not change because just cutting expenses does not make their future better. It might make it worse cause them to lose the game.

Saving A Currency, Not Money

Remember we stated earlier that, after 1971, the U.S. dollar stopped being money and became a currency. That is why in the Information Age a person needs to know how to spend to get rich, not save to get rich. That is why I designed this game to punish savers and reward spenders and debtors.

After 1971, the people who lived frugally and saved money (now a currency) were the losers not the winners. Just look at how much the price of a house has gone up since 1971. My dad purchased his house in 1968 for about $50,000. Today, it is worth millions. There is no way he could have saved

millions of dollars on his salary. One reason why the value of his house went up so much is because the value of the U.S dollar was coming down. As much as my dad tried to save money, he ultimately lost the game because, after 1971, savers became losers. The government was printing money faster than he could earn it — or save it.

Today, many people are saving money in their 401(k) retirement plans. Between 1995 and 2005 they, too, became losers, during the biggest economic boom in history. They lost because they were savers, not investors.

Cheap People With Money

One of the more important lessons designed into the game is the lesson that people need to learn how to spend money wisely, if they want become rich… not just cut expenses and save money, which is what most people do. There are many people who are cheap and think that being cheap will make them rich. In fact, many people actually think that being cheap, cutting expenses, and living below their means is the smart thing to do. While they may accumulate a lot of money, eventually all they become are cheap people with money… and the world despises cheap people with money. In fact many books have been written about cheap rich people. One such book is Charles Dickens novel, *A Christmas Carol*, featuring Ebenezer Scrooge. Another book is *Silas Marner*, another story of a rich cheap man… proving the world loves to hate cheap, rich people.

Even though there are many ways to become rich, I know many people who believe that all rich people are cheap, people who think only of themselves and not others.

In other Rich Dad books, I have written about the fact that rich dad let his son and me know that there are many different ways to become rich. Some of the more popular ways are:

1. You can marry for money. The problem is, if you marry for money, we all know what you become.

2. You can get rich by being greedy. The problem is, no one likes greedy people except other greedy people.

3. You can get rich by being lucky. The problem is, as many lottery winners have found out, luck is hard to repeat after the money is gone.

4. You can become rich by being a crook. The problem is, at the end of the process you're still a crook. On top of that, a crook operating outside the law, can never really trust other people.

5. You can become rich by being born into a rich family. The problem is, you may always wonder if you could have made it on your own.

6. You can become rich by being cheap. I believe this is the most popular of all methods. The problem is, at the end of the process you're still cheap. And, as you know, the world dislikes rich but cheap people the most. That is why there are so many books written about such people.

7. You can become rich by being smart and generous. This is what my rich dad recommended and what I am writing about in this book.

8. You can become rich by being a star, like a rock star, movie star, football star. The problem with being a star is that the money stops if you stop being a star.

9. You can climb the corporate ladder. The problem is, on your way up the view is always the same.

10. You can become rich by trying to get rich quick. The problem is, people who get rich quick often become poor just as quickly.

Although I am not saying one way is better than the other, I am saying that if you want to become rich, you need to find the process that most appeals to you.

Middle Class Values

Growing up in a highly-educated, middle-class family, my mom and dad regularly stressed the importance of saving money, being frugal, living below our means, and keeping our expenses low. In other words, they were trying to get rich by being cheap. My poor dad often said, "A dollar saved is a dollar earned." But no matter how hard they tried to work harder, cut expenses, live below their means and save money, my mom and dad never got ahead financially. In fact, instead of getting ahead, they fell behind financially simply because they did not know the difference between money and a currency, and how to spend money to become rich. All they knew was to work hard and be cheap.

It was because I saw this struggle in my family, the struggle to be cheap and get ahead, that I designed the CASHFLOW game the way I did. For many people, like my mom and dad, learning to spend to get rich is a foreign idea. The idea of borrowing to become rich is even more foreign, since my poor dad often said, "Neither a borrower nor lender be." As you know, he might have done well saving money and being cheap prior to 1971, but after 1971 his financial words of wisdom were as out-of-date as last week's newspaper.

Spending And Borrowing To Become Rich

Learning to spend and borrow to get rich is not easy for many people. That is why I recommend people play the game several times. Each time they play the game, the game will push them out of their comfort zone and open their mind's eye to new worlds of money that they did not see before. Instead of being cheap, they will learn to be smarter with their money.

Back To The Teacher

Getting back to the teacher's profession card and financial statement, the only way the teacher can win this game, even beating a medical doctor with higher pay, is by spending and borrowing.

The teacher's starting financial statement looks like this:

Profession	**Teacher**	Player	**John**

Goal: To get out of the Rat Race and onto the Fast Track by building up your Passive Income to be greater than your Total Expenses

Income Statement

Income

Description	Cash Flow
Salary:	$3,300
Interest:	
Dividends:	
Real Estate:	
Businesses:	

Auditor	**Ryan**

Person on your right

Passive Income= _____
(Cash Flows from Interest +
Dividends + Real Estate + Businesses)

Total Income: $3,300

Expenses

Taxes:	$630
Home Mortgage:	$500
School Loan Payment:	$60
Car Payment:	$100
Credit Card Payment:	$90
Retail Payment:	$50
Other Expenses:	$760
Child Expenses:	
Bank Loan Payment:	

Number of Children: _____
(Begin game with 0 Children)

Per Child Expense: $180

Total Expenses: $2,190

Monthly Cash Flow: $1,110
(Pay Check)

Balance Sheet

Assets

Savings:		$400
Stocks/Mutual's/CDs	No. of Shares:	Cost/Share:
Real Estate:	Down Pay:	Cost:
Business:	Down Pay:	Cost:

Liabilities

Home Mortgage:	$50,000
School Loans:	$12,000
Car Loans:	$5,000
Credit Cards:	$3,00
Retail Debt:	$1,000
RE Mortgage:	
Liability: (Business)	
Bank Loan:	

©1996-2002 CASHFLOW® Technologies, Inc. All rights reserved. CASHFLOW® games are covered by one or more of the following US Patents; 5,826,878; 6,032,957 and 6,106,300. RichDad®, CASHFLOW® and Investing 101® are registered trademarks of CASHFLOW® Technologies, Inc.   G101CTl7

(This financial statement represents the vast majority of people who are working hard, saving money, and trying to get out of debt.)

... to something that may look like this at the end of the game:

Profession	Teacher	Player	John

Goal: To get out of the Rat Race and onto the Fast Track by building up your Passive Income to be greater than your Total Expenses

Income Statement

Auditor: Ryan *Person on your right*

Income

Description	Cash Flow
Salary:	$3,300
Interest:	
Dividends:	
Real Estate:	
3/2 House	$300
4-Plex	$600
Businesses:	
Auto Wash	$1800

Passive Income= $2,700
(Cash Flows from Interest + Dividends + Real Estate + Businesses)

Total Income: $6,000

Expenses

Taxes:	$630
Home Mortgage:	$500
School Loan Payment:	$60
Car Payment:	$100
Credit Card Payment:	$90
Retail Payment:	$50
Other Expenses:	$760
Child Expenses:	
Bank Loan Payment:	$200

Number of Children: ____
(Begin game with 0 Children)
Per Child Expense: $180

Total Expenses: $2,390

Monthly Cash Flow: $3,610 (Pay Check)

Balance Sheet

Assets

Savings:		
Stocks/Mutual's/CDs	No. of Shares:	Cost/Share:
OK4U	600	$20
MYT4U	3000	$10
Real Estate:	Down Pay:	Cost:
3/2 House	$5,000	$95,000
4-Plex	$15,000	$125.000
Business:	Down Pay:	Cost:
Auto Wash	$50,000	$350,000

Liabilities

Home Mortgage:	$50,000
School Loans:	$12,000
Car Loans:	$5,000
Credit Cards:	$3,00
Retail Debt:	$1,000
RE Mortgage:	
3/2 House	$90,000
4-Plex	$110,000
Liability: (Business)	
Auto Wash	$300,000
Bank Loan:	$2,000

©1996-2002 CASHFLOW® Technologies, Inc. All rights reserved. CASHFLOW® games are covered by one or more of the following US Patents; 5,826,878; 6,032,957 and 6,106,300. RichDad®, CASHFLOW® and Investing 101® are registered trademarks of CASHFLOW® Technologies, Inc. G101CTI7

For the teacher to have a financial statement that looks like this, they need to get out of the past and begin investing in the future.

For a person who has been raised thinking that saving money, living below one's means, being frugal, and getting out of debt is the financially smart thing to do, playing CASHFLOW may be a trying ordeal the first few times. But after playing 10 times, they may soon see many more creative ways to get ahead financially, using debt to win the game. The good thing is they can learn by playing with play money.

For many first-time players, the idea of spending money and getting into debt to get rich may be emotionally challenging, even though they are only playing with play money. The reason a player is challenged is because the logical mind knows it is a game played with play money, but the subconscious mind does not. The learning process takes place between the game, the logical mind, and the player's deep-rooted beliefs buried in the subconscious mind. The battle is between the conservative person in you and the risk taker in you. The battle is also between the poor person in you and the rich person in you. Once the battle between logic and emotion is over, the player can play the CASHFLOW game and the game of real life as a new person.

When players can think logically about spending instead of saving, and be comfortable with debt as a means to get rich, they are on their way to becoming better managers of their own money. Instead of being run by their emotions, usually doubt and fear, they begin to think more intelligently about their money. As Warren Buffett says, "If a person cannot control their emotions, they cannot control their money."

Changing Roles By Changing Cash Flow Patterns

Rich dad often said, "I can tell a person's true character by looking at their expense column." What rich dad meant by this was that each of us plays a financial role on this earth. He said, "Many people play poor people in real life. That is their role here on earth. Other people play middle class people. That is their role. And others play the role of rich people; people who are financially smart with money. The only way you can tell which role they are playing is by looking at their expense column."

The Poor Person

This is the cash flow pattern of a poor person. The pattern determines the role they will play in life, regardless of how much money they make.

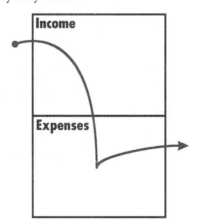

Rich dad said, "Playing a poor person does not mean the person does not earn much money. There are many poor people who earn a lot of money." What he meant was that many people spend everything they make. In other words, it's what they do in the Expense column that keeps them poor, not how much they make in the Income column. These are the people who truly do live paycheck to paycheck.

The Debtor

People who are playing the role of debtors here on earth have a cash flow pattern that looks like this:

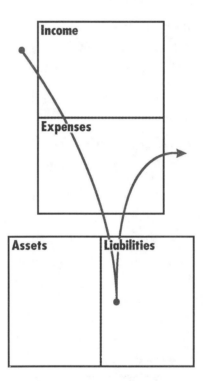

Many people who look like they are playing the role of a rich person have this cash flow pattern. Many people who drive nice cars and live in nice neighborhoods are actually living paycheck to paycheck because their chosen role is the role of a debtor. Much of the middle class is playing the role of the debtor only because they are trying to keep up with the Joneses.

Unfortunately today, with the proliferation of credit cards, many low-income poor people are now playing the role of debtors. Prior to credit cards, many low income people were actually in good financial shape because it was hard for them to get loans. Today with credit readily available, even poor people are playing the role of debtors.

The Saver

Many people play the role of savers during their time here on earth. The following is their cash flow pattern:

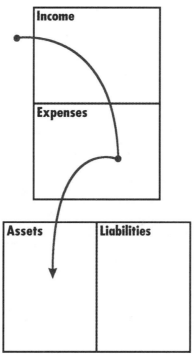

Savers are often collectors of something they think is valuable, such as cash, antiques, mutual funds, coins, art work, etc. The difference between a saver and an investor will be more apparent when you see the investor's cash flow pattern.

The Investor

A true investor's efforts impact the Income Column.

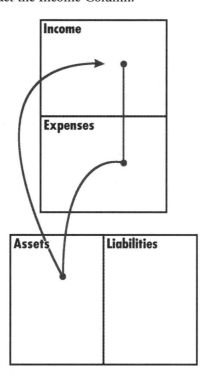

The Smart Investor

The smart investor knows how to use OPM (Other People's Money,) debt or equity, to attain wealth.

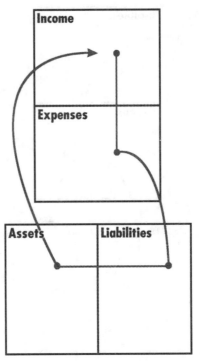

The Rich

The rich have a different pattern. They do not have a job. All they have are assets. *Forbes* magazine defines rich as $1 million or more in income from assets.

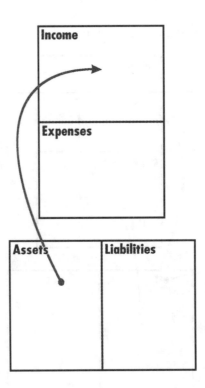

The Gambler/Loser

The gambler is a person who thinks they are investing but no matter what they invest in they never make any money. Instead of winning, they lose money.

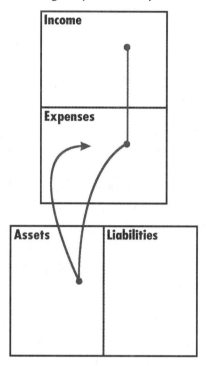

These people are often involved with get-rich schemes, or the newest investment technique like day-trading, the hot technique in the late 1990s. Between 2000 and 2005, the hottest, newest, and latest get-rich-quick investment technique in the real estate market was flipping houses.

The Greater Fool Theory Of Investing

In case you may not know what flipping houses means, it means buying a house for, let's say, $100,000, and immediately marking it up to $150,000. The investor has no plans for living in the house and has no plans on renting it. Flippers invest according to the greater fool theory, as many stock investors do. The greater fool theory of investing means the fool (in this case, the flipper) is hoping for a fool greater than they are to come along and buy the house from them. This investment strategy can work as long as there are greater fools.

Who Are You Talking To?

When I hear financial experts say, "Get out of debt and save money," they are usually talking to someone who is playing a debtor's role and is trying to get them to play a saver's role. When I hear financial experts say, "Invest for the long term and diversify," they are usually recommending that a person adopt the saver's role, not the investor's role.

What Role Are You Playing?

After playing the CASHFLOW game a number of times, a player may want to look at his personal financial pattern and determine which role he is playing in real life. After determining that role, be it the poor person, saver, gambler, or whatever, that players may want to decide to make changes in real life — from the role he is playing to the role the game was designed to teach.

The Desired Role

The CASHFLOW game was created, to teach the role of the smart investor. It was the role my rich dad trained his son and me to play. While it is the hardest of the roles to learn in real life, once that role is learned, real life becomes easier and easier.

Knowing how to responsibly use OPM to create wealth is an important role to learn and to play. Today, because of my training to be a smart investor, my businesses and investments produce many jobs and have created millions in wealth. That is the kind of role I want to play while here on earth.

Why Cheap People Lose

The following are examples of why cheap people lose in the real world.

1. **The cheap real estate investor.** Most of us have seen rental properties where the investor does not spend any money on taking care of the property. As the property runs down, good tenants move out and cheap tenants, often petty criminals, move in. As cheap tenants move in, income to the property goes down. When a property's income drops and expenses increase, due to deferred maintenance, the value of the property declines. In the short term, the cheap real estate investor may make more money, but then loses money on the long-term value of their property.

   Finding properties run by cheap investors is one way rich investors get richer. A rich investors, will buy the property, kick out all the bad tenants, spend money on renovating the property, put in better tenants, increase the income from the property, spend money wisely, and improve the value of the property.

2. **The cheap business owner.** One of the best business opportunities is a business run by cheap owners. Many businesses begin to fail because a cheap business owner thinks cheap. For example, I found a business for sale that needed only to raise the pay to employees. Because the owner paid the employees so little, all he attracted were bad employees. By paying just a few dollars per hour more, better employees came in and the business prospered.

3. **Declining sales.** Many times when sales begin to drop, businesses cut their advertising budget. In other words they save instead of spend. This is true for big companies, small companies, real estate investors and private people. If sales are dropping, the rule is to spend more money on advertising. Do not cut spending.

   Often, when sales begin to drop, owners go into a hole and hide. Fear sets in, bills pile up, and they panic. So rather than promote or market, they cut back on expenses and activities. That is the worst thing they can do. Even if the owners have no money, they need to come out of their shell, start hitting the phones, dialing old customers and friends, letting them know they are open for business. As business comes in and sales increase, they can use some of that money to purchase advertising or spend more on direct mail campaigns to keep the promotion going. I say this because so many times, when a business has enough business, the owner gets cocky and stops promoting. Once the business stops promoting, sales again begin to slide and so does income. Always remember that Sales=Income and sales is a function of promotion, physically and financially.

4. **Lack of knowledge.** In the early 1970s, I was watching a television infomercial about investing in real estate. The author of the book was going to be in town, and for about $30 the public could go listen to him. I was still in the Marine Corps at the time, and I asked several of my fellow pilots if they wanted to attend the evening seminar. Well, no one was interested. Several said, "It's a rip off." One said, "I own a house. What can he tell me about investing in real estate?" A few others just laughed at me wanting to pay money to listen to a con man try and take more of my money. So I went alone.

    During the evening event I signed up for a $385 course to be held that weekend. When I returned to my squadron and told them what I had done, smirks and catcalls of "sucker" were all I got in response.

    Thirty years later, that $385 course has made me millions of dollars. But most importantly, it was a turning point along my journey of learning. Today, I occasionally speak to airline pilots, many who were former military pilots, about investing. Many of these pilots are afraid they will not have enough income to retire on, now that so many airlines are in financial trouble as are their pension plans.

    Today, it is not only pilots who are in financial trouble. Many people are, simply because somewhere along the way they saved a few dollars and scrimped on their education.

5. **On-going support.** At The Rich Dad Company, we televise many of our company meetings to a group of web subscribers known as INSIDERS What we broadcast is a no-holds-barred, no words spared, insider's view of running a business. I got the idea from watching the reality TV show "Big Brother." Instead of just being a show with people talking about nothing, we decided to use similar format to educate. In other words, for people who want to be entrepreneurs and investors. We thought, why not let those who are interested sit in and watch how we operate and grow the business? In my opinion, it is some of the best real world education a person can get. In one of the first programs, I discussed how company sales were declining, why I thought they were declining and how I planned to get sales back up. It was not a pleasant broadcast, yet it was real-world, real-time, and from real people.

    In many ways, the Rich Dad INSIDERS web program is similar to the type of education I got from my rich dad. It was not learning about business from a textbook or a school-teacher. I spent much of my life learning about real life business and investment challenges, as rich dad handled those challenges. For many years, I learned by watching the good and the bad, the successes and failures, and by watching rich dad grow from a small businessman to become one of the richest men in Hawaii.

    The program is not only about me. The program also invites people like my business partner Frank, who did a web broadcast about how he raises money to take companies public through the stock exchange. Another friend of mine, David, is one of the largest mortgage bankers in the U.S. serving the apartment house market. He talked about real estate trends in different parts of the country as well as how to get bigger loans for bigger projects.

Rich Dad's INSIDERS is about on-going support and on-going, real-world education. At this time we only charge $10 a month for a subscription. That's less than a meal at a cheap restaurant. Nonetheless, I hear from cheap people who want the program for free. They actually think $10 is too expensive for information. If they think $10 a month is expensive for real-life business and investment education, from real-world business people and investors, addressing real-world business and investment challenges, in real time, then imagine how expensive a college education is — an education for which you pay high prices to learn about text book problems and often taught by people who have never worked in the real world. That kind of education is not cheap... it's the most expensive kind of education there is... in more ways than just money.

If you would like to look at the INSIDERS program and judge its value for yourself, go to www.richdad.com/insiders. We are considering adding additional programming and have just authorized an additional $100,000 to be spent on our studio so that we can offer higher quality recording and provide in-house editing capability. In fact, we have been advised to increase the monthly fee to $49 per month. So, now is the time to join if you are interested.

Those are some real world examples of why cheap people do not become rich. They may make a lot of money, but many fail to enrich their lives.

Taking Control Of The Expense Column

Control over the Expense column is a very important control to have. Anyone can cut back. Anyone can live frugally or live below their means. Anyone can be cheap and save money. Anyone can invest $50 or more a month to buy mutual funds that return them nothing. Anyone can borrow the equity from their home to pay off credit card debt. In reality, this is using your house as an ATM machine. Anyone can cut up their credit cards. Knowing how to spend, borrow and continue to get richer is a sign of a very high financial IQ, and that is one of the financial lessons I designed into the CASHFLOW game.

Why *Teach To Be Rich* **Works:** Why are so many people struggling financially today? One reason is because there are so many neat things to buy and exciting things to do. My closets are filled with neat things I just had to have, so I bought them. But I rarely use them. Instead of using what is in my closet, it is more fun to go shopping and look for something new. That is why I designed the Doodad card into the game.

The Doodad Cards

Today, one of the biggest businesses in the world is the self-storage business. In the U.S. this is a $17 billion business, larger than the motion picture business. The reason the self-storage business is booming is because people need extra space to save all those precious Doodads.

If we don't want to save those precious Doodads, we throw them away. That is why the U.S. spends more on trash bags than many other countries' entire economies.

So not only is it expensive to buy Doodads, it's expensive to keep them... and throw them away. That is why Doodads were designed so prominently into the game.

After playing the game and understanding the difference between good expenses and bad expenses, many players now go shopping with the word 'Doodads' ringing in their head. Instead of shopping for Doodads, many people report going shopping for expenses that make them rich rather than shopping for Doodads that make them poorer. A sample of several Doodad cards are pictured above.

Author's Note: I am not one of those cheap, frugal people. I personally love my Doodads. I have lots of them, and the richer I get, the more expensive my Doodads become. So you will never hear me say, "Cut up your credit cards, live below your means, and invest for the long term." That is not the financial philosophy I subscribe to. Instead of denying yourself Doodads, I designed the game to teach you how to afford all the Doodads you want, if you want them. All you need to do is learn how to spend and borrow to get rich, instead of spend and borrow to get poor. The game will help you to learn this.

A Baby

Another element designed into the game is the expense of having a baby. After rolling the dice, their marker lands on the section of the Rat Race labeled Baby, the player then checks their profession card to find out how much a baby will cost them. Again, looking at the teachers profession card, on the next page, you will notice that the per child expense is $180 per child.

Going to the player's financial statement, you notice that there is a special shaded box for this entry. If the teacher has two children, the monthly expense is $180 times two. Now I am not saying a child is a good expense or a bad expense. What I was intending to do by putting the cost of children into the game was to bring some real-life reality to the game. Many parents with older children report that this part of the game brings up discussions they were meaning to have with their children but never found the right time to have.

```
┌─────────────────────────────────────────────────────────────┐
│                    Your Profession                            │
│  ┌───────────────────────────────────────────────────────┐   │
│  │              TEACHER (K-12)                            │   │
│  └───────────────────────────────────────────────────────┘   │
│       Please copy all data, excluding 0's, onto your Game Card.│
│       Goal:  To build up your Passive Income to be            │
│              greater than your Total Expenses.                │
```

Income		
Salary:	$3,300	
Interest:	0	
Dividends:	0	
Real Estate/Business:	0	Passive Income: 0
(Interest + Dividends + Real Estate/Business is the sum of your Passive Income)		Total Income: $3,300

Expenses		
Taxes:	630	
Mortgage/Rent Pay:	500	
School Loan Pay:	60	
Car Payment:	100	
Credit Card Payment:	90	
Retail Payment:	50	Per Child Expense: $180
Other Expenses:	760	
Child Expenses:	0	Total Expenses: $2,190

(Note: All Players begin with 0 children)

Monthly
Cash Flow: $1,110

Assets		Liabilities	
Savings:	$400	Mortgage:	50,000
		School Loans:	12,000
		Car Loans:	5,000
		Credit Cards:	3,000
		Retail Debt:	1,000

One parent wrote in and said, "The feature you should have added in is that each year children get more expensive, not less expensive." Another parent wrote in and asked, "Are children assets or liabilities?"

My reply was, "In God's eyes, all children are assets. To your banker, they are liabilities."

By teaching people about the Expense column, you give them the opportunity to take direct and immediate control of their lives… their past, their present, and their future. And that is why teach to be rich works.

Author's Note: Many politicians claim they need to raise taxes because there is not enough money. In reality, there is plenty of money from taxes. So the problem is not the lack of money but the lack of fiscal controls on expenses. If politicians and government workers were better at spending money, we could reduce taxes and perhaps even have a surplus.

Chapter Fifteen

Only Lazy people Use Their Own Money – OR – Taking Control Of The Liability Column

Miss Piggy, that famous Muppet, once said, "The secret to money management is always manage to have enough money." Her profound brilliance has stayed with me and guided me for years.

The secret to taking control of the Liability column is simply to know that there is good debt and bad debt… and if you manage to have lots of good debt, life will be good.

Unfortunately, because our schools do not teach students much about money, all most people know is that debt is bad, which is why financial experts constantly say, "Cut up those credit cards and get out of debt." Or "Take out a home equity loan and pay off those high interest credit cards." While on the surface, such advice may sound like good advice, unfortunately it is not advice that solves the underlying problem. And that problem is most people do not understand debt.

Why The Rich Are Getting Richer

One of the reasons the rich are getting richer is simply because the rich know that debt is really an asset, as well as a liability. In fact, debt could be the biggest asset class in the world. When the U.S., the largest debtor nation in the world, sells a bond, what they are selling is debt, an I.O.U. from the taxpayers of the U.S. that they will repay the principle and the interest. Your home mortgage, a debt to you, is an asset to someone else. When you buy a car, the car is not the asset. You are the asset… your ability and agreement that you will pay the money back.

Recently, several cigarette companies have come out with an anti-smoking campaign. While this makes them look like good corporate citizens, the truth is they do not want you to stop smoking. They simply want you to feel good about the company you are buying your cigarettes from. The same is true for banks. While many banks will say "Get out of debt." in reality, banks need all of us to be in debt. Without credit, debt, and borrowers, this world as we know it would ricochet back to the Stone Age over the weekend. In other words, love doesn't make the world go round and neither does money. What makes today's world go round is debt.

The Balance Sheet

The best way to understand debt or the Liability column is look at the entire Balance Sheet, like the overly-simplified one pictured on the next page.

The reason it is called a Balance Sheet is simply because it must balance. Your net worth is the difference between your assets and your liabilities. Of course, many people have a negative net worth, which means that their liabilities, exceeds their assets. Using an example I have used many times before, let's look at a home mortgage.

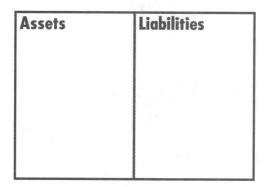

Again, in overly simple terms, rich dad said, "Assets put money in your pocket and liabilities take money from your pocket." In this case, your mortgage takes money from your pocket and puts it in the banks pocket. That is why when a banker says "Your home is an asset," he is not lying to you. He is simply not saying whose asset it is. It is the bank's asset.

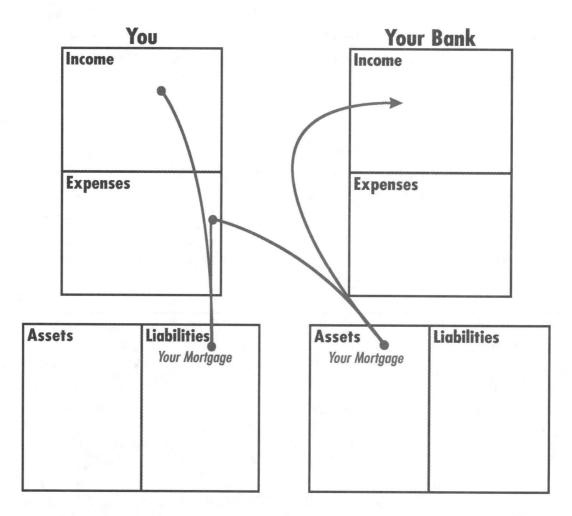

So by simply understanding that for every asset there is a liability and that liabilities are really assets, you will know more than 99% of the people on this earth. You may be more confused, but at least you will know more.

Why The Poor And Middle Class Get Poorer

One main reason why the poor and middle class get poorer is because they do not know that *debt* is an *asset*. So every time they heed the advice of *get out of debt*, they fail to realize that debt can also be something good, something that could make them rich and their lives easier.

My poor dad was a man who always said, "Get out of debt." Obviously he thought debt was bad.

My rich dad often said, "Get into debt. Only lazy people use their own money." To many people, he sounded like a lunatic… especially hard-working people trying to get out of debt, or avoid debt.

In all the years I observed rich dad saying, "Get into debt. Only lazy people use their own money." I never saw one person stop and ask rich dad what he meant. All most people did was glance back at him like he had lost his marbles… or they would laugh, thinking that he was kidding.

Rich dad's explanation to his son and me of why he said, "Only lazy people use their own money" changed the future of my life. This is his explanation.

He said, "The reason most people think debt is bad is because they only know about bad debt… debt they have to pay for. Debt such as their mortgage, car loan, or consumer loans — payments they make every month." At the time he was explaining this to us, credit cards were not in wide use. "Good debt is debt that not only puts money in your pocket, but someone else pays off the debt for you."

Bad Debt

This is the only kind of debt the general public knows. And if this is all they know, then the advice of *get out of debt*, is applicable. Yet, that same advice is not applicable to someone with a higher financial IQ. The diagram below is an example of bad debt, the kind of debt financially smart people don't want.

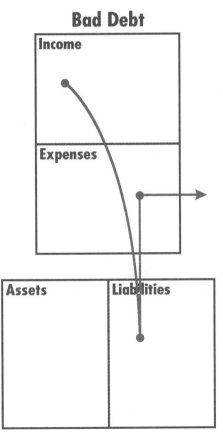

Bad Debt

Good Debt

The diagram below is an example of good debt, the kind of debt financially smart people want. There is a lot of information in this overly-simple diagram.

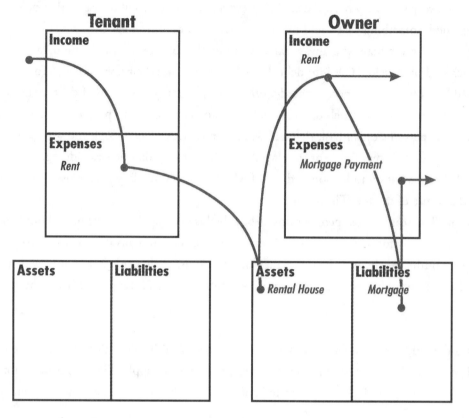

Some noteworthy points are:

1. The tenant has no debt. The owner does. Who will be better off in the long run?

2. With the extra income, from the renter, the owner can buy a second rental property, once again with the help of the banker's money, thus increasing their income.

3. Hopefully, the tenant will some day buy a home. At that point, they will go to the first financial statement, the financial statement of the home owner with bad debt, a home mortgage. If the tenant, now home owner, only knows about bad debt, the new homeowner will then try to pay off that bad debt, instead of look for a second property and acquire good debt.

4. The owner of the rental property is way ahead financially because the owner has a higher financial IQ. Just by successfully owning a rental property, the owner has learned:

    a. How to *borrow* money that makes you money.

    b. How to *manage* a property, people, money, and taxes.

    c. How to *control* income, expenses, assets, liabilities, and insurance.

    d. How to have *money work for them*, both their own money and the bank's money.

    e. Investing for both *cash flow* as well as *capital gains*.

Notice the difference in words. The words most people know are, "Work hard, save money, get out of debt, invest for the long-term, and diversify." To most people, those words are indicative of the financially smart thing to do. Yet, when compared to the words a person who has invested in just one property uses, the vocabulary, the words they use are very different. Instead, the property owner uses words such as *borrow*, rather than get out of debt; *manage*, rather than turn your money over to a money manager for the long term so they can collect their fees; *control*, instead of diversify; *investing*, rather than saving; and knowing the difference between cash flow and capital gains, are words most people with 401(k)s or standard retirement plans, really do not know.

In other words, just by buying one small rental property, or a business, the financial IQ of the person is far ahead of a person with a portfolio or retirement plan filled with paper assets such as mutual funds. Even if the investor makes mistakes, which are learning opportunities, and loses money occasionally, they are far ahead in the financial IQ category than an 'A' student with a normal retirement plan filled with stocks, bonds, mutual funds. At least, that is how my rich dad, a school drop-out, beat my poor dad, an 'A' student, in the real world. One had a high academic IQ and one had a high financial IQ.

Only Lazy People

One of the hardest things I had to learn was how to borrow or raise money, and that is why rich dad said, "Only lazy people use their own money." What he meant was that it is very easy to work hard or borrow money you will have to pay back yourself. It takes a higher form of financial IQ to borrow money and then have the money work hard for you and on top of that, have someone else pay off the loan.

I still remember shaking nervously as I applied for a loan to buy my first rental property. I was about 25 years old. I already owned my own home, a condominium on Waikiki Beach. I was still in the Marine Corps, a low-paid lieutenant with flight pay. When the same banker who gave me my loan for my home asked me how I was going to make the down payment for my rental property, I handed him my credit card. "I want you to extend the limit on my credit to $2,000."

"You're going to make the down payment with your credit card?" asked the banker in shock. "You only make $1,000 a month. You just bought a home."

Needless to say, I was turned down. The banker did not extend the credit limit on my credit card.

This is an example of what rich dad meant by "only lazy people use their own money." At this point, I could have quit, which many people do, or worked a second job to raise the money. Instead, I hit the streets looking for a banker that would say "Yes." About three weeks later I found my banker in a little obscure branch office. Not only did he say "Yes," he encouraged me to buy two more properties in the same development.

The reason he said "yes" was because I had written a simple proposal, using the diagram you are by now familiar with. See the diagram on the next page.

What I was looking for was a $2,000 loan or a credit card with that limit. The purchase price of the property was $18,000, Another lender was offering 90% financing. All I had to do was come up with $1,800 plus closing costs, which is why I asked for $2,000. My real job was to prove to the banker the property was worth $30,000 and that I could pay back the $2,000 on my credit card from the monthly cash flow. I did this by showing him actual rental income and operating expenses from other condominiums in the complex.

As you can see from the example, I valued the property higher than the market. I did this by using rental income as a guide to property price. My rule of thumb is monthly rental income times 100. In this example, $325 X 100 = $32,500. In this example, I knocked the valuation down a little because the area was a little depressed.

"How did you find this property?" asked the banker.

Income
$325

Expenses
$245

Assets	Liabilities
$30,000	$18,000

"I just kept looking and asking," I replied. "Almost every real estate broker I asked said what I was looking for did not exist."

"That's why most of them are real estate brokers and not real estate investors," said the banker.

"All I need is the down payment," I said. "All I need is about $2,000, because another bank is financing 90%.

The banker nodded. "Here fill this out. This is an application for a credit card with a line of credit of $6,000."

"Why $6,000?" I asked. Since I only made a little over a $1,000 a month, to have a line of credit six times my monthly income was a little frightening.

The banker smiled and said, "If this project is as good as you say it is, then buy two more.

A few months later, the market turned. The island of Maui became hot with California tourists. I put my properties on the market for $48,000 each and they sold in less than a month. With my $30,000 gross profit from each condominium, I paid off my credit card loans and went looking for new investment opportunities with nearly $80,000 in tax-deferred capital gains.

At the time, I was making about $12,000 a year as a Marine Corps pilot, before taxes. In less than a year, I had made over six times my 'E' quadrant income, and paid no taxes because I was earning money in the 'I' quadrant. That is why when my poor dad recommended I go back to school to get my masters degree so I could get a good job with the government. I politely told him I had other plans for my life.

What I Learned vs What I Earned

Making approximately $80,000 from three properties is no big deal. Today, $80,000 is chump change. What is important is what I learned, more than what I earned. The following are some of the things I learned.

1. How to borrow money

2. How to manage an investment

3. How to minimize taxes

4. How to minimize risk

5. How to get high returns on someone else's money

Today, whenever I hear people say, "I got an 8% return on my money." I just nod my head and say "That's great." Silently I'm saying, "The problem is it's your money, the risk was too high, the return too low, the tax consequences are horrible, show me the money, how do you know it's 8%, and what are the fees?"

Taking that little real estate investment course I wrote about in the previous chapter and that first little $18,000 investment were my real life foundation, not in money, but in financial skills. Today, rather than work for money, I raise capital… millions of dollars instead of just $2,000. Instead of turning my money over to money managers, I hire managers to manage my properties and my businesses. Most importantly, that little $18,000 investment taught me how to control the income, expenses, assets, liabilities, insurance, and management of an investment. You do not get that kind of *return on investment*, a return on your financial IQ, when you buy a stock, bond, or mutual fund.

Rich Dad's Advice

When rich dad advised his son and me to get into debt, he was advising two things. They are:

1. **Get as much good debt as possible.** In other words, use debt to make you rich. Good debt was one reason why he loved real estate. He would say, "Instead of saving my money to buy mutual funds, I would rather use my banker's money to buy real estate." And he often ended with his wise remark of "Ask your banker if he will lend you money to buy mutual funds."

2. **Learn how to turn debt into an asset.** For example, he would buy a piece of property for let's say $100,000. He would then sell the property for $150,000 on terms. In this example, he increased the value of the property by $50,000 and sold the $50,000 as debt. The buyer would sign an I.O.U. and begin payments on the entire $150,000. The transaction looks like this.

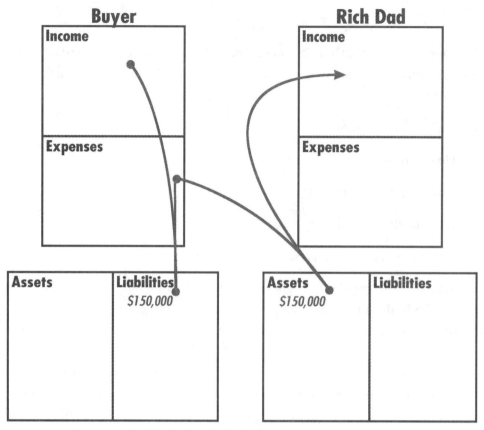

You may notice this example of cash flow looks very similar to the cash flow pattern of a banker and a homeowner.

As stated in the previous chapter, my poor dad often said, "Neither a borrower nor lender be." My rich dad would say, "If you want to be rich, you need to know how to be a borrower and a lender."

Real Life Example

In July of 2005, Kim and I were shopping in a tourist shop in a little town, in the Arizona desert. Out of the blue, the shop owner said, "You should see this piece of land I saw for sale the other day. It is the most beautiful piece of land I have ever seen."

"If it is so beautiful, why don't you buy it?" I asked.

"Oh, it's just too expensive," said the shopkeeper. "Besides the seller wants cash and won't offer terms."

Without hesitation, I got directions to the property, rounded up the so-called local land expert real estate broker (who did not know of the property) and headed off to take a look. Just as the shop owner said, the land was spectacular. Since the so-called land expert did not know about the property, he did not know the price. On our way back to his office to find the listing, I drove around the neighborhood and did some market research. All around the property were large homes selling for over a million dollars, which is very expensive for that town. Also, there were half-acre lots selling for $60,000.

Arriving back at the office, we found the listing and the asking price of $170,000 for 28 acres, cash only. Immediately, we offered $140,000 cash and a week later the offer was accepted.

The reason the land was so cheap, especially when compared to lesser quality land selling for $60,000 per half acre, was because the seller wanted cash. Since Kim and I always have more than enough cash flow coming in, we had more than enough cash. Rather than keeping it in the bank in

savings, it made more sense to me to buy the land, increase the price of the land, and sell it off in smaller parcels for 20% down and 10% interest.

At present, our plan is this: We are going to divide the 28 acres into 4-acre lots and sell each of the 4-acres parcels for $100,000 each. Since a half acre lot, 400 yards away is selling for $60,000, asking $100,000 for four acres is still a bargain… and on top of that, the views from the property are breathtaking. Seven lots times $100,000 equals $700,000. That means we took our $140,000 and increased it to $700,000, an increase of $560,000. Try doing that with your bank.

Collecting 20% down, we bring in $140,000 in deposits. Notice the return of our initial investment of $140,000. We pay a 10% commission or approximately $70,000 for the sale so we do not get all of our money back. We pay a higher commission (standard commission is 6%) because we want our real estate brokers excited about selling our properties. Being generous, rather than greedy, is one of the better ways of getting rich. Anyway, we get back approximately 50% of our initial investment.

If everything goes as planned (which it never does… sometimes things go better) after commissions are paid the net transaction looks like this:

This means after all the 4-acre parcels are sold, we should receive $63,000 a year in interest at

10% from the investment. That means, once sold, we should have almost all of our initial $140,000 back after the first year and collect $63,000 a year in interest payments each year after that. Obviously, we do not want or need the buyers to cash us out, since we already have our money back and want the cash flow from the interest payments.

If we had left our $140,000 in the bank at 3% interest, we would be receiving $4,200 a year in

interest. On top of that, since the money is really a currency, the $140,000 is going down in value. In 50 years, that $140,000 may not even buy you a nice dinner in a fancy restaurant, the way things are going.

If things go as planned, our $140,000 will come back to us and is available to go work at acquiring another investment somewhere else. Meanwhile, we continue to receive $63,000 a year in income, as long as no one gets the silly idea of paying off their debt.

This is an overly-simplified example of turning debt into an asset.

What Is An Asset... REALLY?

Most of the poor and middle class only know of one kind of debt and that is bad debt. To them, all debt is a liability. Many of the poor and middle class borrow money to get further in debt or invest in something that produces no income. For example, if you watch television you'll see banks advertise, "Take out a home equity loan and fix up your kitchen, or buy that big screen TV, or pay for your child's college education, or pay off high interest credit cards." So they use debt to tread water, not increase income.

On top of that, the poor and middle class actually think the object they are buying, say the home, or the car is the asset. Banks do not want your home, your car, your remodeled kitchen, or your big screen TV. All they want is this:

What the banks want is your promise to pay the money back at a certain percentage rate. The only

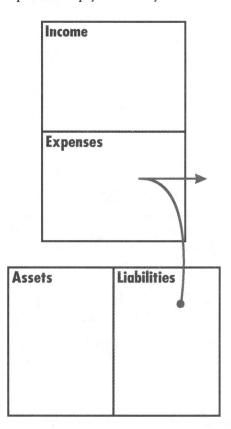

reason they make such a fuss over the car or the real estate is because you make a fuss over it. If they can take back what is near and dear to you, you might be more motivated to pay. So, the car, kitchen, TV set, or real estate is not the asset. You are the asset.

Why The Rich Are Getting Richer

One of the reasons the rich are getting richer is simply because they know how to use debt to acquire assets, assets that put money into their pocket. They also know how to turn debt into an asset. It takes a higher financial IQ to be able to do this.

Instead of learning how to use debt, the poor and middle class work and try to save as much money, either in a bank or in their retirement accounts, often stuffed with mutual funds. Why do they do this? While there are many reasons, one reason is because it is easy to do. You don't have to think too hard, you don't have to study, and you don't have to work too hard. Just go to work, pay your bills, and if you have any extra money, all you have to do is turn your money over to a total stranger, someone who claims to be an investment expert. Then you can go fishing, play golf, shop 'til you drop, or watch TV. As rich dad said, "Only lazy people use their own money."

Why *Teach To Be Rich* Works: Teaching people to take control of their Liability column is a very important task, especially today.

One of the reasons why the U.S. economy exploded after 1971 was because the dollar became an instrument of debt. It is due to debt that we have attained such a high standard of living. While debt has done a lot of good, it has also done a lot of bad. The U.S. has become the largest debtor nation in the world, and Americans have become the most heavily indebted people on earth. If we are to solve this debt crisis problem, we need to have better financial education. To simply say to people, "Cut up your credit cards, take out a home equity loan, and pay off those credit card bills" is very low financial intelligence quotient advice. It may solve the problem in the short term but may not solve the problem in the long run. Also, it is a sad state of affairs when more young people declare bankruptcy than graduate from college.

In 2008, the first of approximately 75 million baby-boomers in the U.S. begin to retire. The baby boomers retirements will put a tremendous strain upon the U.S. government. Look at it this way, once again using the financial statement as a way of explaining the problem:

Obviously, I would not want to be running for President in 2008, when 75 million assets start becoming 75 million liabilities.

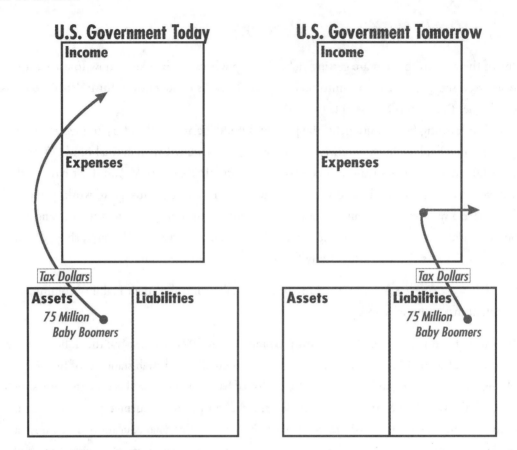

How To Solve The Problem

In my opinion, the best way to solve the problem is to not be part of the problem. I do not want to be one of the 75 million who expect the government to take care of me, or expect to live off of my company pension, or 401(k). In fact, I want to get as far away from the problem as possible.

Just look at how big the problem potentially is, just in terms of the cost to the U.S. government. See the diagram on the next page.

If each baby boomer costs the U.S. government just $1,000 a month in Social Security and Medicare costs, per month the cost per month will be $75 billion dollars. If you think we are in debt now and think the dollar has gone down as far as it can go, I think you should think again. If I were a gambling man, which I am not, I would bet that the U.S. government needs to speed up its printing presses so it can make some of the payments it owes these retirees. If you think the pension plans of GM, United Airlines and other big companies are in trouble today, just wait until millions of new people start withdrawing money from their retirement plans. For you younger people, those born after 1974, who think Social Security taxes are high now… just wait.

So since I have no plans to run for President, and since I have no idea on how to solve this looming problem beginning in 2008, I think it best to heed my rich dad's advice and simply not be a part of the problem. Instead of trying to save the world, I think it best to try and save myself and anyone else who sincerely wants to be saved from the coming financial meltdown. That's why teaching myself and others to be rich makes sense, at least to me. As a preacher friend of mine says, "The best way to help poor people is to not be one of them. It's hard for a poor person to help another poor person financially."

U.S. Government

Income
Expenses

Assets	Liabilities
	75 Million Baby Boomers

What To Learn And What To Teach

Looking at the balance sheet from the CASHFLOW game, when you look closer at the Liability column, you will notice that most of the liabilities are bad liabilities… liabilities that take money from your pocket, not put money in your pocket.

Also, you may notice that the liabilities are the liabilities of the middle class and many of the working poor. One reason this group cannot get ahead is because their monthly payments, from those liabilities, eat up much of their monthly income, via the Expense column.

Balance Sheet

Assets			Liabilities		
Savings:			Home Mortgage:		
Stocks/Mutual's/CDs	No. of Shares:	Cost/Share:	School Loans:		
			Car Loans:		
			Credit Cards:		
Real Estate:	Down Pay:	Cost:	Retail Debt:		
			RE Mortgage:		
Business:	Down Pay:	Cost:	Liability: (Business)		
			Bank Loan:		

Instead of getting ahead, many people today are working harder, some holding down two and three jobs, but working for the wrong kind of income… earned income. When they get into trouble, they may borrow against the equity in their home, if they have a home, or get a new credit card that appears in the mail.

On a macro-economic scale, not only are blue collar jobs going overseas, so are white collar jobs, the jobs of those who went to college. Today, college educated, white-collar workers in developing nations are competing with white collar workers in the U.S. Japan, and Europe.

So it is tough to get ahead simply by going back to school, working harder, saving money, and getting out of debt. And that is why today, the U.S. is facing a financial crisis simply because so many millions of people, even college educated people, do not have enough money to live on once they retire.

Baby Boomer's Baby

While many millions of baby boomers will be facing a tough retirement, so will the children and grand children of the boomers. The generation I am very concerned about is the generation that was born after 1974. I often wonder how they will get ahead if their incomes do not increase as fast as the baby boomers incomes did. I wonder how they can expect pay raises when technology allows third world college educated workers to compete, even for a medical doctor's job.

How can the generations following the baby boomers afford to buy homes at such high prices? In major cities such as San Francisco, New York, London, Sydney, many first-response professions, such as police, fire, and hospital staff cannot afford to live in the cities where the more affluent live.

What will happen to the babies of baby boomers when their boomer parents move in with them? What will happen when babies of baby boomers are expected to pay up to 50% of their income for Social Security and Medicare to care for the baby boomers when they retire? This is in addition to any income taxes they will need to pay.

The Cure For High Prices

In Hawaii, where housing is very expensive and wages are low, many homes now have two to three families living in one home. As beautiful as Hawaii is, I would rather save my money and move to where housing is more affordable, and I believe that is what will happen. Rich dad said, "The cure for high prices is high prices. The cure for low prices is low prices." In other words, in cities where homes are too expensive, soon people and jobs will move to where life is more affordable. Suddenly, the retiree's expensive home starts going down in value. People and business will move to parts of the country where life is more affordable.

In this chapter, I wrote about the 28 acres of land I purchased and plan to sell. One of the advantages of this land is that life in this quaint desert town is still affordable. On top of that, less than a half-mile away is a very large and growing hospital. There is also a college less than twenty miles away. So life goes on and so do investment opportunities.

In my opinion, one of the ways to get out of this mess of low wages, high prices, high taxes, and higher living expenses is via financial education. Instead of getting deeper and deeper into bad debt to support a lifestyle, you may want to raise your financial IQ so you are better able to use debt to acquire assets and learn to create debt as an asset. This requires a much higher financial IQ than someone who simply invests in mutual funds, picks stocks, or buys bonds.

Debt To Acquire Assets

The diagram below is a completed balance sheet of a player who used debt to acquire assets, assets that provided cash flow.

Balance Sheet

Assets			Liabilities		
Savings:			Home Mortgage:		$50,000
Stocks/Mutual's/CDs	No. of Shares:	Cost/Share:	School Loans:		$12,000
OK4U	600	$20	Car Loans:		$5,000
MYT4U	3000	$10	Credit Cards:		$3,00
Real Estate:	Down Pay:	Cost:	Retail Debt:		$1,000
3/2 House	$5,000	$95,000	RE Mortgage:		
4-Plex	$15,000	$125.000	3/2 House	$90,000	
			4-Plex	$110,000	
Business:	Down Pay:	Cost:	Liability: (Business)		
Auto Wash	$50,000	$350,000	Auto Wash	$300,000	
			Bank Loan:		

Notice how many of the real estate transactions used debt in the Liability column to acquire the asset.

Now look at the entire financial statement on the next page. Notice how debt in the Liability column, acquired an asset in the Asset column, which then provided cash flow to the Income column, at the same time making the loan payment in the Expense column.

This is just one example of one transaction… a transaction in which debt was used to acquire an asset that provided income. In the game, there are many other ways debt can be used to win the game. All it takes is a little higher financial IQ. And that is why teaching others can help them as well as you, grow richer. Once you open up their minds to the power of debt, both as a liability and as an asset, you bring more power to them, to you, and to the world at large.

This is worth repeating: "The best way to help poor people is to not be one of them. It's hard for a poor person to help another poor person financially." In other words, if you are financially poor or have a low financial IQ, it's hard to be generous with money or knowledge in accordance with Golden Rule #1.

Profession	**Teacher**	Player	**John**

Goal: To get out of the Rat Race and onto the Fast Track by building up your Passive Income to be greater than your Total Expenses

Income Statement

Auditor	**Ryan**

Person on your right

Income

Description	Cash Flow
Salary:	$3,300
Interest:	
Dividends:	
Real Estate:	
3/2 House	$300
4-Plex	$600
Businesses:	
Auto Wash	$1800

Passive Income= **$2,700**
(Cash Flows from Interest +
Dividends + Real Estate + Businesses)

Total Income: **$6,000**

Expenses

Taxes:	$630
Home Mortgage:	$500
School Loan Payment:	$60
Car Payment:	$100
Credit Card Payment:	$90
Retail Payment:	$50
Other Expenses:	$760
Child Expenses:	
Bank Loan Payment:	$200

Number of
Children: _____
(Begin game with 0 Children)

Per Child
Expense: **$180**

Total Expenses: **$2,390**

Balance Sheet

Monthly Cash Flow: **$3,610**
(Pay Check)

Assets

	No. of Shares:	Cost/Share:
Savings:		
Stocks/Mutual's/CDs		
OK4U	600	$20
MYT4U	3000	$10

Real Estate:	Down Pay:	Cost:
3/2 House	$5,000	$95,000
4-Plex	$15,000	$125.000

Business:	Down Pay:	Cost:
Auto Wash	$50,000	$350,000

Liabilities

Home Mortgage:	$50,000
School Loans:	$12,000
Car Loans:	$5,000
Credit Cards:	$3,00
Retail Debt:	$1,000
RE Mortgage:	
3/2 House	$90,000
4-Plex	$110,000

Liability: (Business)	
Auto Wash	$300,000
Bank Loan:	$2,000

©1996-2002 CASHFLOW® Technologies, Inc. All rights reserved. CASHFLOW® games are covered by one or more of the following US Patents; 5,826,878; 6,032,957 and 6,106,300. RichDad®, CASHFLOW® and Investing 101® are registered trademarks of CASHFLOW® Technologies, Inc.

G101CTI7

Chapter Sixteen

ARE YOUR ASSETS FOOL'S GOLD OR REAL GOLD? – OR – TAKING CONTROL OF YOUR ASSET COLUMN

In early 2005, a friend called and said, "My daughter and her husband just realized the home they bought three years ago has gone up nearly a quarter million dollars. Imagine that — $250,000!"

"That's great," I replied. "That's a lot of money."

"Well, my question is, what should they do now?" asked my friend. "Should they take out the equity and invest in more real estate?"

"Don't know," I replied. "How good are they at investing? How much experience do they have?"

"Well, they just made $250,000," said my friend with a hint of cockiness. "How many kids in their twenties have that kind of money? They must know something. They must have done something right."

"Just because the real estate market went up doesn't mean their financial IQ went up," I replied gently. "And they really haven't made $250,000 yet. All of that is a paper gain, not a real gain."

"So are you saying they should sell and take the money?"

"No, I'm not saying that. I just want to know what their investing experience and education is. The market is very high. Some say it is a bubble. This is not the time to be jumping into the real estate market if you do not have much education and experience."

"So what should they do with the money they made? Just let it sit there?" my friend demanded. "You don't get these opportunities everyday you know."

"I know," I replied quietly. "But I will say it again: Prices are high and they may be late to the party. Generally, when prices are high, the professionals are selling and the amateurs are buying. This is true for any market. So if they have no experience, I wouldn't be starting my real estate investing career at this time."

"I told you, they just made $250,000. They know something. They did something right. So how can you say they have no experience or education? The market is hot so why not invest more?"

"OK," I said. "I hope you're right. As always, I recommend education and experience before risking a lot of money. But it's their money so they are going to do what they're going to do. Let me know what they decide to do."

A few months later, I ran into this same friend on the golf course. He smiled and said, "They talked it over with their real estate broker, the one that sold them their first home, and she convinced them to sell their home and take the equity."

"Oh," I replied hesitantly. "And then what happened?"

"Well, instead of $250,000 they netted $305,000. They said that buyers were bidding the price up. It was quite a frenzy."

"And what have they done with the money?" I asked.

"Their broker found them a bigger house in town, so they bought that. And they bought a beach house. Well, it's not really a beach house… it's a condominium in a beach town. But even if it's not beach front, it's not bad for kids in their twenties? And they tell me the prices have gone up since they bought them. What do you have to say now? Still think they need more education and experience?"

"No," I replied. "They're going to get that education and experience one way or another. My question is how are they going to afford two homes?"

"Oh, they're young. They'll work harder and soon their pay raises will make up for the higher mortgage payments. So what do you think?" asked my friend.

"I think their education has begun," I said softly. "I hope they appreciate the experience that comes with it."

Creating Two Liabilities Not Two Assets

For those of you who have read *Rich Dad Poor Dad*, you may already know why I feature this example of financial mismanagement. For those of you who may not know why, the reason I use this example is because this young couple took their home equity and created two more liabilities, not two assets.

While things may go well, as long as the dollar continues to decline in value, interest rates stay low, the economy stays strong, and real estate prices keep going up. My point is that if they had a little more financial education and experience, they could have used their $305,000 and made life easier. Instead, now they have to work harder in order to make the payments on two mortgages. Instead of using their $305,000 in gains and turning it into assets that generate passive income, they used the money and increased their monthly expenses.

This example is hardly a rare or isolated example. One of the reasons why so many people who suddenly come into money go broke is simply because they take their new-found money and buy liabilities instead of assets. Instead of becoming richer, they increase their risk. Even rich people make the same mistake, as the example below will illustrate.

Asset Rich And Cash Poor

Years ago, rich dad introduced me to an acquaintance, a man who was, at one time, very rich.

"What happened?" I asked rich dad as we drove away from the meeting. "He lives in a big house and he seems rich. Yet he was asking you for a loan."

Rich dad nodded as he gazed over the steering wheel of the car, watching the road and oncoming traffic. "I wanted you two boys to see this early in your life," said rich dad. "I wanted you to see what happens to someone who is asset rich and cash poor."

"Asset rich, cash poor?" asked Mike. "What does that mean?"

"It means he owns a lot of valuable things, such as land and beautiful homes, but he has very little cash. So he calls me every so often to borrow some money."

"Why doesn't he borrow from the bank?" I asked.

"Because he already has," said rich dad. "The bank won't lend him anymore money."

"Why doesn't he sell something?" Mike asked.

"Because the economy is depressed. The price of his land has gone down, not up, which is another reason why the bank won't lend him more money. So he and I have private meetings every so often."

Rich dad explained that this man had inherited his land, a sugar plantation, from his grandparents.

When sugar prices went down because of foreign competition and his labor costs went up, he was forced to shut down his sugar mill. Now he had all this land and no income from sugar. Even though the land was producing no income, he still had loans and taxes to pay. He was shifting to a new crop, macadamia nuts, but growing those trees was taking time and money... a lot of time and money.

The idea that even the rich had money problems was a shock to me. Only in high school at the time, I had always thought that being rich meant not having money problems, like my family did. When we arrived back at rich dad's office, he said, "I wanted you boys to see what you just saw, early in your life. You see his problem is when his grandparents died they passed the plantation on to him, but they did not pass on their wisdom. As a rich kid, he has very little real life financial education, although he went to the best schools. He doesn't know how to take nothing and turn it into something. He doesn't know how to take a dollar and turn it into one hundred dollars, as his grandparents did. Since he has no real life financial education, this tough financial experience, is now his teacher. He is learning from the school of hard knocks. Instead of growing the family asset, his lack of education and experience is devaluing the asset. His family asset is now a liability. He is asset rich and cash poor."

The two above examples are examples of real gold being turned into fool's gold.

America's Greatest Fear

One of the reasons the greatest fear in America is running out of money during retirement is because many people know that once retirement begins, their lack of education and experience will cause their assets, their financial nest egg to shrink, not grow. Instead of turning liabilities into assets, many will take assets and turn them into liabilities, as the person who sold their house and bought two houses did and the plantation owner did.

Taking Back Control

Rich dad spent a lot of time teaching his son and me about controlling the assets inside the Asset column. He would say, "You must know the difference between good assets and bad assets. People with little financial training do not know the difference. That is why they tend to invest in bad assets. Instead of investing in gold, they invest in fool's gold."

Looking at the Asset column from the CASHFLOW game, you will see a few different asset classes. They are: savings, paper assets, real estate, and businesses. Obviously, there are many more different types of assets subset classes. For the sake of the game, I kept the classes limited to the broadest of categories.

Assets		
Savings:		
Stocks/Mutual's/CDs	No. of Shares:	Cost/Share:
Real Estate:	Down Pay:	Cost:
Business:	Down Pay:	Cost:

Now look at this example, the profession card of the Teacher (K-12). Notice all this person has is $400 in savings in their Asset column to start.

Your Profession

TEACHER (K-12)

Please copy all data, excluding 0's, onto your Game Card.

Goal: To build up your Passive Income to be greater than your Total Expenses.

Income

Salary:	$3,300
Interest:	0
Dividends:	0
Real Estate/Business:	0

(Interest + Dividends + Real Estate/Business is the sum of your Passive Income)

Passive Income: 0

Total Income: $3,300

Expenses

Taxes:	630
Mortgage/Rent Pay:	500
School Loan Pay:	60
Car Payment:	100
Credit Card Payment:	90
Retail Payment:	50
Other Expenses:	760
Child Expenses:	0

(Note: All Players begin with 0 children)

Per Child Expense: $180

Total Expenses: $2,190

Monthly Cash Flow: $1,110

Assets / Liabilities

Assets		Liabilities	
Savings:	$400	Mortgage:	50,000
		School Loans:	12,000
		Car Loans:	5,000
		Credit Cards:	3,000
		Retail Debt:	1,000

The object of the game, is for the teacher to invest, acquire assets, gain passive income, and escape from the Rat Race with more passive income than monthly expenses, as the example on the next page shows.

In the process of playing the game, the school teacher had to play the game as a professional investor, not a professional school teacher.

The more a person plays the game, the more comfortable they become at recognizing good assets from bad assets. Also, they learn when to buy a paper asset, such as a stock, as well as when to sell the paper asset and possibly buy a piece of real estate or a business.

Repeating what I said earlier, it's important to remember that when most advisors recommend you diversify, they are not really diversifying. They are generally recommending you invest in only one asset class, paper assets. And as a person becomes more comfortable with the game, they begin to understand that different assets have different strengths and weaknesses. In order to win the game, the teacher had to invest in different assets, playing on different strengths and weaknesses, rather than simply diversify into one asset class.

Profession	Teacher	Player	John

Goal: To get out of the Rat Race and onto the Fast Track by building up your Passive Income to be greater than your Total Expenses

Income Statement

Income	
Description	Cash Flow
Salary:	$3,300
Interest:	
Dividends:	
Real Estate:	
3/2 House	$300
4-Plex	$600
Businesses:	
Auto Wash	$1800

Auditor	Ryan

Person on your right

Passive Income= **$2,700**
(Cash Flows from Interest +
Dividends + Real Estate + Businesses)

Total Income: **$6,000**

Expenses	
Taxes:	$630
Home Mortgage:	$500
School Loan Payment:	$60
Car Payment:	$100
Credit Card Payment:	$90
Retail Payment:	$50
Other Expenses:	$760
Child Expenses:	
Bank Loan Payment:	$200

Number of Children: _____
(Begin game with 0 Children)
Per Child Expense: **$180**

Total Expenses: **$2,390**

Monthly Cash Flow: **$3,610**
(Pay Check)

Balance Sheet

Assets		
Savings:		
Stocks/Mutual's/CDs	No. of Shares:	Cost/Share:
OK4U	600	$20
MYT4U	3000	$10
Real Estate:	Down Pay:	Cost:
3/2 House	$5,000	$95,000
4-Plex	$15,000	$125.000
Business:	Down Pay:	Cost:
Auto Wash	$50,000	$350,000

Liabilities	
Home Mortgage:	$50,000
School Loans:	$12,000
Car Loans:	$5,000
Credit Cards:	$3,00
Retail Debt:	$1,000
RE Mortgage:	
3/2 House	$90,000
4-Plex	$110,000
Liability: (Business)	
Auto Wash	$300,000
Bank Loan:	$2,000

©1996-2002 CASHFLOW® Technologies, Inc. All rights reserved. CASHFLOW® games are covered by one or more of the following US Patents; 5,826,878; 6,032,957 and 6,106,300. RichDad®, CASHFLOW® and Investing 101® are registered trademarks of CASHFLOW® Technologies, Inc.   G101CTI7

When designing the game, this feature of investing in and out of different asset classes was an important aspect of the game. Not only did it require the player to think in terms of multiple assets, the player also had to know when to invest for cash flow and when to invest for capital gains. Also, the game rewards the player that can anticipate market trends and acquire the appropriate assets waiting patiently like a race car driver for the right opening, the right opportunity and then stepping on the gas.

Author's Note: If you are uncertain about the difference between investing for *capital gains* or investing for *cash flow*, the following are some of the differences. First of all, most investors invest for capital gains. That is why most people think investing is risky. Investing for capital gains is simply buying low and hoping to sell high. For example a person may buy a stock at $20 and hope to sell at $30. If the stock price goes up and the person sells at $30, the person has realized a $10 capital gain. Or in real estate a person buys a house for $100,000 and sells it for $150,000, they have realized a $50,000 capital gain, before expenses.

A person who invests for cash flow is different. If they buy stocks, they purchase stocks that pay a dividend. For example, they buy a stock for $20 and the stocks issues a $1 *dividend*, then that $1 is cash flow. If they purchase a house for $100,000 and they make $50 a month, net rental income after all expenses, then they have a $50 a month cash flow.

The reason so many people think investing is risky is because most people invest for capital gains. The risk comes from being out of control over the sales price of the asset. You see these people watching the financial TV programs, feeling good when the price of their stock goes up and feeling bad when it goes down. They are out of control and the market is in control.

A person's net worth is based a lot on capital gains. For example, you may list your home's value at $200,000 and you owe $130,000. In this example, your home has contributed $70,000 to your net worth. The problem with a person's net worth is that, more often than not, it is worth less, not worth more. The reason is because a person often includes so-called assets, which are not really assets, such as cars, jewelry, clothing, furniture, valuables in your attic, and art work, into this figure… and you and I know what we think our clothing is worth much more than the price you will receive at a garage sale. This is why rich dad preferred to measure a person's cash flow rather than net worth. He said, "I can accurately measure cash flow. I cannot accurately measure the value of your used car, unless I sell it, or the valuables stored in your attic."

When a financial expert advises investing in growth funds when you are young, they are generally recommending investing in stocks that will go up in value, which means you are investing for capital gains. When you are older, they may recommend you convert your growth funds to income funds, stocks that pay dividends, and bond funds. In other words, invest later in life for cash flow.

That is an overly-simplified lesson on the differences between investing for capital gains and investing for cash flow. When playing the CASHFLOW game, the player is challenged to begin thinking between investing for capital gains or investing for cash flow. In order to win the game, a player must know how to invest for both types of returns on their investment dollars.

When You Come To A Fork In The Road

Yogi Berra, the famous New York Yankee baseball player is often quoted as saying, "When you come to a fork in the road, take it." Personally when I invest, I do not invest just for capital gains or just for cash flow. When I invest, I want both, both — capital gains and cash flow. When I come to a fork in my investment road, I take both. That is the primary reason why my investments are very low

risk. As long as I have cash flowing in, I can sleep at night, whether the market is going up or going down.

Not Just Real Estate

One more point worth remembering is that I am not just an investor in real estate, as some people think. One of the lessons rich dad stressed was that we learn to trade in and out of different assets, which meant we had to study the different assets. For example, we had to know the strengths and weaknesses of paper assets, real estate, commodities, businesses, and cash. By knowing the strengths and weakness, we could take advantage of different market conditions. For example, when real estate was down, buy. When real estate was high, sell and buy oil if it was low. When stocks were high, sell. When gold was low and dollars high, trade your high dollars for low gold. This active buying and selling of different asset classes is what I designed into the CASHFLOW game.

Diversified Only Into One Asset Class

Rich dad did not want us blindly turning our money over to a financial advisor who claimed to diversify your investments, yet your investments were all in only one asset class, paper assets. He also said, "The main reason most advisors only put you in paper assets is because that is the only asset class they can make a commission on. Why would they recommend you buy a business or an apartment house if someone else got the commission?" For example, if you have $100,000 to invest, very few mutual fund sales people will advise you to buy an apartment house or a franchise business with that money. In most cases, they will recommend you put all of that $100,000 into a well-diversified portfolio of stocks, bonds, REITs, and mutual funds.

Real World Advantages

So, one of the big advantages of the CASHFLOW game is that it opens up the player's mind to true diversification, that is using different asset classes to reach your financial goals. One advantage to this type of financial education is that, if a person has only a little bit of money to invest, they may want to start off in stocks, or start a small business before investing in real estate or commodities.

Often I hear people say, "I can't afford to invest in San Francisco. Prices are too high." My response is, invest in stocks first… or buy a small business and grow it." Instead of saying, "Thank you, what a great idea." Most say, "But I want to get into real estate. How do I get the money?" The cause of such limited thinking is not knowing how to use different asset classes for different objectives. The CASHFLOW Game was designed to teach people to think in a truly diversified way, a much more flexible way.

Growing up in Hawaii, I saw real estate prices go from cheap to super expensive. If I were in my twenties, without much income, instead of trying to invest in real estate in Hawaii, I would start a business, grow the business, and then, with the cash flow, buy real estate.

In fact, even if you can afford to invest in real estate, I still recommend starting with a business. Why do I recommend this? The reasons is because all investments, regardless if they are in stocks, bonds, real estate, commodities, or currencies, are about investing in business. So the better you are at understanding business and entrepreneurship, the better investor you will be, regardless of what you invest in.

In my opinion, one of the reasons why so many people invest in fool's gold rather than gold, is

because they have been trained by the school system to be employees, not entrepreneurs. That is why so many employees buy mutual funds rather than invest in the hard assets such as a business or real estate or commodities. They invest in fool's gold rather than real gold.

Later in Part IV of this book, I will explain why entrepreneurs make better investors than employees. It is a matter of education, control, and knowing what is important and what is not.

My Personal Asset Column

In my personal Asset column, I have millions of shares of stocks, because I started a business. Also, I have millions of dollars in real estate, because I started a business. Although I do not believe in diversification, at least not in the way most financial planners recommend, I am diversified. But, I am diversified not as a *defensive* strategy, which is the reason most people diversify... I am diversified as an *offensive* strategy. I diversify to gain more and different assets with less risk, in a short period of time. That is the mental mindset I designed into the CASHFLOW Game. If you want the more popular way of *defensive diversification*, which is not really diversification, then listen to your traditional financial advisor.

Do You Need To Diversify?

Another question I am asked is, "Do I need to invest in all the different asset classes?

My answer is "No, you do not. The reason I designed different asset classes into the game is to open up the player's mind to the different classes and learn how to use the different assets to achieve their financial goals." I go on to explain that investors such as Donald Trump invests primarily in real estate and Warren Buffett invests primarily in businesses, not stocks. My point is, you can become very rich on just one asset, even stocks, bonds, and mutual funds, if you know what you are doing. If you simply turn your money over to experts, then you will probably never understand what you are doing.

The Most Expensive Asset

When you look once again at the school teacher's profession card on the next page, you may notice that the only thing this person has in their Asset column is $400 in savings.

Rich dad often said, "Savings are your most expensive asset." The reason he said that is because in order for this teacher to save $400, they would have to have earned approximately $800 in gross income. As you already know, as an employee in the 'E' quadrant, this teacher would have to have paid a lot in taxes before he or she could net the $400.

On top of that, this saver would have received less than 1% interest on that $400 between 2000 and 2004 due to low interest rates. And, even that 1% would have been once again taxed at one of the higher tax rates. To make matters worse, the value of that $400 would have dropped by nearly 40% against the Euro, making the value of the $400 even less.

In spite of the fact that savings are your most expensive and least-leveraged asset, so called financial experts continue to insist that you save more money. The following is taken from a book written by one of the leading financial experts in America. I won't mention his name for obvious reasons. He says "Start saving early. If it doesn't hurt you're probably not saving enough." My head hurts every time I read or hear these financial experts recommend that we save more money.

Your Profession
TEACHER (K-12)
Please copy all data, excluding 0's, onto your Game Card.

Goal: To build up your Passive Income to be greater than your Total Expenses.

Income

Salary:	$3,300		
Interest:	0		
Dividends:	0	Passive Income:	0
Real Estate/Business:	0		
(Interest + Dividends + Real Estate/Business is the sum of your Passive Income)		Total Income:	$3,300

Expenses

Taxes:	630		
Mortgage/Rent Pay:	500		
School Loan Pay:	60		
Car Payment:	100		
Credit Card Payment:	90		
Retail Payment:	50	Per Child Expense:	$180
Other Expenses:	760		
Child Expenses:	0	Total Expenses:	$2,190

(Note: All Players begin with 0 children)

Monthly Cash Flow: $1,110

Assets

Savings:	$400

Liabilities

Mortgage:	50,000
School Loans:	12,000
Car Loans:	5,000
Credit Cards:	3,000
Retail Debt:	1,000

The Least Expensive Investment

If our savings is our most expensive investment, then real estate is the least expensive investment. While there were many reasons why rich dad thought real estate was the least expensive investment, the main reason was because real estate cost the least amount of his money. The majority of his acquisition cost came from the bank. As rich dad often said, "I love real estate because my banker loves it." This is also why rich dad often said, "Ask your banker if he will lend you money to buy mutual funds."

As most of us know, today we can quite easily get a 90% or even a 125% loan (which I do not recommend) to acquire a property. Rich dad often said "Instead of using my money to get rich, I use my banker's money. I don't have to work for it and it's tax-free money."

In other words, instead of being the person standing in line to save money at the bank, rich dad was the guy sitting at the banker's desk borrowing the money the saver was depositing. Why does the saver stand in line while the borrower sits at the banker's desk? The reasons are simple. Bankers need to lend out the saver's dollars twenty or thirty times and bankers make money on borrowers, not savers.

Kim's Lessons

When I met my wife, Kim, in 1984, she was a very diligent saver. She took pride of the money sitting in her savings passbook. It took me awhile to explain to her why savers are losers. Finally, she got the idea and bought her first property, a two-bedroom / one-bath home for $45,000. She put $5,000 down and was shaking all through the process. All she could think about was being $40,000 in debt – learning how to find renters and manage the property.

She soon got over her nervousness and was buying more and more properties. Her goal was 20 properties in 10 years. In less than 18 months, she had accomplished her goal. She was up to her eyeballs in debt. She had very little in savings.

In 1994, she sold most of her properties and had made $275,000 in tax-deferred gains. "I could never have saved that much money," she said. Immediately, she rolled that $275,000 into two properties worth over a million dollars each. On top of that, her income from those two properties was well over $10,000 a month, again at a very low tax rate. She could never have done that with her savings. On top of that, she would never have learned what she had learned if she had continued to be only a saver.

Today, she is borrowing tens of millions of dollars and earning tens of thousands of dollars a month from rental income. She is richer than most men. When she talks, especially to women's groups, she often says things such as, "I borrowed $8 million dollars for my last investment. That one investment pays me about $30,000 a month in income. My question is how long would it take you to save $8 million dollars? If I had waited till I saved $8 million dollars to buy this property, I would never have purchased it."

In other words, one of the reasons the rich are getting richer is because they are *borrowers* not *savers*, which is one more reason why savers are losers.

The Secret To Investing In Real Estate

Now I can hear some of you saying, "Oh, that is so risky. What if the market crashes? What if the tenants stop paying? What if… what if… what if? And those are valid 'what ifs' so I will let you in on the secret to borrowing a lot of money.

The secret to borrowing money to invest in real estate is to first find a good real estate investment. If you know how to find a great investment, your risks are low. If you do not know how to find a good real estate investment, then your risks are high, and you should not borrow that much money. So before you borrow, learn how to find great real estate investments, one that cash flows and has a built in *cushion of capital* gains… in other words you bought it at a good price.

The reason I mentioned the young couple that took their $305,000 in capital gains and purchased two more properties is because, in my opinion, they borrowed money to invest in bad real estate investments. That is why I said they turned an asset into two liabilities. It is also why I kept asking about their education and experience as real estate investors.

Obviously, many real estate investments are bad investments. Also, most real estate investors start off as bad investors. That is why I recommend you play the CASHFLOW game a lot, teach it a lot, and then start with small deals, just as the game suggests, before trading up to big deals.

Look at the picture of the CASHFLOW game board below.

Notice that between the Rat Race and the Fast Track are two types of deals… Small Deals and Big Deals. This was intentionally designed into the game. In the real world, I strongly suggest you start with small deals and do a lot of small deals until you become an expert at small deals. Then move on to bigger deals… not only in the game but in the real world. After you are an expert at the bigger deals, then you can move on to the Fast Track, if you want to. In the real world, you can become very rich with just small deals. All you have to do is be good at small deals. I met one young man who came to my seminar who owned 800 small single-family houses. He had over a $150,000 a month in positive cash flow. He attended my seminar to find out what he was doing wrong. He wanted to know if he should invest in bigger properties. My suggestion was, "Don't change unless you really want to change. If he wanted to change, I suggest he keep investing in small deals anyway. He was an expert at them."

It takes a bit of education and experience to be able to find investments that will cash flow, pay off the mortgage, earn some money every month, and increase in value. When you find a property that does all those things, borrowing money is not that risky. If you do not have all those advantages, the investment risk is higher and so are the borrowing risks.

This small deal to big deal process is true for all asset classes. I am not saying that it only works for real estate. What I am saying is to start small and stay small until you are good at it. Then if you want to move on, move on. You can even be an expert at mutual funds and do very well. The lesson is, when looking for gold, the first thing to learn is how not to be a fool. That is why I recommend starting small, because we start out as fools before we find real gold.

How To Find Great Real Estate Investments

One of the *advanced financial educational products* we at The Rich Dad Company have produced is a video, audio, and workbook program titled, *Rich Dad's 6 Steps to Becoming a Successful Real Estate Investor*. This program is a real-world, hands-on, step-by-step program that shows you the six-step process my rich dad taught me for how to find great real estate investments.

The 6 steps are:

Step 1: Decide to become an investor.

Step 2: Find an area to concentrate on.

Step 3: Find Properties that meet your criteria.

Step 4: Negotiate the deal.

Step 5: Put the deal together.

Step 6: Manage the property.

Other Real Estate Products

There are other educational products from The Rich Dad Company that are important to anyone wanting to become a better real estate investor:

1. ***How To Increase the Income from Your Real Estate Investments.*** This is an audio program with workbook, put together with Ken McElroy, an investment partner and Rich Dad's Advisor. Ken founded one of the largest property management companies in the Southwest United States. Ken also founded a real estate development company that builds apartment houses or takes large, existing apartment complexes and converts them into condominiums.

   This product, *How to Increase the Income from Your Real Estate Investments*, is the final step in the investment process… just before the investor commits the money. This is where the investor does their due diligence on the property. The workbook in this product includes many of the due diligence checklists that Ken uses as a property manager and as an investor. On the audio, Ken shares his trade secrets such as how to make sure the property is sound, what the costs will be to manage it, how to find good tenants, how to keep the properties occupied and other essential lessons that improve the income and the value of the investment.

   For those of you who are looking for the nitty-gritty detail that is essential to being a great investor, this product is priceless. I estimate that it would take a novice investor at least 10 years of trial and error mistakes before they could put together a comparable due diligence checklist. Not only will this product save you time, money, and heartache, it can also make you a lot of money. That is why it is titled, *How To Increase the Income from Your Real Estate Investments*.

2. *How To Get Your Banker to Say "Yes."* This is an audio program with Scott McPherson, a mortgage banker who has funded some of the biggest real estate acquisitions in the Western U.S. In this educational program, Scott shares with you the banker's view on the subject of lending money. He tells you what bankers look for and what turns them off. The program gives you inside tips on how to prepare your proposal for a loan, even if the property is bad or if you have bad credit. It is a very informative program on an essential step, raising capital, in the real estate process.

3. *The ABCs of Real Estate Investing.* This is a Rich Dad's Advisor book, written by Ken McElroy. Again, since Ken is a property manger, he views a real estate investment from the inside out. Many books on real estate investing are by people who play games with financing, fix up properties, or flip properties. Ken's book is not that kind of book. It is about the fundamentals of running, acquiring and managing properties for long term cash flow while increasing value of the property. It is the philosophy of real estate investing that Kim and I subscribe to.

If you would like more information on any of these educational products please go to www.richdad.com.

Low Financial IQ = High Risk, High Costs And Low Returns

Whenever I hear financial advisor say such things as, "Save money and invest for the long term in a well diversified portfolio of funds" in my mind they are talking to someone with a low financial IQ. As you can tell by my example on why savers are losers, saving money, a low IQ activity, is not a great way to get ahead financially. The same is true for mutual funds. In my opinion, these assets are designed for people who may be well educated, but are not financially educated. Assets such as savings and mutual funds are for people who want the easy answers, the short cuts to investing, and with few management challenges. With a lower financial IQ, they invest in investments that are higher risk, higher costs, lower returns, less efficiencies, higher taxes, and fewer controls. These types of investments for these types of investors are often the most elegantly packaged and most advertised, often stating high returns that are deceptive. That is because such investments are really fool's gold waiting for fools.

The World Is Filled With Assets

The world is filled with assets. Anything — be it a business, a piece of real estate, an oil well, a gas station, a stock, a bond, an insurance policy, a retail store, an airport or a taxi cab — can be an asset. Cash is always flowing. That is why the saying goes, "Money makes the world go around." In order to be rich, all you need to do is find an asset that flows money into your pocket, not out of your pocket. The next time you are out for a drive, look at all the assets around you. Look at the television stations, banks, radio stations, the delivery trucks, the parking meters, the parking lots, the office buildings, apartment houses, health clubs, the telephone lines, the electrical lines, the water lines, the hamburger franchises, and even surfboards that can be assets. A friend of a friend's family owns one of the beach concessions on Waikiki Beach. They rent surfboards to tourists. The surfboards (now made in China) cost them about $60 each since they buy in volume. They rent a surfboard for $10 an hour, which means they may pay for the board in one day, depending upon business. The boards last about a year,

which means after one day, two days max, the rest of the income per surfboard is all gross profit. If a surfboard can be an asset, what else can you turn into an asset that pays money for the long-term?

For me personally, when I write a book I am paid royalties for years. So a book can become an asset. Also the brand *Rich Dad* is an asset that brings in millions of dollars a year in royalty payments. Businesses from all over the world pay The Rich Dad Company for the rights to use our brand name. In other words, Kim, Sharon, and I took two words, *Rich* and *Dad*, put them together and turned it into a multi-million dollar asset, known as intellectual property… proving it does not take money to make money. If we can make millions of dollars by turning two words into an asset, what can you do? Keep buying mutual funds for the long term and trying to save money? By now, I believe you're smarter than that.

Why The Rich Are Getting Richer

All of the above listed items are examples of assets. Simply put, *an asset is something that takes money from some one and then delivers that money to someone else.* Unfortunately, due to poor financial education at home and at school, many people *only* think in terms of their home, savings, and mutual funds as assets. It is due to this lack of financial information that most of the poor and middle class are the people *the assets* are taking money from and then transferring the money to the rich. That is what real assets do and that is one more reason why the rich are getting richer.

Real Fool's Gold

When you look at savings, personal residences, and mutual funds, many people think they are assets. Yet, if you observe how the cash really flows, for most people their savings, homes, and mutual funds are really liabilities, since their money flows out of their pockets and causes more money flow into the pockets of the rich. In other words, most people do not have real gold in their asset column, they have fool's gold.

Not knowing the difference between real gold and fool's gold is another reason why the rich get richer, the poor get poorer, and the middle class works harder, gets deeper in debt, and pays more in taxes. Working harder, getting deeper in debt, paying more in taxes, and investing in expensive, low-return investments, is the price of a low financial IQ.

If our schools would teach students just a little about money, then more people would know the difference between real gold and fool's gold.

A little financial education would point out the differences between an asset, a liability, and knowing where the cash is flowing… from whom and to whom. As we all know by now, cash flows from the fool, through the gold (the asset), and into the pockets of the rich. I am not saying this is right or wrong. This is a reality of life. All I am saying is that we have the choice of being the fool who owns fool's gold or being the person who owns the real gold. And that is what the Asset column tells us… is it fool's gold or real gold?

In Conclusion

In conclusion, the world is filled with assets. Yet, if a person has a limited financial education the only types of assets they know of are assets that make the rich richer. While the investor may receive some kind of return, the return is minimal when compared to the returns to the rich.

Why *Teach To Be Rich* Works: Teaching someone to take control over their assets and their Asset column is essential for long-term financial security. Without a sound financial education, people must follow the advice of save money and invest for the long term, primarily in mutual funds. Again, for people without much financial education, saving money in a bank or saving money in mutual funds is sound advice. It sure beats doing nothing or saving money under a mattress.

When you look at the Asset column from the financial statement of the CASHFLOW Board game, you notice the four types of assets most people invest in.

Assets		
Savings:		
Stocks/Mutual's/CDs	No. of Shares:	Cost/Share:
Real Estate:	Down Pay:	Cost:
Business:	Down Pay:	Cost:

The object of the game is the same as the financial object of life. That is to acquire assets that provide cash flow to the Income column. If the player follows the popular financial advice of save money, get out of debt, invest for the long term, and diversify, they will never win this game. Instead of investing in gold, which cash flows money to the Income column as pictured:

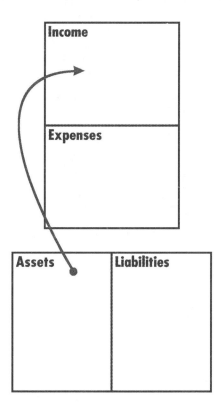

...many people invest in fool's gold as pictured below.

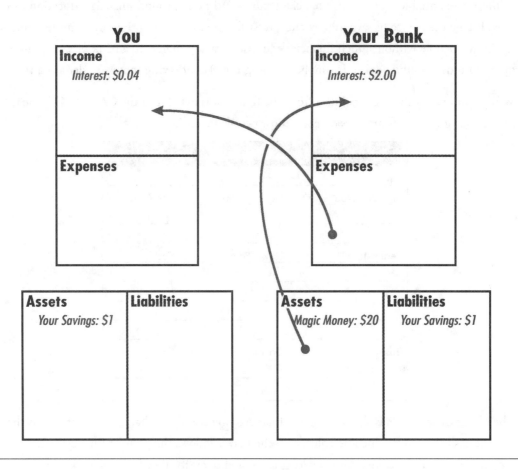

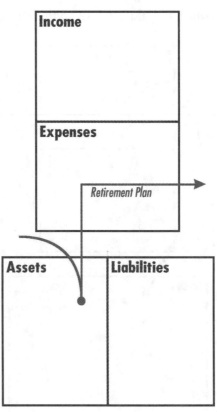

Your Greatest Asset

One of the greatest challenges this game poses is the challenge to a person's greatest asset, their brain. Simply by playing this game, the brain is forced to think in new ways, to see truths, to make changes, to see new worlds of financial possibilities. The game was designed to challenge our brains and then awaken the rich person sitting inside each of us.

And that is why teaching works. It is not about giving them advice or answers. True education is about letting each of us use a part of our brains many of us have never used before. It is about awakening that financial genius that is in every one of us. Once the genius is awakened, then the person does not need to purchase neatly-packaged investment products, supported by glossy brochures with lots of intelligent sounding words, nice clear graphs, with pictures of the CEO, and presented to you by your friendly financial advisor. To my rich dad, anytime an investment was presented with glossy brochures by well-dressed investment advisors, he knew the investment was probably not gold, but fool's gold.

Rich dad liked to look at investments that were hairy, a little messy, and filled with problems. He would say, "I get rich solving problems. If you want to be rich, you need to know how to control the asset and solve the problems. That is what a high financial IQ is for… it is to be able to solve financial problems."

You Learn By Solving Problems

One of the purposes of the board game is to raise your financial IQ by solving problems. The more you play the game, the more problems you will learn to solve. The more problems you solve, and the faster you can solve them, the stronger your financial genius becomes.

Once your financial genius is strong, educated, and experienced, you can put together your own deals, create your own assets and keep the lion's shares of the returns for yourself and your family. You will not be looking for investments with nice brochures. You will be looking for investments that most people consider risky or riddled with too many problems. Instead of seeing them as risky, you will see them as liabilities ready to be turned into assets. After all, that is what a high financial IQ is for… finding liabilities, solving problems, and turning the liability into an asset.

Raising my financial IQ, and putting my own deals together has given me control of my life and my financial future. This is what taking control of the asset column meant to my rich dad, to me, and hopefully for you. All it takes is a little dedication and a little financial education. And that is why teaching yourself and others works. With a high financial IQ you can turn fool's gold into gold. With a low financial IQ, all gold is fool's gold.

Chapter Seventeen

WOULD YOU DRIVE A CAR WITHOUT INSURANCE? – OR – CAN YOU CONTROL INVESTMENT RISK WITH INSURANCE?

We all know that markets go up and markets go down… and history shows that market crashes come in cycles. Advising people to invest for the long term, primarily in mutual funds, an asset that is tough to insure, is almost criminal. That advice is more than risky, it is financial suicide.

Whenever I hear someone say, "Investing is risky." I know the person is not a professional investor. Investing is risky for people who:

1. Do not have any financial training.

2. Do not have control over the investment.

3. Do not have insurance.

Even paper assets such as stocks can be insurable. As far as I know, mutual funds are not. If you would not drive a car without insurance, why would anyone risk their financial security on an asset that is uninsurable?

When I purchase a piece of real estate, my banker requires that I have all sorts of insurance. After all, the banker is my money partner. Yet, when a financial advisor tells you to invest in mutual funds, they do not require you to buy insurance. I've always thought that was strange, don't you? If they were really your advisor, wouldn't they want your investment to be insured?

As a business owner, I provide health insurance for my employees. Why do I do that? I do that because my employees are important to me. So if a financial advisor's clients are important to them, why do they sell them investments, such as stocks, bonds, and mutual funds, without insurance?

You Can't Buy Insurance When You Need It

One reason why insurance is an important control and needs to be addressed prior to investing in anything, is because you cannot buy insurance when you need it. If you are in an auto accident, you cannot call your local insurance agent and say, "You know that auto insurance policy we were talking about? Can I purchase it now?" Or, after you die, your spouse cannot call up your life insurance agent and say, "I would like to take out a million dollar policy on my spouse. Can you meet me at the funeral home? I'll sign the papers on the casket."

Between 2000 and 2004, millions of investors found out too late, that they were investing without insurance. When the market crashed, as all markets do, millions of investors lost trillions of dollars. Why? Because they were investing without insurance.

Many financial experts believe that a well-diversified portfolio is a form of insurance. Well, if you

look at the aftermath of the market crash, diversification did not save millions of investors from trillions of dollars in losses. Many investors will never get their money back.

Many people today think that Index Funds, such the S&P 500 Index or Exchange Traded Funds are safer investments. Unfortunately, that is not true. When the stock market crashed, the S&P 500 and many other index funds went down also.

Why I Don't Have A 401(k)

One of the reasons why I don't have a 401(k) retirement plan filled with mutual funds is simply because I can't insure it. Why would I want to invest in something I can't insure? That is really risky.

Rich dad said, "There are no risky investments. There are only risky investors." One of the greatest risks is to lack the financial education and not know that investments can be insured. It is the lack of financial education that is risky… not investing.

Who Does Diversification Protect?

Many people think that diversification is smart because it protects the investor. If you step back and look at the bigger picture, you may see that diversification really protects your advisor. If your advisor had control over the investments he recommended, he could be more confident about recommending them. But like you, your financial advisor has no control over the investments they recommend, so to protect themselves and make more money by recommending an array of products, they protect themselves. For example, let's say the advisor feels especially bullish about Enron and had recommended you put half of your available cash into Enron, they would have probably been fired. But if you had a well-diversified portfolio, with only a small percentage in Enron, they would have been praised for having you in a well-diversified portfolio. So when a financial expert recommends diversification, it is to protect themselves as much, if not more, as it is to protect the investor.

All investments have risk. All investment markets, including real estate, experience booms and busts, which is why insurance, or hedging, as it is more commonly known in the investment world, is a very important control.

Even Gamblers Buy Insurance

If you have every played Blackjack in a casino, when the dealer turns over an ace, the dealer will ask the table, "Insurance?" If I have two twenty-five dollar chips on the table, the cost of my insurance will be one twenty-five dollar chip. In other words, insurance costs me 50% of my bet. If the dealer has 21, then I keep my entire three chips, a $75 position. If the dealer does not have 21, the dealer takes my $25 insurance chip. My point is: Even gamblers are smart enough to gamble with insurance. How can so many millions of investors risk their financial future without insurance?

Every time I invest, I know I could be wrong. I know I could lose my money. That is why knowing how to hedge my bet, or insure my position, is a vital control. How millions of investors can be conned into thinking that diversification, by simply buying more of the same asset class, is a smart way to invest is one of the biggest hoaxes played on unsuspecting and naïve people.

Knowing how to control risk, insuring against losses or mistakes, is a very important segment in a person's financial education. Rich dad spent a lot of time with his son and me on this subject. The following are some of the other ways investors insure against losses.

Insurance For Real Estate

A number of years ago, Kim and I had one of our properties burn down. It seems one of the tenants had left the lights on their Christmas tree on and went shopping for more presents. When they returned home, not only was their unit on fire, so were the other seven apartments in that building. The good news is that everyone got out and all eight families found new homes that night. On top of that, our insurance company paid to have all eight units repaired to better-than-new condition and pay us for lost rent. So in spite of the fire, we had no financial losses.

One of the reasons I do not worry about investing in real estate is because of insurance. The following are some of the insurance policies I carry on each and every property.

1. **Property Insurance:** All my real estate investments have insurance in the event of fire, flood, or other acts of nature.

2. **Liability Insurance:** Lawsuits are a way of life, especially in America.

3. **Preferred mortgage insurance:** If my down payment is too small, banks may require that I purchase PMI, to protect them from me, in case I cannot make my payments.

4. **Legal entities:** As a professional real estate investor, all of my properties are held in some form of legal entity such as an LLC (Limited Liability Corporation) or an LP (Limited Partnership). These are the only two entities our advisor, Garrett Sutton, recommends for holding property.

About six years ago, a tenant claimed to have stepped on a rock and fallen. The tenant was not injured but filed a complaint to the property manager. Five months later, Kim and I found out that the tenant was filing a law suit against the limited partnership. The tenant did not know our names or how many properties we owned because of the legal entity, in this particular case, a limited partnership. Once the tenant's attorney realized the property was held inside a limited partnership, he knew the litigation could be a long and expensive battle. Instead of taking the case, the attorney asked the tenant for a retainer. The tenant dropped the case because they did not want to risk paying for a long, expensive court battle.

Protection For The Rich

One of the reasons personal injury attorneys do not like suing limited partnerships is because even if they win, they may lose. An example of how they may lose even if they win the lawsuit is as follows: Jane wins a lawsuit against Fantasy Apartments LP, claiming she was promised a 10% interest in ownership as a limited partner as of January 1, 2005. The management of Fantasy Apartments LP decides to make no distributions to the partners for 2005. To her surprise and dismay, Jane receives a K-1 for 2005, attributing $100,000 of income for her 10% interest, meaning that she must pay $40-50,000 in taxes on her personal tax return on the $100,000 income from her 10% interest. As a result she received no money but had to pay $40-50,000 out of her personal assets. Did she really win?

The Rich Own Nothing

My poor dad was proud to say, "Our house is in my name." In fact, everything was in his name, including his car.

My rich dad wanted nothing in his name. He did not want to *own* anything. Instead his legal entities owned everything. This was another form of insurance protection.

In the real world, many of the poor and middle class own everything in their name. They, too, are proud of "ownership," which unfortunately makes them easy targets for personal injury attorneys.

I believe that if we had held the property in our names personally, the tenant's attorney would have eagerly come after us personally and all the other properties we own. We might have lost millions. Having the legal entity protected us from losing everything. According to Garrett, many personal injury attorneys do not like going after legal entities. They find it much easier to sue people who keep their investments in their names. As I said earlier, professionals invest with insurance and amateurs invest without. It is those amateurs who lose in the stock market as well as in real estate.

Diversify Your Entities

As I stated earlier, I do diversify, but not in the same way most financial planners recommend diversifying. Instead of simply buying more of the same asset class, one way I diversify is to diversify our entities. Since we have so many different properties, we hold different properties in different entities, which means we have multiple LLCs and LPs. If a tenant sues us and wins, then the damage is limited to one property in one entity. This makes it very difficult for the tenant to go after the other properties protected in different entities.

Entities such as LLCs, LPs, 'S' Corporations, 'C' Corporations, sole proprietorships, and partnerships, are a vital subject for anyone serious about attaining wealth. Entities protect the rich from two things: lawsuits and taxes. Garrett Sutton, my legal advisor on entities has written a Rich Dad's Advisor book titled *Own Your Own Corporation*. You can find this book in bookstores everywhere and it is an important book for your financial library. Garrett also has a companion book, with the same title, written specifically for the Australian market.

Investing Naked

When an investor simply buys a stock, let's say 1,000 shares of IBM, and does not purchase insurance, that is known as *investing naked*. Once again, amateur investors invest naked, without insurance, and professionals are cognizant of the importance of insurance. When a professional investor invests with insurance, they say, "I'm covered" which means they are insured.

During the dot-com bubble, I was in the stock market knowing the crash was near. Because prices of all stocks were high, I knew I had to cover, hedge, insure every stock I had. I did not want to invest naked. The following are two of the insurance strategies I used.

1. **Stops:** A stop is simply an order given to my broker to sell my shares if the stock fell below a certain price. For example, let's say I purchased a stock for $10 and it climbed to $30. Not knowing if the price is going to go up or down and wanting to protect my gains, I might ask my broker to "Stop me out at $28." If the stock price dropped to $28, my broker would sell, hopefully at $28, thus protecting my gains. This is what Martha Stewart claimed she did with her broker. Obviously, the courts did not agree with her.

2. **Options:** There are two basic types of options. *Call options* and *put options*. In overly simple terms, this is how they are used.

   Call options. Let's say a stock is priced at $10 and I feel it is about to go higher. In this case I might buy a call option for let's say $1. My hunch turns out to be correct and the stock jumps to $15. My $1 call option allows me to buy the stock at $10, even though the price is now $15. So a call option is an insurance policy against higher prices.

   Put options. Let's say a stock is at $30 and I am concerned it might go down in value. Rather than lose sleep at night, or watch the financial TV network day in and day out, I can simply buy a put option, for let's say $1, which allows me to sell my stock at $30. A month later the stock market crashes and the stock goes to $5. That $1 insurance policy — my put option — allows me to sell my stock at $30 a share.

A Market Unto Itself

There is an entire market for buying and selling options. You can buy or sell options for almost anything in the financial world. In fact, many people only trade options, and never get into the asset. For example, an options trader may trade options and never invest in orange juice or oil or a particular company's stock.

A down payment for a piece of real estate is an option. Let's say the property is $100,000 and you put up $10,000 as a down payment. That down payment can be viewed as a call option, since the reason most people buy a piece of real estate is because they want to control the price of the property and the down payment protects them from a price increase… it also allows them the right to sell the property at a profit.

During this last real estate bubble, people who were flipping properties were technically using a down payment as a call option, fixing the price and then hoping to *flip* it for a higher price. One of the problems with real estate is that I do not know of a way to use *put options* to protect your position in case the market crashes.

Since I do not play the *flipping* game, I tend not to use a down payment as a *call option* play.

Learning To Control Insurance While Investing

The subject of risk and insurance control is such an important subject, that I created an advanced version of the CASHFLOW 101 game and named it CASHFLOW 202. Actually, both games started out as one game. The problem was that there was so much to learn, a game teaching fundamental investing and technical investing (which option investing is known as) was far too much to learn. So, the games were split.

After a person has played CASHFLOW 101, at least 10 times, and feel they understand the fundamentals of investing, then they may want to move on to CASHFLOW 202. The picture on the next page is one of the additional worksheets from the CASHFLOW 202 game.

CASHFLOW® 202

Player _____ Auditor _____

OPTIONS WORKSHEET

Call Options *(You expect the stock price to go up.)*

Stock Symbol	# of Shares (a)	Cost of Option/Share (b)	Total Amt. Paid (a x b)	Strike Price (c)	Today's New Price (d)	Price Gain (d – c)	Amount Receive (d – c) x a	Turn Count
								1 2 3
								1 2 3
								1 2 3
								1 2 3
								1 2 3
								1 2 3

Put Options *(You expect the stock price to go down.)*

Stock Symbol	# of Shares (a)	Cost of Option/Share (b)	Total Amt. Paid (a x b)	Strike Price (c)	Today's New Price (d)	Price Gain (c – d)	Amount Receive (c – d) x a	Turn Count
								1 2 3
								1 2 3
								1 2 3
								1 2 3
								1 2 3
								1 2 3

Turn Count: To keep track of your 3 turns before your options expire, mark off each number as that number turn passes.

SHORT SALES WORKSHEET *(You expect the stock price to go down.)*

Stock Symbol	# of Shares (a)	Sale Price Per Share (b)	Total Sales Amount (a x b)	Cost Per Share (c)	Total Cost (a x c)	Total Gain/Loss (a x b) – (a x c)

For examples of how to record your Call Options, Put Options and Short Sales, please refer to pages 6, 7 and 10 in the CASHFLOW® 202 rule book.

©2000, 2002 CASHFLOW® Technologies, Inc. All Rights reserved. CASHFLOW® games are covered by one or more of the following US Patents; 5,826,878; 6,032,957 and 6,106,300. CASHFLOW® is a registered trademark of CASHFLOW® Technologies, Inc.   G202CTI3

Other Forms Of Insurance

There are other forms of insurance controls available, including:

1. **Life Insurance:** Many people use life insurance as a hedge against the possibility they may pass on before they have built their nest egg for their families. I have several friends who have multi-million dollar policies to provide for their families. Also, it is important to note that there are insurance policies for the rich and for everyone else. Some of the insurance schemes the rich have available to them reassures me that Golden Rule #2 is alive and well in the insurance industry.

    If you would like more information on some of these different insurance schemes, just find an insurance agent who caters to the rich, tell him or her that you make millions of dollars, and they will share with you the insurance policies of the rich. Since most of the poor and middle class only know of term or whole life insurance, this little venture into insurance for the rich should be eye-opening.

2. **Disability Insurance:** If you have not yet built your nest egg and you still need to work to earn money, then please consider some additional disability insurance.

3. **Health Insurance:** The best form of health insurance is to take care of your health. Of course you already know that. Unfortunately, many people know this yet fail to take care of their most important asset, their health. One reason why taking care of your health is so important is because in the U.S. it is not Social Security that is the biggest problem, it is the government-sponsored medical programs, such as Medicare. If you are expecting the federal government to take care of your health, I think you may be disappointed.

4. **Death Insurance:** Many people die poor, leaving nothing but bills. The rich also want to die poor. The difference is, they want to die owning nothing and leaving everything as they direct it. They do this by structuring the ownership of their assets into vehicles like trusts that will prevent those assets from going through probate after their death.

    Just the other day, a friend came to me and said his dad passed away. His estate was now being taken apart by attorneys and the government. My friend said, "Dad looked into setting up a trust, a trust that would have protected his estate. But he thought the fees for setting up that trust were too high. Now most of his estate is going to attorneys and the government, not his kids and grandkids." That is another example of how being cheap on expenses can in the long run be very expensive.

    At minimum, regardless if you are rich or poor, each of us needs to have a will which clearly defines what we want done with the assets we spent our lives accumulating.

5. **Marriage insurance:** I have had the pleasure of sharing the stage with Donald Trump on several occasions. Each time, during his talk, he has stressed the importance of prenuptial agreements. So if you are uncertain about your future husband or wife, and have wealth or plan on being wealthy, then his advice may be good advice.

Kim and I do not have a prenuptial agreement. There are several reasons why. Reason number one is because I seriously doubt we would ever split up. I am certain we are soul mates. The second reason is because we had nothing when we were married. Everything we have today is due to a joint effort. And the third reason is because we both know how to create our own wealth. Many times a person who wants a piece of the action is afraid that they may not have the skills to create their own fortune. Kim and I are confident that, even if we lost it all, we would make it back, as a couple or as individuals. In other words, the best insurance is to have a high financial IQ.

6 **Trend insurance:** We all know markets go up and down. That is why professional stock investors use tools such as call and put options, or stops to protect their investment. These tools are forms of insurance to protect the investor against a change in trends, i.e. from a bull market to a bear market or a stock price heading down instead of up.

There are other kinds of trends that professional investors watch. And those are long-term historical trends. One of those long-term trends is the cycle between equities (stocks) and commodities (gold, oil etc.). This trend shows that equities go up for approximately 20 years at the same time commodities are going down for 20 years. Then the trend reverses and stocks go down for 20 years and commodities go up for 20 years. In 1980, the price of gold headed down from an all time high of nearly $800. At the same time the price of equities (stocks) started to rise. In 2000, as expected, equities headed down from all time highs (dot-com bubble) and commodities headed back up. That is why in 1996 I got out of equities and began investing in gold, silver, oil and gas, when they were at all-time lows. Back in 1997, oil was $10 a barrel and gold was below $270 an ounce. Like clock work, when the year 2000 rolled around, the long-term trend changed.

If you would like more information on this trend, Jim Rogers has written a book titled *Hot Commodities*. Until I read his book, I always thought the trend was a 20/10-year trend. By that I mean, I thought equities went up for 20 and down for 10 and commodities went up for 10 and down for 20. In his book, Jim Rogers has new data on this important trend. Millions of investors lost trillions of dollars when the trend from equities to commodities occurred in the year 2000. Even worse than losing money, they failed to make money when the trend changed.

If this trend holds true, that means equities should drift down until around 2020. At that point, the investors will finally give up hope, the equities market may crash, as I wrote about in my book *Rich Dad's Prophecy*, and after the crash, the next boom in stocks will take off… just as the amateurs finally give up all faith and hope in equities. That is when the professionals will come back in. What may alter this 20-year trend is the growing financial power of China and India.

In real estate, I watch demographic trends. For example, as baby boomers retire, they will tend to move from colder climates to warmer climates. That is one reason I am in Arizona, one of the top three states that boomers will be moving to. Another demographic change is that populations will continue to increase. The population of the U.S. was

approximately 280 million in the year 2000. It is expected to grow as high as 400 million by the year 2025. They will all need to live, work, shop, and play somewhere.

Also in real estate, I watch for hot new corridors, where growth will accelerate whether the real estate market is up or down. One of those corridors is between Houston, Dallas, and Oklahoma City. Another growth corridor is between Sierra Vista, Tucson, Phoenix, and Flagstaff, Arizona. In Australia, the growth corridor I watch is between Sydney, Brisbane, and Cairns. In Canada, the growth corridor I watch is between Calgary and Edmonton and between Vancouver and Whistler, BC. While people are fighting it out with high prices in cities like San Francisco, Los Angeles, Sydney, Vancouver or New York, I would rather keep my eyes on where people are moving to, not where they already are. That is why I prefer to watch and invest in the new growth corridors, regardless if the real estate market is up or down.

In these two examples, the insurance is to watch the historical, long-trends, have a big picture view, and be patient. There is a saying that states that demography is destiny. In other words study what people do and where they are going — and invest accordingly. More specifically, never be part of the thunder herd, but invest in what the thundering herd is doing and where they are going. The reason you do not want to be a part of the thundering herd is because the herd is generally headed for the slaughterhouse. That is why knowing and studying *long-term trends*, rather than being a *long-term loser* in the stock market, blindly following the investment advisors advice of *invest for the long-term*, can be one of your best forms of insurance.

7. **Investment insurance:** The insurance industry puts out a form of investment insurance known as annuities. There are two basic types of annuities, fixed and variable. Fixed annuities act like a CD (Certificate of Deposit) and variable annuities protect your investment in mutual funds. An annuity basically assures the investor that they will receive an income for life as well as protect the investor from market fluctuations or disasters. In theory, I like the idea of annuities but they can be very expensive. Annuities are great products for the person who does not want to invest in their financial education. The returns on investment are lower and they are a little bit more expensive, but that is the price of insurance. The task of the investor is to find a reputable insurance company that will stand behind their product.

In Conclusion

Simply said, professional investors invest with insurance. Amateurs don't. So when I hear someone say, "Investing is risky," I know the person is an amateur because investing is not risky if you know what you are doing.

Why *Teach To Be Rich* Works: The reason I created two games, CASHFLOW 101 and CASHFLOW 202 is because a person with a high financial IQ understands the *fundamentals* of investing as well as the *technical* side of investing. The technical side is the up and downs of the market. Another word for the *ups and downs* is *market volatility*. It is due to *market volatility* or

unexpected changes in the market that professional investors need to understand how to use insurance as asset protection. That is another reason why CASHFLOW 202 was created separately from 101.

When most financial experts talk about investing they often use averages, not specifics. They will say such things as, "On average, mutual funds have gone up by 8% a year." Using averages is a way of covering up the harsh realities of market volatility. The use of averages soothes the amateur's timid little heart and gives them comfort that they are doing the right thing by investing in averages.

A professional investor, while also enjoying the comfort of long-term average growth, also likes market volatility. Market volatility gives them buy signals and sell signals. For example, a down market is an opportunity to buy and a high market may be an opportunity to sell. In fact, professional investors make more money in down markets. Personally, I love market crashes. That is when bargains can be found.

Amateur investors hate market crashes. It frightens them. It disturbs them. That is why they take comfort in the words of advice that say, "On average mutual funds have gone up by 8% a year. That is why you should invest for the long-term. Do not go in and out of the market. That is risky and dangerous." What the advisor is really saying is "If you go in and out of the market, you disturb my steady commission check."

Now, on the other hand, stock brokers love short-term investors. These investors are constantly in and out of the market, which means the broker collects a commission coming and going. They buy when a hot stock moves up and sell when it comes down. I see these guys all the time. One day they are up and the next day they are down. The first speed dial number on their cell phone is to their stockbroker not their wife. At social gatherings you hear them say such things as, "My broker says XYZ is about to launch a new product. So I bought a few shares and the stock price went up." Or "I made a little money so I sold and took my profits. You know you don't go broke making a little money." The sad realities are, most of these in-and-out investors rarely make any money. The ones who make the most money are the broker and the brokerage house.

By the way, people do these short-term trades in all financial markets. In real estate these people are known as *flippers*. In the stock market, the really short-term investors are known as *day-traders*. While they both may be making profits, their profits will be taxed at the highest rates if they haven't owned the assets more than a year.

So rather than be a turtle and leave your money in the market for the long-term without insurance, allowing the hyenas to take a bite out of your money every day, or a grasshopper, jumping in and out of the market, terrified of every market up and down, why not learn to use insurance vehicles and strategies to protect your asset and your money… for the long-term. By understanding the use of insurance, the chances are you will make more money and sleep better at night. That is why teaching others about insurance and growing rich for the long-term with less risk… works.

Chapter Eighteen

Never Let A Hungry Dog Guard Your Smokehouse – OR – Taking Control Of Your Management/Education

Rich dad often said, "If a person cannot control their money, they have very little chance of becoming rich, no matter how much money they make." He also said, "A poor person has no chance of becoming rich if they continue to handle money like a poor person. Worst of all, if you hire a poor person to watch your money, you will probably wind up poor."

One of my favorite religious preachers is Reverend Ike. He is first of all a man of God; secondly, a wise man with money; and thirdly, a stand up comedian. Any time I find myself taking myself too seriously and need a laugh, I pop in one of my Reverend Ike tapes or CDs and begin laughing.

He makes fun of the inner conflicts many of us experience between God and money. Some of his lines I have committed to memory are:

1. "If you think money is dirty and evil and will come between you and God… then put all your money in the offering plate."

2. "Do you know how much you can love the Lord sitting in the back seat of your Rolls Royce limousine?"

3. " I don't spend money… I use money… because when I use money it comes back to me multiplied."

As you can tell, his message from the pulpit ruffles a few feathers. Nonetheless, if you need some comic relief when it comes to religion and money, then you can contact his organization at www.revike.org. If you do not think money, religion, and humor should be mixed, then please do not contact his organization.

One of Reverend Ike's sayings I keep close to me is, "Never let a hungry dog guard your smokehouse." These are great words of wisdom since when it comes to money the world is filled with hungry dogs.

Are You Doing Business With A Hungry Dog?

When I bring this subject up in my seminars, almost everyone knows one or two hungry dog stories. In one class a person shared how her brothers and sisters fought over their parents' fortune and today the brothers and sisters no longer talk to each other. Another person told a story of how his business partner ran off with his company's treasury and has never been found. Another story was of a person investing in a hedge fund and the hedge fund turned out to be a scam costing the person several million dollars. Between 2000 and 2005 the world news has been filled with stories of

companies such as WorldCom and Enron which are stories about CEO millionaires and their executive staff stealing from their own companies and lying to investors. While all these stories are sensational and some even make the news, hungry dog stories are a common every day experience.

Earlier in this book I wrote that mutual funds companies are not required to issue financial statements to investors. As you already know, they do not teach people to fish. They sell fish. While they do send out reports to investors, they are not transparent… which means they do not have to disclose everything a professional investor would want to know. Why is that? Again, the answer is because most mutual fund investors are not professional investors and most have limited financial training. Basically, whenever I look at a mutual fund annual report I see it as a sales document, a "feel good" brochure.

Again, there are times when I will buy a mutual fund, but only in certain instances and only at certain times. Two reasons why I am cautious about buying mutual funds, above and beyond the fact that they are not required to be transparent, are:

1. **Dividend Declaration Date.** If a mutual fund issues a dividend on a certain date, and you are not aware of this date and purchase the fund, you may have taxes to pay on that dividend. For example, let's say you purchase the fund in October and the fund's dividend declaration date is November, you may have to pay taxes immediately after purchasing the fund, wiping out much of your potential capital gains. In some ways it is like buying a 2005 model car in October of 2005 and paying full price for the car, while smart buyers know that in October every dealer is discounting their cars heavily to make room for the 2006 models. While a car sales person will tell you of the end-of-year discount, most mutual fund sales people will not inform you of a dividend declaration date and they don't have to.

2. **Embedded Capital Gains.** If a mutual fund company purchases 10 million shares of a stock at $1 and five years later they sell those 10 million shares for $11, they have a $100 million capital gains taxable event which is passed straight through to the investor, which means an investor may have to pay taxes even though the investor has made no money.

While these two events do not affect an investor who buys a mutual fund inside a tax-deferred retirement plan too badly, it does adversely affect an investor who purchases the mutual fund with after tax dollars. So buying mutual funds outside a retirement account is really risky since I have no control over the mutual fund, I cannot purchase insurance against market crashes, and, purchased outside a retirement plan, they are tax inefficient. In other words, there are better investments for better investors.

My point is that most mutual fund sales people often will not tell you these facts. Why… because it might affect their commissions or they simply do not know these facts themselves. Which leads to the question, are you doing business with a hungry dog or a stupid dog?

I Like Paying High Commissions

Once again, I feel it important to say that I am not against paying commissions. In fact I like paying high commissions. For example, in real estate, I have paid as high as a 35% commission. Why… because the deal is a great deal and I can make 40% to 70% on my money after paying taxes, insurance, and commissions. So I am willing to pay a higher commission for a better investment.

My point is not to take away a sales person's commissions. Personally, I find it reprehensible when someone wants to cut the salesperson's commissions. After all, commissions are how a salesperson earns their income and in many ways, we are all on some sort of commission plan. Traditional employees call their commission a salary and a professional person such as an attorney may call their commission their hourly rate.

My main point is to illustrate the price of the lack of financial education in our school systems. How else can we have so many millions of people trusting their retirement to fund managers who cannot beat the S&P 500, taking huge salaries in spite of this lack of performance; charging fees the investor does not know are being charged, sending out reports without transparent financial statements, investing without insurance, not understanding the tax consequences of the dividend declaration date or embedded capital gains or the tax consequences upon exit from the retirement plan, and many times not even knowing the person or the company they blindly turn their money over to? In simpler terms, many investors do not even know the hungry dogs they do business with or how hungry they are. And these hungry dogs are supposed to be guarding their future retirement next-egg and long-term financial security once their working days are over.

Are You The Hungry Dog?

We have all heard stories of professional athletes or rock stars becoming very rich in their twenties and being broke by their thirties. One reason for that is because they become a hungry dog or their friends and families become hungry dogs. A friend of mine who is a financial advisor to many of these very rich young athletes says that, "I can counsel the athlete about managing their money responsibly, but I cannot manage their friends and family. Often," she goes on to say, "I can get the young star athlete to calm down and manage their money. But it is not long before the star's mother, while at the beauty shop, is asked by the beautician, 'So, has your son bought you a new house and car yet?' Or the father is at work and his co-workers ask, 'Why are you still working? Can't that millionaire athlete of yours pay for you to stop working?'" My friend the financial advisor goes on to say, "That is when the pressure to spend the nest egg begins. Soon, not only does the athlete have a new house and three cars, so do mom and dad. I had one client who gave in to the pressures of friends and family and now travels with an entourage of over 20 people. He is no longer my client and I am afraid he will be broke within five years after his career ends, even though he makes millions today." In other words, the pro athlete became a hungry dog surrounded by a pack of hungry dogs.

One of the great concerns I have is the inevitable rude awakening… when the baby boomers begin retiring and suddenly find out how much money they have in their nest eggs. I wonder if they will then be able to manage their nest egg for the rest of their lives? In other words, when the retiree suddenly sees the size of their retirement nest egg, will they, too, turn into a hungry dog? Or if not them, will their friends and family turn into hungry dogs?

One story I read about was of a couple who realized they had nearly a million dollars in their retirement plan when they retired. Suddenly their dreams of sailing the world became a possibility. Immediately, they took out nearly half of their money, bought a large sailboat and began to live their dream. It was not long before they realized why people say a boat is a hole in the water that you pour money into. While they had calculated the price of the boat, they had not figured in the expenses of running and maintaining the boat. By the time they finally sold the boat, their million-dollar nest egg was down to nearly $300,000 in less than a year. This story illustrates my concern. If people have poor management skills and a limited financial education, they may become foolish hungry dogs when they retire.

The reason for this concern is that it has only been since the creation of the *defined contribution* plan (i.e. 401(k) plans) that so many people have been put in charge of their retirements and long term financial security. Prior to these *defined contribution* pension plans, most workers were covered by a *defined benefit* pension plan, which took care of them for as long as they lived. They never saw the lump sum that they had put away or realized that it was all they were going to receive during retirement. Within the next few years, we will begin finding out how many hungry dogs are out there.

Boomer Dogs

As a civilized society, we have never been down this path before since it has only been since the creation of the 401(k) plans that we suddenly began requiring workers to take responsibility of their finances. In 2008, the first baby boomers begin to retire. This is the first generation that the pension change hit, just when their working careers began. So we do not yet know what will happen when they retire. So far this generation's financial track record does not look good. Not only does this generation have the highest debt burdens in history, it also has the lowest savings rate in history (about 1%) and only 8.4% of this generation has made the maximum allowable contribution to their retirement plan according to the Center for Retirement Research at Boston College. On top of that, my age group, those between 50 and 59 today only have an average account balance of $88,000 saved for retirement in their plans. Not much of a nest egg for a hungry dog to guard.

Talking about hungry dogs who like to consume rather than invest or save, boomers began consuming ever since the movie about Davy Crockett began selling coonskin caps to us in the 1950s. I know because I bought one. Today, every new movie must have its merchandise sold through fast food franchises and retail super stores. Boomer dogs were the first consumer dogs, which may make them rabid hungry dogs when their working days are over. Some boomer dogs may try selling their old memorabilia such as coonskin caps or Star Wars light sabers they have spent years and fortunes collecting. It might be difficult to earn a living that way.

The Big Dogs

Even the big dogs have trouble managing their money. A study by the National Center for Policy Analysis found that the Big Dogs' 401(k) plans of companies such as Citigroup, Merrill Lynch, Morningstar, and Prudential – big dogs who make a lot of money selling their financial advice, under-performed the index funds, such as the S&P 500 by 3% to 11%. If these financial big dogs cannot manage their own retirement 401(k) plans for their own employees, what chance does the average company or person have? On top of that, if these big dogs are doing a poor job guarding their own employees' smoke houses, how can they sell their investment advice and expertise to millions of people? If management/financial education is a key control, who put these big dogs in control of the

financial future of millions of people? Is it Golden Rules #2 and #3 in action again? Is it a case of blind guard dogs leading other blind dogs? If matching the performance of the S&P 500 is like getting a 'C' in school, how can these high-priced 'A' students, the funds hire to invest your money, perform at 'D'- and 'F'-student levels in the real world of money? Smells like hungry dogs to me… big ones.

The Super Dog

The biggest hungry dog in the world is the U.S. government. In 1971, when we shifted from the gold standard to a fiat currency policy, the U.S. went from being one of the richest creditor nations in the world to being the biggest debtor nation in the world. In 1971, the U.S. became the super dog of hungry dogs. As a people, we are the biggest debtors in the world consuming far more than we produce. But as a nation we are a super consumer and we pay for our consumption with IOUs rather than with real money. Not only do we owe the rest of the world a lot of money, we owe our own people a lot of money.

When Social Security was created in the 1930s, Franklin Delano Roosevelt admitted that it was created as a way to gain more of the popular vote since we were in the midst of a Depression. That may be why he was elected to four terms as President. Ever since then, Social Security has become the most popular of all benefits in America and any politician that attempts to change it faces stiff opposition… even though most of us know that we, as a people, cannot afford to pay for these campaign promises. But the Social Security problem is not the biggest financial problem we face. There is a much bigger one.

The Biggest Debt Of All

In the 1960s, socialized medicine entered the U.S. and today is known as the Medicare and Medicaid programs. Of all the mass benefit programs, these are the worst, financially speaking. As of 2004, two economists, Jagadeesh Gokhale and Ken Smetters, estimated that the bill for Social Security was $10.4 trillion and the bill for the Medicare was $62 trillion for a total IOU of $72.4 trillion.

When looking at the financial statement of the U.S. government, the diagram looks like this:

The U.S. Government's Financial Statement

Income
Expenses

Assets	Liabilities

I.O.U.
$72,400,000,000,000

The reason the $72.4 trillion is shown off balance sheet is because that is exactly what it is. It is a debt that the federal government is allowed to accrue without accounting for it. If you or I did this, we would go to jail for fraud.

What does this debt mean? It may mean many things. First of all, it means people born after 1970 will have much higher taxes to pay. It may mean the U.S. dollar will continue to lose value, which means savers will lose. It may lead to a financial disaster the likes of which we have never experienced before… since no country in history has ever been in so much debt before. Whatever happens, it will affect not only the U.S. but the world.

How Much Is A Trillion?

A problem with such large numbers is that most people cannot comprehend the difference between a billion and a trillion. When a person has a mind that operates in thousands… millions, billions, and trillions all sound alike. To give context to these numbers, we need to compare them to something. A good comparison is the world stock and bond markets. In the year 2000 the total value of all publicly-traded companies in the world was $36.1 trillion and the value of every bond traded in the world was $31 trillion for a total world value of $67.1 trillion.

That means if the rest of the world cashed in all their stocks and bonds and turned all of their money over to the U.S. government to pay for the retirement and medical benefits of Americans, the U.S. would still be $5.3 trillion short. In other words, the national debt is only about $4 trillion but the U.S. debt to its people is beyond comprehension. This means the children and grandchildren of the baby boomers will be working hard to pay for campaign promises made years ago.

Yet, even with the comparison of how much $72.4 trillion is compared to the world financial markets, the number is too big. So it is best I break down the number to even smaller terms and we can all comprehend. Another example is, if you begin to count dollar bills at the rate of one a second for 24 hours a day it would take you nearly 12 days to count $1 million. At the same rate, it would take you 32 years to count a billion dollars. And it would take you 32,000 years to count a trillion dollars.

By now you may realize why 1971 was such an important date and why I invest in real estate, oil, silver, and gold. I invest in these asset classes because I suspect the super hungry dog guarding the world's smokehouse is out of control. When the U.S. government was allowed to print fiat money at high speed, the world changed. How can we as a people be expected to manage our money when the federal government does not do a good job managing the world's richest economy?

In late 2004, the *prescription drug benefit program*, which once again increased the debt of future IOUs was instituted making the previous debt figures of $72.4 trillion obsolete. The debt keeps climbing, we as a nation keep spending, and politicians keep making promises they cannot keep.

Today, as I write, we are experiencing the biggest financial bubble in the history of the world. Will it continue? Will the world keep accepting the U.S. dollar as an honest currency? If the world loses faith in the U.S dollar, what will happen next? I leave the answer to that question to you.

Financial Immaturity

One of the reasons that we're facing this financial fiasco goes back to the fact that our schools do not teach us much about money. As a nation, we lack financial maturity. One reason these debts go unchecked is because this massive financial crisis is not shown on the books of the federal government. In other words, the very things that brought Enron down — not listing all liabilities on its balance

sheets — the U.S. government is guilty of doing. Just as mutual funds do not present a true picture to investors, neither does the U.S. government present a true picture to its people.

My rich dad often said, "Politicians aren't lying. They're just not telling us the truth." One of the deceptive slight of hands is this subject known as *inflation*. Lately, as oil prices went from $10 a barrel to over $60 a barrel, the news from the federal government is that there is no inflation. How can this be? Also, in 1994, a house down the street from me sold for $495,000. It sold again a month ago, a little over ten years later, for $2.9 million. And still the federal economists say, "There is no inflation." How can this be? Are we that naïve?

One of the reasons for this confusion is caused by the fact that the Federal Reserve Banks are only responsible for keeping *consumer* prices under control… not *asset* prices. And since China has come to market, consumer prices have dropped… but asset prices have gone through the roof. So when the federal government says to us that inflation is running at less than 2% or whatever figure they come up with, they are not lying… they simply are not telling us the truth. If people actually knew how high inflation really was they might withdraw their savings, earning less than 3% from the bank, and the whole system would come crashing down.

Again, this is Golden Rule #2 in action and one more reason why it is important for each of us to take control of our education and financial training. If you do not know the truth, it's tough to manage your own money. If you do not know the truth, you might actually believe that working hard, saving money, getting out of debt, investing for the long term and diversifying is the smart thing to do.

A Nation Of Poor People In A Rich Country

It seems strange that the U.S., once the richest country in the world, is now the biggest debtor nation in the world. I wonder how this could have happened. While it is easy to point the finger at politicians, I believe the real problem lies in our educational system. My question is: How can we spend so much on education and have so many educated people so financially needy at the end of their lives? Why do we have so many people willing to vote for the politician or political party that promises to take care of them when they retire? How is it that we have so many educated, poor people in such a rich country? Again I believe the answer is found in New York State's Teacher of The Year, John Taylor Gattos' comment which I repeat, underlying the points I think most applicable:

> *"The secret of American schooling is that it doesn't teach the way children learn — nor is it supposed to. Schools were conceived to service the economy and the social order rather than kids and families — that is why it is compulsory. As a consequence, the school cannot help anybody grow up, because it's prime directive is to retard maturity. It does this by teaching that everything is difficult, that other people run our lives, that our neighbors are untrustworthy, even dangerous. School is the first impression children get of society. Because first impressions are often decisive ones, school imprints kids with fear, suspicion of one another, and certain addictions for life. It ambushes natural intuition, faith, and love of adventure, wiping these out in favor of a gospel of rational procedure and rational management.*

My thoughts are that most people leave school needing to have a company, the government, or a financial expert take care of them simply because our schools conveniently omit the study of money from their curriculum. Instead of learning to be financially independent dogs, most people learn to

entrust their money to hungry dogs. And that is why, today, the great country of the United States has become the biggest debtor nation in the world, owing money not only to the world but to its own people. In other words, financially illiterate and financially naïve people will ultimately cause a rich nation to become poor.

A Perfect Storm Is Brewing

Learning to manage money is a fundamental life skill. It is an important life skill, especially in today's world. As rich dad said, "Rich or poor, smart or not-so-smart, we all use money." Yet so many people still have some kind of quasi-religious attitude about money… thinking that money is the root of all evil and should *not* be discussed, especially at home, at school, and in many churches. To me, money is not evil… the lack of education is. Rich dad said, "It's not money but how you make your money that is good or evil." You can be rich by being a good person doing good things for the world and you can become rich doing bad things for the world, bad things such as not telling people the truth or not teaching people what they need to know to survive in this world. That is evil." As Reverend Ike says, "The love of money is not the root of all evil. The lack of money is." Unfortunately in our world today, we have many highly-educated, highly-paid poor people teaching us about money. That is a primary reason why we as a nation are financially naïve.

Rich dad also said, "Money itself is not evil. But people who need money can become evil." When Hurricane Katrina hit New Orleans and the Gulf Coast region, and life support was cut off, many good people suddenly became dangerous people. As I watched the violence and looting on TV, I wondered if I was watching a picture of the future. What happens if or when our government's social systems break down because our financial systems have broken down? Instead of tens of thousands of people needing food, shelter, and medical care, what happens to the richest country in the world when there are millions of aging baby boomers, many who are broke and in need of food, shelter, and medical care? A perfect storm is brewing and it is only a few years away. In spite of this perfect storm, our school systems still pretend all we need to survive in today's world is a job. Our school systems are living in the past, in the Industrial Age, a time when companies and governments were financially solvent enough to take care of people. In the next few years, we will find out how obsolete that thinking is.

Today in school we have driver's education and sex education, but no financial education. Instead of teaching young people about the financial realities of a real world, the school system ignores a *fundamental life skill*, the skill of knowing how to manage your own money. We leave school financially illiterate, unable to read financial statements… which makes us unable to know the truths, which is why Enrons can occur, mutual funds do not need to be transparent, the U.S. government can leave nearly one hundred trillion dollars in liabilities off the books and, on top of that, tell us there is no inflation. Instead of teaching us to read and become financially literate so we can manage our own money, we as a nation are taught to let someone else manage our money for us. How can we manage our own money when we leave school highly-educated but financially illiterate? To me, this is an educational crime against our nation and our children. This must change if we are to survive as a civilized nation and as a civilized world.

Why *Teach To Be Rich* Works: When you look at the financial statement from the CASHFLOW game pictured on the next page, you are looking at empty financial boxes, labeled Income, Expense, Assets, and Liabilities. The CASHFLOW game was created to teach people to be financially literate

because being able to read numbers is the basis of financial education and the building blocks of a person's financial IQ.

A proper financial education would teach a person what each box means — how the boxes are related. To a person without a financial education, which is most people, this financial statement and its empty boxes means very little.

Profession _____ Player _____

Goal: To get out of the Rat Race and onto the Fast Track by building up your Passive Income to be greater than your Total Expenses

Income Statement

Income

Description	Cash Flow
Salary:	
Interest:	
Dividends:	
Real Estate:	
Businesses:	

Auditor

Person on your right

Passive Income= _____
(Cash Flows from Interest +
Dividends + Real Estate + Businesses)

Total Income: _____

Expenses

Taxes: _____
Home Mortgage: _____
School Loan Payment: _____
Car Payment: _____
Credit Card Payment: _____
Retail Payment: _____
Other Expenses: _____
Child Expenses: _____
Bank Loan Payment: _____

Number of Children: _____
(Begin game with 0 Children)
Per Child Expense: _____

Total Expenses: _____

Monthly Cash Flow: _____
(Pay Check)

Balance Sheet

Assets

Savings: _____
Stocks/Mutual's/CDs   No. of Shares: Cost/Share:
Real Estate: Down Pay: Cost:
Business: Down Pay: Cost:

Liabilities

Home Mortgage: _____
School Loans: _____
Car Loans: _____
Credit Cards: _____
Retail Debt: _____
RE Mortgage: _____
Liability: (Business) _____
Bank Loan: _____

©1996-2002 CASHFLOW® Technologies, Inc. All rights reserved. CASHFLOW® games are covered by one or more of the following US Patents; 5,826,878; 6,032,957 and 6,106,300. RichDad®, CASHFLOW® and Investing 101® are registered trademarks of CASHFLOW® Technologies, Inc.   G101CTI7

By investing time to learn how to fill in the boxes and teaching others to do the same, you are teaching others to be financially literate and, more importantly, take control of their lives. The more control you give others, the more control you receive. It's simple physics.

Newton's Law

In physics class we learned from one of Newton's Laws that *for every action there is an opposite and equal reaction.* The same law applies to money management. For example, if a person does something in the expense column, like have a baby, it affects the other three columns in some way. Once a young person or an adult understands the impact of each and every one of their actions, they will know how those actions affect the different boxes and their financial future. Once a person learns about the impact their actions have on their financial life they have a better chance of taking control of their financial future.

Instead of blindly turning their money over to someone they think is a financial expert, they may decide to become their own financial expert and take care of themselves and their money. Rather than expect a company or the government to take care of them in their old age, they may decide to take care of themselves early in life, retire young and get on with their real life. That is the power of teaching someone, young or old, to become their own financial expert, learn to manage their own money, and take control of their financial future.

Knowing How People Steal From You

Earlier in this book, I quoted Warren Buffett's statement on diversification. He said,

"Diversification is required when investors do not understand what they are doing."

One of the purposes of teaching a person about money management is to assist them in their understanding of money and how it works. Today, when I look at an investment, I look at the same diagram of a financial statement on the next page.

Looking at the investment, I must honestly ask myself if I understand how to increase my income and decrease my expenses or whether I need to increase my expenses; control my debt and liabilities, and increase the value of the asset. That is what a sound financial education really teaches someone.

Also included in my *understanding* of how money works, I need to know how people steal from me, legally and illegally. For example, let's say I decide to open a small convenience store. Not only do I need to know how to make money, I also need to know how customers as well as employees could steal from me. All of this knowledge is essential to the word *understanding*. One of the reasons people do not know how people are stealing from them, legally or illegally, is simply because they are not taught how to read the numbers. Once a person learns how the numbers are related, it is easy to sense or detect if money is legally or illegally disappearing. It is also easy to know if someone is lying or telling you the truth.

Running On Empty

Using the automobile example again, let's say you go out to your car and you find your gas tank empty and you know you filled it up last night. Right away you would suspect that either there was a hole in the gas tank, which would need to be fixed, someone siphoned gas from the tank, or someone has been joy riding in your car without you knowing about it. When it comes to their money, many

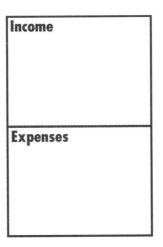

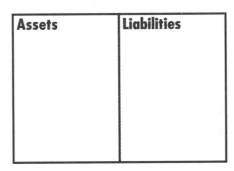

investors do not know how many legal thieves have been joy riding with their money simply because they do not understand the business of money. Many hard-working people are running on empty simply because they do not know how many hungry dogs are joy riding in their financial car.

Big Legal Thieves

Recently several high profile CEOs have been in the news for stealing from their companies. And it's likely that there are many more who have not yet been caught. As we know, not all crooks go to jail even though they have broken the law.

Some of the biggest thieves I know are legal thieves. These are often employees, from CEOs on down to secretaries, who legally drain the company of resources. These are some of the most infuriating of all people. Over the years, I have hired and fired several company presidents and CEOs who were legally stealing from the company. If not for my business training and my ability to understand the numbers, I might not have caught the holes in the company.

One of my more painful learning experiences was an oil company I was a partner in. The CFO suddenly decided to make a financial decision (that affected the liability column) without checking with the board of directors or the petroleum engineers. When his decision went sour, the entire company nearly came down. When we asked him to resign, he asked for a severance bonus even though he knew the company's treasury was depleted because of his blunder. I could not believe his greed and audacity. His actions nearly cost everyone in the company their jobs and he wanted a bonus plus severance pay. In my book, that guy is a legal thief.

Another example of legal thieves is a person who approaches you and says, "I want to help. " After years of experience, some of it painful, I have learned to ask, "Are you here to help me or to help yourself?"

When watching the looting after Hurricane Katrina, I thought of some of the people I have done business with over the years. Although I still become angry when I think about their legal thievery, I am also grateful because they helped me gain real world experience, which added to my better *understanding* of the real world of business.

One of the greatest benefits of gaining business experience in the real world and teaching others is that I have been able to meet a lot of people. Eighty percent are great people who sincerely want to do a good job. Still, there is that 20% who come not to help you or your company but only to help themselves. These are often the people who steal legally.

In other words, not only do we have to learn to manage money as part of a strong financial education but we must learn to manage people, too. Rich dad often said, "It is tough doing business with poor people, greedy people, and incompetent people. While we all want to do business with good, honest, and competent people, the only way we find out what they really are is by doing business with them." He also said, "The best way to learn about managing money and people is by doing it and learning from each experience."

One of the problems of turning your money over to an expert is that you really will not know if they really were experts until you retire. On top of that, if you simply turn your money over to someone else to manage for you, you learn nothing… and knowing nothing about managing money and people, at the end of your working life, is not the best time to start learning. So rather than learning with real money, I suggest using a game such as the CASHFLOW game and teaching yourself and others to play the game using play money. To me, that makes more sense than simply hoping the person you have entrusted your money with is really an expert and not a hungry dog.

In conclusion, as Reverend Ike said, "Never let a hungry dog guard your smokehouse." The reason you want to learn to manage your own money and teach others to manage theirs is to recognize hungry dogs early and not be a hungry dog yourself. That is why teaching to be rich works.

Chapter Nineteen

THE FINANCIAL BENEFITS OF BEING IN CONTROL

In 1999, Kim and I realized that we had outgrown our accountants. They were good when we were small... but our wealth had grown and we needed more sophisticated advisors. Just as you shop for a car, we began shopping for new accountants.

One firm came highly recommended and we met with them. After the meeting, we left our financial records and they said they would get back to us after reviewing them in about three weeks. So we set an appointment, shook hands and left their office.

Three weeks later, we met again. Their findings were informative and it seemed they could really help us save a lot of money on taxes... far more than our old accountants were able to. As the meeting drew to a close, one of the senior partners said, "We have some concerns about your investments."

"Oh," I said. "What are you concerns?"

"Well, we just happen to have our senior investment officer here from New York today and we think it best he tell you what he has found."

"OK," I agreed. "Let's meet with him."

In walked a handsome, Ivy League-preppy young man who sat down and got straight to the point. This young man looked like he stepped out from the pages of *Gentleman's Quarterly*, down to the techie wire-rimmed glasses. Adjusting his glasses he began by saying, "I find you are too heavily investing in real estate, gold, silver, oil, and gas."

"Yes," I replied. "Kim and I own the companies or are controlling investors in the businesses."

"Yes... but you're too heavily weighted in real estate and hard commodities," the good-looking preppy said.

"So what do you recommend?" I asked.

"I recommend you sell your real estate and commodity holdings and invest in a well-diversified portfolio of mutual funds."

"Really?" I replied. "What kind of mutual funds do you recommend?"

"I love the high tech sector," he said with a smile. "After all, we are in the Information Age and your investments are Industrial Age investments. You might want to invest in the true blue chip stocks but also look at some of these high-flying dot-com stocks. I might be able to get you into an IPO. Not with a lot of money, but just a few shares to test the market. You know diversification is the way to go."

To this day, I cannot believe I almost believed him. After all, he was from an Ivy League School, top of his class in finance. He looked good and sounded convincing... and his talk about getting into a dot-com IPO tickled my greed button. In other words I was being sucked in.

"How does this sound to you?" asked the senior partner. "I think we can save you a lot of money

in taxes and get you more diversified in your investments."

With the word *diversified*, I snapped out of my haze and said, "Thank you. Let us think about it and we'll call you when we've made our decision."

Three days later I called and said we were passing on them as accountants and as investment advisors.

As I said, I wanted to believe what I was hearing. I was very impressed by the well-educated and smartly-dressed young man. He sounded like he knew what he was talking about. Also, managing your own money and investments is time consuming and often trying. So the idea of turning over our investments to well-educated experts was enticing. Yet when he said the word *diversification*, I snapped out of my dream state.

One of the reasons the word *diversification* snapped me out of my dream state is because I learned early in life that you do not win by diversifying. As stated earlier, diversification is a defensive strategy, not an offensive investment strategy. Instead of diversifying, rich dad had taught his son and me to focus… focus on winning. He said, "Great athletes focus. Very few athletes can be all-stars in many different sports." If you take Michael Jordan as an example, he is one of the greatest basketball players who ever lived… yet when he tried out for professional baseball, he was not as great. In other words he won when he focused and lost when he diversified.

The other day, while on vacation in Hawaii, I came across an advertisement for Winners Camp, a camp I had dealings with years ago when I first began my quest to learn more about education. Winners Camp designed a life skills curriculum for young people, to fill the gap left by traditional education. It does a great job for most young people, especially if the young person wants to make changes in their life. In their ad in the in-flight magazine, Winners Camp stressed that they taught young people to focus and use the word focus as an acronym standing for:

F = **Follow**
O = **One**
C = **Course**
U = **Until**
S = **Successful**

Rich dad would have applauded Winners Camp for teaching young people to focus… because that is what he taught his son and me to do. Rich dad did not care what we did as long as we focused, which to him meant doing something until we were successful at it. In other words, set a goal and keep going until you achieve your goal. Don't be a quitter… be a winner.

When I said to rich dad I wanted to learn to invest in real estate, he insisted I focus… until successful. When I wanted to become an entrepreneur, he insisted I focus… until successful. When I began working on my own IPO, like my gold and silver companies, I focused… until successful.

> *"(John Maynard) Keyes essentially said, 'Don't try and figure out what the market is doing. Figure out a business you understand and concentrate."*
>
> –Warren Buffett

When I started my own oil and gas company I focused… until successful. In between setting the goal and eventually becoming successful, there were many failures, many dark moments, many disappointments… yet I kept focusing until successful. My gold company took nearly seven years of focus and millions of dollars, until it finally went public and was successful.

When that young Ivy League financial expert advised Kim and me to diversify, I realized we did not share the same reality on investing. I did not gain my financial experience in school. Kim and I gained our investment knowledge in the real world by managing our own money and focusing until successful. We turned down their services because Kim and I realized that our financial intelligence came from financial challenges, struggles, failures, disappointment, and successes. We did not become financially successful by diversifying… we became successful by focusing.

While it is possible to achieve financial success by diversifying, I was not willing to throw away all I had learned by focusing… and diversifying. Instead of diversifying, Kim and I decided to focus even harder. From 1999 to the present, our wealth has increased at least a 100 times and so has our financial knowledge.

If we had diversified as the young man suggested, we would have lost millions in one of the biggest market crashes in history, the crash that started in 2000 and from which, as of this writing, the world has not yet recovered. Instead of our wealth going up by many millions, our wealth would have come down by many millions, even if we had diversified.

Although the word *diversification* woke me up, it was my rich dad's lessons on the six financial controls that ultimately made our decision. As much as I wanted to turn my money over to this young expert and be rid of the problems of managing my money, I realized that he was recommending we put our money in investments we had no control over.

Now, I may not have done as well in school as this young man did, but I do know the difference between investing with control and being out of control. In the end, we decided not to go with this accounting firm simply because Kim and I had not spent so many years of our lives learning to be in control and then turn our money over to people who invest our money in investments none of us had control over. I may not have done well in school, but I am certainly not that stupid.

An Example Of Controls

Once again, the following are the six basic controls a sophisticated investor wants over an investment:

1. Income

2. Expense

3. Asset

4. Liability

5. Financial education / management

6. Insurance

Sometimes I do invest in investments where I am not in control. For example, in one of my oil and gas investments, I am not in control of the day-to-day operations. Yet, I am in control of one of the controls and it is control over the management. If I do not like what I see happening or my monthly checks are not big enough, I simply get on the phone and call the CEO of the company. Since I am one of his largest investors, he takes my call.

Most mutual fund investors cannot personally call the CEO of a mutual fund. For example, if you have invested in Berkshire Hathaway, most investors cannot call Warren Buffett and talk directly to him. In most instances, they will only talk to the investor relation secretary.

In my Chinese gold company, although I am not in control of the day-to-day operations, I am the third largest shareholder and the CEO takes my calls. Once again, that is an important control: control over management.

Why *Teach To Be Rich* Works: One of the advantages of focusing on gaining more control over the controls is that your financial IQ and your wealth go up, while your risks go down. To me, it makes more sense to be in control rather than diversify into assets neither your advisor nor you have any control over.

When you teach someone to FOCUS… to *Follow One Course Until Successful*, you are teaching them as well as yourself to focus on taking control of your life. Instead of quitting when things get tough — which is what losers do — you teach them to focus, to keep going, keep learning, keep persevering until they become winners. Also when you teach someone to focus, you teach them and yourself *to see worlds others never see* and it is what you can see that others do not see that really makes you rich. As rich dad said, "If money is not in your head, it won't be in your hands." That is the power of focus and *why teaching to be rich works*.

Too Much Money Coming In

In 1985, Kim and I were broke and out of money. By 2005 our wealth had grown to beyond our wildest dreams. We have more money coming in than we can possibly spend. Those dreams would not have come true if we had worked hard for a steady paycheck, tried to live below our means and save money, worked to be debt-free, turned our money over to experts who invested in assets they nor us had any control over, and diversified into paper assets. Instead we got there by starting small, *focusing* instead of *diversifying*, and continually increasing our financial IQ on how to control assets.

In Part IV of this book I will share with you how I learned to personally *focus and win* as well as teach others to *focus and win*. I believe you, too. can have the problem of too much money coming in if you will *focus to win* rather than *diversify to avoid losing*.

Robert Kiyosaki

Robert Kiyosaki, author of *Rich Dad Poor Dad* - *USA Today's* #1 Money Book for 2004 and international runaway bestseller – is an investor, entrepreneur and educator whose perspectives on money and investing fly in the face of conventional wisdom. He has, virtually single-handedly, challenged and changed the way tens of millions, around the world, think about money.

In communicating his point of view on why 'old' advice – get a good job, work hard, save money, get out of debt, invest for the long term, and diversify – is 'bad' (both obsolete and flawed) advice, Robert has earned a reputation for straight talk, irreverence and courage.

Rich Dad Poor Dad ranks as the longest-running bestseller on <u>all four</u> of the lists that report to *Publisher's Weekly* – *The New York Times, Business Week, The Wall Street Journal* and *USA Today* – and has held a top spot on the famed *New York Times* list for over five years.

Translated into 45 languages and available in 90 countries. the Rich Dad series has sold over 25 million copies worldwide and has dominated best sellers lists across Asia, Australia, South America, Mexico and Europe. In 2005, Robert was inducted into the Amazon.com Hall of Fame as one of that that bookseller's Top 25 Authors. There are currently 12 books in the Rich Dad series.

Robert writes a bi-weekly column – 'Why the Rich Are Getting Richer' – for Yahoo! Finance and a monthly column titled 'Rich Returns' for Entrepreneur magazine.

Prior to writing *Rich Dad Poor Dad*, Robert created the educational board game CASHFLOW® 101 to teach individuals the financial and investment strategies that his rich dad spent years teaching him. It was those same strategies that allowed Robert to retire at age 47.

Today there are more than 1,600 CASHFLOW Clubs – game groups independent of The Rich Dad Company – in cities throughout the world.

Born and raised in Hawaii, Robert Kiyosaki is a fourth-generation Japanese-American. After graduating from college in New York, Robert joined the Marine Corps and served in Vietnam as an officer and helicopter gunship pilot. Following the war, Robert went to work in sales for the Xerox Corporation and, in 1977, started a company that brought the first nylon and Velcro 'surfer wallets' to market. He founded an international education company in 1985 that taught business and investing to tens of thousands of students throughout the world.

In 1994 Robert sold his business and, through his investments, was able to retire at the age of 47. During his short-lived retirement he wrote *Rich Dad Poor Dad*.

In Robert's words, "We go to school to learn to work hard for money. I write books and create products that teach people how to have money work hard for them."

Sharon Lechter

A life-long education advocate, Sharon Lechter is co-author of the international bestselling book *Rich Dad Poor Dad* and the Rich Dad series of books as well as one of the founders of The Rich Dad Company. She is a CPA, entrepreneur, philanthropist, educator, international speaker, and Mom.

She graduated with Magna Cum Laude honors from Florida State University with a degree in accounting, then joined the ranks of a Big Eight accounting firm. Sharon held various management positions with computer, insurance, and publishing companies while maintaining her professional credentials as a CPA.

She has been a pioneer in developing new technologies to bring education into children's lives in ways that are innovative, challenging and fun and remains committed to education – most especially, financial literacy.

"Our current educational system has not been able to keep pace with the global and technological changes in the world today," Sharon states. "We must teach our young people the skills – both scholastic and financial – that they need to not only survive but to flourish in the world."

The Rich Dad Company has grown into an international powerhouse more than 20 books, board games, website, CDs, audio cassettes, seminars, and coaching services. *Rich Dad Poor Dad* has been on The New York Times Bestseller List for over five years and is available in over 50 languages and sold in more than90 countries.

Sharon's speaking topics range from educating children and adults on taking control of their personal finances to the entrepreneurial business strategies she used in building Rich Dad's international success. She shares the spectacular history of this mega-hit and how *Rich Dad Poor Dad* was originally designed to be a brochure for their CASHFLOW board game.

A committed philanthropist, Sharon also gives back to the world communities as both a volunteer and a benefactor. She directs the Foundation for Financial Literacy, is an active member of Women's Presidents Organization, and serves on the national board of Childhelp USA, a national organization founded to eradicate child abuse in the United States. In 2002, Childhelp honored Sharon and her husband, Michael, as recipients of that organization's "Spirit of the Children" Award. In 2004, Sharon and Michael were recognized as an Arizona "Power Couple." In addition, Sharon was recently named as a 2005 Woman of Distinction by the Crohn's & Colitis Foundation of America.

Sharon's co-author, business partner and friend, Robert Kiyosaki, says "Sharon is one of the few natural entrepreneurs I have ever met. My respect for her continues to grow every day that we work together."

Rich Kid Smart Kid.com

Money is a life skill — but we don't teach our children about money in school. We are asking for your help in getting financial education into the hands of interested teachers and school administrators.

RichKidSmartKid.com was created by The Rich Dad Company as a free innovative and interactive Web site designed to convey key concepts about money and finance in ways that are fun and challenging… and educational for young people in grades K through 12.

AND, schools all across the world may also register at www.richkidsmartkid.com to receive a FREE download of our electronic version of CASHFLOW for Kids at School™.

Join Us

Play CASHFLOW® for KIDS™ and CASHFLOW 101 with family and friends and share the richkidsmartkid.com Web site with your local teachers and school administrators.

By taking financial education to our schools, together we can better prepare our children for the financial world they will face.

Thank you!

Rich dad said, "Spiritual Money is not about money. It is about doing something that must be done and it disturbs you that no one else is doing it."

Are You Serious?

If you are serious about becoming a successful entrepreneur, we recommend you carefully study the B-I Triangle.

The B-I Triangle:
The key to a successful business

In **Rich Dad's You Can Choose to Be Rich™**, we provide a more in-depth analysis of the B-I Triangle, with *experts* from each level offering their experience and insight. They will help you jumpstart your business and more importantly — avoid the pitfalls that many new business owners encounter.

Learn how the rich, the poor and the middle class think...and then choose which path you want to follow. **Rich Dad's You Can Choose to Be Rich** is a must for anyone serious about becoming a successful entrepreneur.

For more information about this product,
please visit **www.richdad.com/choosetoberich**

Get Started Today!

Rich Dad's Coaching

Working with a Rich Dad Coach will help you begin to change your understanding of how the rich get richer and how you can start leveraging your own resources to achieve wealth.

Your Rich Dad Coach will help you:

- **Expand your Context**
- **Achieve your Plan**
- **Write your own Rules**
- **Get what you want!**

Call today to receive a free introduction
to Rich Dad's Coaching
1-800-240-0434
ext 5001

To contact Rich Dad

visit *www.richdad.com*
or call *1-800-308-3585*

To order books

visit *www.twbookmark.com*

For more information:
The Rich Dad Company
4330 N. Civic Center Plaza, Suite 100 Scottsdale, Arizona 85251
TEL: (800) 308-3585 • Fax: (480) 348-1349 • E-mail: service@richdad.com

Australia/New Zealand:
Rich Dad® Australia™
4-6 Mentmore Avenue • Rosebery NSW 2018 Australia
TEL: 1300 660 020 • FAX: 1300 301 988 • E-mail: info@richdad.com.au